A Family Systems Guide to Infidelity

A Family Systems Guide to Infidelity offers an explanatory model and concrete techniques, enabling therapists and counselors to treat the core of a couple's relationship problems instead of merely applying a therapeutic bandage. Chapters give therapists proven techniques to help couples redevelop trust, rebalance power, increase satisfaction, and recover from the wounds that infidelity causes. This text uses case studies from clinical practice, examples of public or historical figures, and scenarios from popular movies to illustrate concepts, and it provides a systemic explanatory model for understanding infidelity, one that focuses on marital dissatisfaction, power imbalances, unfulfilled dreams, and the discovery of infidelity.

Paul R. Peluso, PhD, is Professor and Chair of the Department of Counselor Education at Florida Atlantic University and the Past President of the International Association of Marriage and Family Counseling (IAMFC). He is also the author/coauthor of six books—including *Changing Aging, Changing Family Therapy: Practicing With 21st Century Realities*—and the past editor of the journal *Measurement and Evaluation in Counseling and Development.*

Family Systems Counseling: Innovations Then and Now

Series Editor: Paul R. Peluso, PhD, *Florida Atlantic University*

This series is aimed at both current practitioners and students who wish to learn about the historical power and boldness of the family systems approach but who also need to see it applied to current problem situations. The books in this series will reflect on the pioneering elements of family systems approaches and how they might have been used previously with a particular issue or population.

A Family Systems Guide to Infidelity: Helping Couples Understand, Recover From, and Avoid Future Affairs
Paul R. Peluso

For more information about this series, please visit www.routledge.com/Family-Systems-Counseling-Innovations-Then-and-Now/book-series/FSCTN.

A Family Systems Guide to Infidelity

Helping Couples Understand, Recover From, and Avoid Future Affairs

Paul R. Peluso

NEW YORK AND LONDON

First published 2019
by Routledge
711 Third Avenue, New York, NY 10017

and by Routledge
2 Park Square, Milton Park, Abingdon, Oxon, OX14 4RN

Routledge is an imprint of the Taylor & Francis Group, an informa business

Library of Congress Cataloging-in-Publication Data
Names: Peluso, Paul R., author.
Title: A family systems guide to infidelity : helping couples understand, recover from, and avoid future affairs / Paul R. Peluso.
Other titles: Family systems counseling: innovations then and now.
Description: New York : Routledge, 2018. | Series: Family systems counseling: innovations then and now | Includes bibliographical references and subject index.
Identifiers: LCCN 2018007122 | ISBN 9780415787765 (hardcover : alk. paper) | ISBN 9780415787772 (pbk. : alk. paper) | ISBN 9781315225739 (e-book)
Subjects: MESH: Couples Therapy—methods | Interpersonal Relations | Family Conflict—psychology | Models, Psychological | Extramarital Relations
Classification: LCC RC488.5 | NLM WM 430.5.M3 | DDC 616.89/1562—dc23
LC record available at https://lccn.loc.gov/2018007122

ISBN: 978-0-415-78776-5 (hbk)
ISBN: 978-0-415-78777-2 (pbk)
ISBN: 978-1-315-22573-9 (ebk)

Typeset in Minion
by Apex CoVantage, LLC

This book is lovingly dedicated to the memory of Jon Carlson, EdD, PsyD (1945–2017), for his hard work and commitment to the field of couples and family therapy, as well as for his devotion, mentorship, and friendship to me over the past 20 years.

Contents

Series Foreword

Family Systems Theory, or Systemic Family Therapy (and everything that followed from it), was based on a "crazy" idea. No, literally, it was. In the 1950s Murray Bowen and his team attempted to work with the one condition that neither the Freudian Psychoanalysts or the Skinnerian Behaviorists were able to effect any change: schizophrenia. He decided that the disease was formed and maintained within the emotional processes (or "system") of the family and that only by changing the family system could the individual patient's schizophrenic symptoms (delusions, hallucinations, etc.) be abated. *That* was the crazy idea, and it sparked a movement that revolutionized the way that children, couples, and even individuals (to say nothing of families) were treated.

One of the guiding forces for Bowen (and subsequently other practitioners) was the work of Gregory Bateson in General Systems Theory. Ideas like feedback and homeostasis took practitioners away from the focus on strict, linear "cause and effect" and instead ushered into the practice of psychotherapy and counseling the idea of circular causality, where each member of the system impacts other members (and vice versa). The search for a person to "blame" for a family's problems was replaced with an exploration of system-wide communication, disrupting problematic interactions and creating collaborative solutions that required everyone's cooperation.

The methods that these early pioneers would employ were equally as radical. Some would do literally *anything* to disrupt a family's dysfunctional processes and try to effect change. From Salvador Minuchin watching families with anorexia eating meals together, to Carl Whitaker pretending to fall asleep while couples bickered, to the Milan group calling families in between sessions and giving homework "rituals" for families to complete, to Jay Haley prescribing "ordeals" for clients, or to Virginia Satir physically moving family members around to communicate more clearly or experience a perspective change, these were all radical uses of systems theory to help families in pain. These clinicians were creative, courageous, and, at times, counter-intuitive. And while some of their practices might seem odd, outlandish, or even borderline *unethical* to us today, the underlying principle was to disrupt the family's unhealthy systemic functioning and replace it with a healthier systemic functioning. They wanted everyone to change altogether, not just make individual change. They recognized that this required a boldness and a commitment to the principles of systems theory that underlie all couples and family therapies today.

However, today many practicing couples and family therapists do not fully understand or embrace the systemic approach that gave family therapy its power. This is in part due to the rise of the cognitive-behavioral approach, which emphasized individual thought over systemic communication. Related to this, the rise of the evidence-based movement made studying systemic change more difficult than individual change (which Cognitive Behavioral Therapy was able to do well). Last, there was the rise of "managed care," which changed the way practitioners were paid by insurance companies by emphasizing limits on individual sessions (and virtually eliminating reimbursement for family therapy sessions). These movements, taken together over the last 25 years, have drastically changed the training of couples and family therapists as well as the practice of couples and family therapy. It has taken away much of the original systems focus (and thus the power) of family therapy approaches. At the same time, many private practitioners and agency providers find that they frequently have situations that call for them to provide family therapy, couples counseling, or some type of consultation for parenting or relational issues. Often they have to "wing it" and try to apply individual therapy models to family systems work; however, this is ultimately frustrating to clinicians and leads to poor outcomes for clients.

This series is aimed at both current practitioners and students who wish to learn about the historical power and boldness of the family systems approach but who also need to see it applied to current problem situations. The books in this series will, where possible, reflect on the pioneering elements of family systems approaches and how they might have been used previously with a particular issue or population. Where some of the historical approaches might be unacceptable by today's standards, authors will be asked to provide a contextually based discussion of relevant issues from all sides of the approach (in favor of and opposed to) in the hopes of synthesizing a dialectical solution that reflects the original intent of systemic change.

Paul R. Peluso
Boca Raton, FL
January 2018

Acknowledgments

I would like to thank all the people at Routledge, but especially Mr. George Zimmar, who was instrumental in the creation of this text, as well as for believing in this new series. I would also like to thank Ms. Elizabeth Graber, who helped in the creation of the series, for her encouragement to me during its early formation. She has been gracious, fair, gentle, thoughtful, and honest in her helpfulness, and for that I am most grateful. In addition, I would like to thank my family, especially my wife, Jenny, and my daughters, Helen and Lucy. I spent many hours cooped up to complete this, and they gave me the time and space to do so. Thank you! I am also grateful for my colleagues in the Department of Counselor Education at Florida Atlantic University. I am also indebted to the students of the Alliance Lab at FAU (the "Avengers"), who have been my encouragers and collaborators in many endeavors. Finally, I would like to express gratitude to my mentors, who have given me their wisdom and guidance. They include Roy Kern, Gus Napier, Jon Carlson, Jeffrey Kottler, Paul Ekman, and John and Julie Gottman. I am also indebted to the countless couples with whom I have worked over the years who were instrumental in shaping my thinking and approach. These nameless individuals were the inspiration for the clinical case examples contained in this book.

CHAPTER 1

Introduction and Overview

Consider the following . . .

- *A young couple married less than 10 years decide to separate following the discovery of multiple affairs on the part of the wife, including the night before their wedding.*
- *A former presidential candidate admits he had a sexual relationship with a woman, and fathered a child with her, while his wife was battling terminal cancer.*
- *A couple that has been married for over 20 years, in a shocking disclosure to their friends and close family members, announce that they are divorcing after discovering that the husband has had an ongoing affair.*
- *A governor whose rise to power was tied to a career as a federal prosecutor fighting corruption is caught in a prostitution ring, reportedly using multiple call girls for sexual encounters.*
- *A woman reconnects on Facebook with a former lover that she has not seen in 15 years and admits that all throughout her 12-year marriage, she has never stopped loving him. She has a sexual affair and leaves her husband.*
- *Another governor who came to office promoting "traditional family values" is reported missing and unreachable. At first he is described as "alone hiking the Appalachian Trail." However, when he is found, he discloses that he has been having an affair with a woman in Argentina, whom he calls his "soul mate," despite his 20-year marriage to his wife.*
- *A married couple, with a 2-year-old child, separate after the husband has an affair with a co-worker. He states that the pressures of parenthood and the changes to his wife no longer made her attractive to him.*

How could these things happen? Is there any way to understand what makes a couple that look so happy to many people take this step to risk personal shame and ridicule? Infidelity—affairs, cheating, "emotional affairs," "Internet/cyber affairs"—are all devastating to a relationship. It is just as corrosive to a relationship as spilling an acid or liquid chlorine on a piece of clothing—it eats it away. It tears away the trust between two people and leaves them feeling lost and vulnerable.

One reason couples feel this way is because after an affair you can't go *back* to the way things were before. That part of their life is (suddenly) over, and the dreams that went with it are shattered. Often couples want to know *how* it could have happened or *why* it happened.

Another reason couples in a relationship feel lost and vulnerable is because the offended spouses don't know if they can *trust* anyone, anymore. They can no longer trust their partner—usually the person they were able to confide in (or so they thought). Often, they can't trust the world around them because nothing seems dependable anymore. And finally, they cannot trust themselves because they blame themselves for failing to recognize that their partner was slipping away from them and into the arms of another person.

Last, after an affair the couple doesn't know *how* to move forward. Partners don't even know if they can. After learning that the person they loved has done one of the most *hurtful* things that they can imagine, it can be overwhelming and downright scary for the other partner to think about moving on—regardless of whether they break apart or stay together.

The Need for This Book

Couples Counseling's Dirty Little Secret About Infidelity

So what is a person to do? Many couples will (sometimes reluctantly) go to couples counseling. Unfortunately, the odds here aren't very good. Many couples counselors aren't specifically trained—and don't feel very comfortable—treating couples where infidelity is the primary issue. What's even more amazing is that they don't feel comfortable and are not specifically trained to treat infidelity *even though it is the most common reasons for couples coming into counseling*. That is like going to a medical doctor who cannot treat for the common cold! It makes no sense (Labrecque & Whisman, 2018; Softas-Nall, Beadle, Newell, & Helm, 2008; Whisman, Dixon, & Johnson, 1997).

Why is this the case? First, they are not specifically trained to understand or treat infidelity issues. Despite all of the news reports and tell-all books, there are only a handful of professional couples counselors who *really* know how to treat infidelity. The rest never get any training on the subject and are forced to "figure it out" (usually at the expense of the couples they are trying to treat). Second, many therapists fail to use the couple's emotional responses. The raw emotional energy that is released when an affair is discovered can be used to power *real* change in a relationship, if it is properly used. Unfortunately, many couples therapists try to diffuse this emotion, thinking that it is destructive and hurtful to the relationship. Paradoxically, if it is not directed properly, it usually *does* damage the relationship. But, if this energy is wasted, most relationships will either freeze in place (and bury the underlying issue that drove them toward the infidelity) or will disintegrate and break apart under the weight of the doubt and mistrust.

In other words, couples dealing with infidelity feel lost, the couples counselor feels lost, and, eventually, all hope is lost and any chance for healing is squandered away.

But It Doesn't Have To Be That Way

This book addresses the issue of treating infidelity. Over the last decade, this topic has continued to grow in magnitude and impact for couples and for clinicians. From high-profile cases, to the advent of the "Ashley Madison" website (and others) that explicitly helps married individuals have an affair, infidelity remains the number one issue that couples present with, and it is the issue that clinicians feel the least prepared to treat. Researchers have shown that clinicians who have the ability to provide a systematic conceptualization that helps the client understand the causes of infidelity, and then have a planned method of treatment that they can readily articulate to couples, have significantly better outcomes with clients. By taking a family systems approach, this book outlines a three-step model which can provide both an *explanatory* model and a *treatment* model for clients. We will discuss these in detail in the chapters that follow. But, first, we need to define the scope of the problem and the terms that will be used.

Statistics on the Prevalence of Infidelity

So what is the story on infidelity? Do we have a good handle on its prevalence? The reality is that statistics on infidelity in couples vary widely. Some reports have estimates that range from 25% to over 50% of individuals reporting engaging in an extramarital affair (Starratt, Weekes-Shackelford, & Shackelford, 2017; Weiser & Weigel, 2015). In the dating population, these figures can rise from as high as 70% for women and 75% for men (Shackelford & Buss, 1997). And estimates in gay, lesbian, and bisexual relationships also can be widely varying. However, there is a problem with some of the figures that are thrown around as "definitive." First, they are usually based on a very limited convenience sample (web-based surveys, surveys of individuals in treatment, etc.). Second, many are based on samples that are not randomized or drawn from the general population. Third, if studies are not anonymous, individual respondents may be less willing to be truthful with their answers. As a result, the generalizability of the findings is very limited (Labrecque & Whisman, 2017).

The best information comes from large, national surveys. The University of Chicago conducts the General Social Survey, a multiwave survey that has sampled households in the United States every two years since 1972. Each wave of participants is new and represents a cross-section of the general adult population (18 years and older). The questions range from general health to relationship issues. Labrecque and Whisman (2017) examined over 13,000 responses from nine waves spanning from 2000 to 2016 to see how people's responses to questions related to extramarital sex have changed, or remained the same, over the last 16 years. Overall, 3% of married individuals in a given year will report having extramarital sex. Lifetime rates of infidelity for married couples range from 22%–25% of men and 11%–15% of women. Tafoya and Spitzberg (2007) conducted a meta-analysis of 50 studies and found that 24% of women and 34% of men have engaged in extramarital sexual activities.

An interesting trend that has emerged is that the prevalence of infidelity increases as people age. Williamson and Brimhall (2017) reviewed the General Social Survey waves that spanned from 1991 to 2006 (15 years of data). They found that the lifetime rate of infidelity over the age of 60 was 28% in 2008 (up from 20% in 1991). For women, the increases were even sharper, rising from 5% in 1991 to 15% in 2006. They speculated:

> While many potential explanations exist, many scholars wonder if this increased rate of infidelity is one reason that recent statistics indicate that divorce rates have doubled among persons aged 50 and older and that 25% of the divorces in 2010 included a person over age 50.
>
> (Williamson & Brimhall, 2017, p. 233)

In addition, they posited four potential reasons for these findings, including changes in values and interests amongst the couple, adjusting to illnesses and other physical changes, loss of identity post-retirement, and social isolation and loneliness. These findings and explanations are significant considering that the American population is living longer, which puts increased stress on relationships (Peluso, Watts, & Parsons, 2013).

Underscoring the significant societal pressures on individuals who have affairs, an overwhelming majority of people (91%), according to a 2013 Gallup poll, stated that they felt that having an affair is morally wrong. However, in the General Social Survey, the percentage of adults who reported that extramarital sex was "always wrong" significantly declined from 79.4% in 2000 to 75.8% in 2016 (Labrecque & Whisman, 2017). At the same time, the percentage of respondents who reported that extramarital sex was wrong "only sometimes" significantly increased from 7.1% in 2000 to 8.7% in 2016, while the percentage of individuals who thought it was "always wrong" and "never wrong" remained constant (11.8% and 1.9%, respectively).

So the bottom line is that there are some subtle shifts in the rates and perceptions of infidelity. There is some reason to believe that the lifetime and per-year rates of infidelity remain relatively stable. The *perceptions* of infidelity in the general population have shifted as well, with people generally thinking that infidelity is wrong, although there does seem to be some softening of the absolute view of infidelity as wrong. Last, it seems that there are increases in older populations (over age 60) in the rates of reported infidelity. But there is a human story here as well.

Definition of Infidelity

There are some areas of clear agreement and disagreement when it comes to the definition of infidelity. According to Moller and Vossler (2015), the disagreement about what constitutes infidelity is the single greatest reason for the wide discrepancies in the rates of infidelity that are reported in the literature (from as little as 1% to as much as 86%). They suggest that definitions for infidelity that are used by researchers commonly fall into one of three categories: (1) infidelity as sexual intercourse, (2) infidelity as extra-dyadic sexual activities, and (3) infidelity as emotional betrayal. Each of these will be discussed in the following.

Infidelity as Sexual Intercourse

On the one hand, this might be the most self-evident definition of infidelity, and there would be little disagreement that this *is* at the center of infidelity. If one person in a committed relationship engages in sexual intercourse with another person outside of that relationship, then it is infidelity. At the same time, however, there are several groups of individuals who would dispute this as *the* definition of infidelity. Polyamorous couples may not define sexual intercourse as infidelity as long as agreements that are made about sexual contact are kept (Rassmussen & Kilbore, 2007). In some same-sex couples (particularly male same-sex couples), open arrangements are common, with negotiated rules around safety (Shernoff, 2007). Put simply, some couples do not agree that commitment and sexual activity with other people are incompatible with one another. Indeed, contextual and cultural factors also play a role. According to Moller and Vossler: "sexual intercourse may not be very helpful for understanding what infidelity actually means to people" (2015, p. 488). As a result, a strict definition of infidelity as sexual intercourse may be too restrictive.

Infidelity as Extra-Dyadic Sexual Activities

If the aforementioned definition tightly defines infidelity, broadening it to include other sexual behaviors (that do not include penetrative sex) exposes a wide continuum of possibilities. Extra-dyadic sexual activities includes behaviors like "masturbating in the presence of another, performing oral sex, engaging in sexual play, kissing, flirting, visiting strip clubs, watching pornography, and having sexual fantasies about a person other than the partner" (Moller & Vossler, 2015, p. 488). In addition, including Internet activities like cybersex, sexting, online flirting, and online pornography introduces a whole new realm of issues. Some people argue that since these activates explicitly do not include intercourse, then they can be wholly consistent with the idea of remaining *faithful*. On the other hand, there are many people who consider any or all of these activities, outside of the primary relationship, to be a violation of the relationship. The problem comes when each person in a couple has contradictory views. The failure to agree can create tremendous conflict when one partner discovers the other engaging in activity they feel is inconsistent with a faithful relationship, but the other person does not think it is "that big of a deal." Sometimes people caught in extra-dyadic sexual activities want this to be true (that it isn't a "big deal") so they don't have to admit to doing something wrong in their relationship. Sometimes it is the other partner who wants to believe this because then they don't have to deal with the issue of being "cheated" on (after all, it *wasn't* sex . . .). The biggest problem is that these perspectives are not discussed by the couple explicitly or ahead of time. Often, issues of sex and sexual behavior are buried and "go underground." As a result, one partner may do these activities (whether it is going to a strip club or watching porn online) secretly without the other person knowing. That is where the third definition comes in!

Infidelity as (Emotional) Betrayal

"Emotional infidelity" is a loose term that is used to describe relationships where significant emotional connection is formed with another person outside of the primary relationship but has not (yet) become sexual (and may not *ever* become sexual). According to Moller and Vossler (2015):

> Emotional infidelity has been operationalized in various rather vague ways, including "deep emotional attachment" and "falling in love with another person" . . . ; feeling "deeply connected". . . ; an investment of romantic love, time, and attention in a person other than the primary partner . . . ; sharing intimate details; discussing complaints about the primary partner and meeting for an alcoholic drink.
>
> (p. 488–489)

The common element is the secrecy of the relationship or the secrecy about the depth of the emotional connection. Often, the partner knows of the relationship, and may know the other person, but may not know the significance of the connection. In addition, if the significance of the relationship was revealed, the partner would likely feel a sense of betrayal. The downside to this definition of infidelity is that it can be too broad, since any activity or relationship that is secretive in nature can constitute a betrayal. One concern is that the term *infidelity* and the meaning of the term becomes overly "watered down" and begins to lose its significance. On the other hand, many researchers and practitioners prefer to define infidelity in terms of behaviors that violate couple norms or break a couple's contract and circumvent agreed-upon assumptions about exclusivity in the relationship (Hertlein, Wetchler, & Piercy, 2005).

So What Is My Take?

My experience is that it is a "merry-go-round" question. You can go 'round and 'round but you'll never get a good answer about what *is* and *isn't* infidelity. I prefer to think of it like a tumor (sorry, I know it is a rough metaphor, but bear with me). Some tumors are benign—an abnormal growth of cells that is not spreading or life threatening. Other cancers are malignant—they have spread to other areas of the body and may be life threatening. Most malignant cancers started out benignly but were not detected and began to spread. The point is that both types—benign and malignant—need attention: the benign ones to protect them from becoming malignant, and the malignant ones to prevent them from being life threatening. And while no one would deny that cancer is serious (no matter what type), infidelities—no matter what type, sexual or non-sexual—are a serious threat to a relationship.

For the couples counselor, there are two issues to be cautious about. The first is not to be caught in a triangle with the couple. Getting caught in a debate about what "is" or "is not" infidelity is one of those "no-win" clinical situations that can sabotage counseling. The best strategy (unless you have a firm position about this) is to allow for the couple to wrestle with this with each other. Letting them come to a decision about how each of them define infidelity can be a good diagnostic tool about the overall functioning of the couple (for example: Do they fight fair? Do they avoid conflict and are deferential but sweep discord under the rug? And so on.). The second "trap" is the couple looking to you to be the "referee" who rules what is "in bounds" and what is "out of bounds." The problem with this (similar to the first problem) is that instead of being an "honest broker," the counselor gets aligned with one partner or the other. And while the partner that gets the "support" may feel vindicated, it is a pyrrhic victory because it will mean that the therapy will go nowhere as the other person feels that the counselor does not support them or "have their back." When this happens, the chances of the therapy being successful are all but lost.

So what is the answer? Focusing on the couple as a system is the key! This is the major thesis of the book and will be discussed in greater detail in Chapter 2 (and beyond).

Common Questions/Myths and Facts About Infidelity

Before we begin, there are four common questions/myths to get clear about infidelity.

1 Are All Affairs Equal(Ly Bad)?

The reality is that it is a common myth that infidelity spells an immediate and automatic end to a relationship or marriage. While many relationships do dissolve in the wake of an infidelity, research shows that the majority of relationships where there is an infidelity remain intact. The reality is that there are many relationships that are sexual satisfying to the partners, but for various reasons (that will be detailed later), an outside relationship is pursued. There are *some* types of infidelity that are indicative of individual issues (sexual addiction), regardless of what the spouse does. Those issues need specialized treatment. In addition, there is a myth that in relationships where there is an infidelity, the sex is bad. The more important question is whether the couple's relationship is changed as a result of the experience (and some good couples counseling!) and if the underlying issues that allowed the infidelity to occur are sufficiently addressed (see Chapter 2 for more details).

2 Who Is to Blame for Affairs? The Cheater, the Partner, or the "Other Person"?

Is the answer to this "multiple choice" question A, B, or C? This is actually a trick question! The reality is that for systems-oriented therapists, the answer is "all of the above." Again, from a systems perspective, this is a key principle that all of the individuals are responsible and none are to blame. There will be more about this in Chapter 2 as well.

3 Does the Relationship With the "Other Person" Have to End?

The answer to this is complicated: yes and no. The relationship with the "other person" does not necessarily have to end. Depending on the goals of the couple in the primary relationship (Are they working improve the relationship? Do they refuse to work on the relationship? Or are they trying to end the relationship?), there may be a compelling reason to continue the relationship with the "other person." There may also be compelling reasons why the relationship *can't* be broken off (the person is a co-worker and leaving a job is impossible). However, unless the relationship with the other person is *radically* changed, there isn't much hope that the primary couple's relationship can be helped with treatment. For some couples, the primary relationship may be beyond repair, and the "other person" may represent a significant emotional attachment. There may be practical reasons to keep a relationship with the "other person" (if they become the next spouse or there are children that need to be co-parented). Again, it will depend on the goals of the primary couple relationship following the disclosure of the affair.

4 Can a Relationship Be Healed After an Affair?

Often I am asked, "Can a marriage really be saved after an infidelity?" Frankly, that is not an easy question to answer. It really does depend on the couple and their willingness to work on healing the marriage. However, it is possible for a marriage to get even stronger following an infidelity. The best analogy to describe this is what happens to broken bones. These are painful injuries that can incapacitate a person, and it is not a simple healing process. Think of what you need to do when a bone is broken. First, it has to be set—that is, jarred from its broken place into its proper place. That is a sharply painful process, but it lets the healing begin. Then you need to place the limb with the broken bone in a cast to immobilize it. This means you have to do things you would not normally do with it (generally can't shower with it unless it is wrapped in plastic, may need help getting clothes on, etc.). You also can't do the things you would normally do with it (can't play sports or any strenuous activity, mobility is limited, etc.). However, if the bone is set properly, and allowed to heal, the bone is often stronger at the breakpoint than it was before the break. I think that this is true of marriages (or relationships in general) when there is an infidelity.

The Current Book

This book attempts to cover the issue of infidelity and its treatment by couples counselors. Specifically, the text views infidelity (and its treatment) from a systems theory perspective. It utilizes case studies drawn from clinical practice (although with key information obscured, changed, or amalgamated to prevent any disclosure) to illustrate various concepts. In addition, two other elements are included: using case examples from public or historical figures and using scenarios drawn from popular movies. Consider the following movie example.

Movie: *A Walk on the Moon*

In the 1999 movie *A Walk on the Moon*, Diane Lane plays Pearl, a middle-aged housewife in the summer of 1969. She is married with two children (an adolescent daughter and a middle school–aged son). Her husband, Marty, a TV repair man (played by Liev Schreiber) is devoted to her but preoccupied with work. They live in New York City but spend the summer at a summer camp in upstate New York (close to the site of the Woodstock music festival). Marty must work during the week, so Pearl is left alone with the children and her mother-in-law. It is revealed that Pearl and Marty were forced to marry when Pearl was 17 because she got pregnant. She always felt like she missed out on her youth because of the responsibilities of being a wife and mother.

A traveling blouse salesman, Walker (played by Viggo Mortensen), arrives into town, and she begins a relationship with him. First, he flatters her by getting her to try less matronly looking blouses, and soon she begins to think about what her life could have been like. When the moon landing creates a big business opportunity for Marty, he stays in the city, and Pearl begins a sexual affair with Walker. Immediately she resolves to break off the relationship, but Walker pursues her. The next significant event is the Woodstock festival, which prevents Marty from getting to the summer camp. Pearl attends the festival with Walker, and they continue the affair, after which Walker invites Pearl to move to California with him. She experiences personal freedom (through the use of drugs at Woodstock and her continued affair with Walker) and begins to imagine a life apart from her family. Ultimately (after the affair is disclosed to Marty), she must choose between her life at home with her children and husband, and her dreams of a life apart where she pursues her passions. However, when Walker sees her with her family, both she and he know that their relationship was just a fantasy and that she cannot go with him.

In the movie example, a common theme in an infidelity is captured: the power of fantasy and freedom. Often an the affair has tremendous power over someone because it offers them the chance to break free of what they thought was "imprisoning" them (namely their home life/primary relationship). However, for many people, the cost of the "freedom" is not a price they want to pay, as in the case with Pearl. At the end of the move, it is hinted that Marty and Pearl's relationship *may* get better as she finds a way to incorporate some of her desires and passions into her relationship with Marty. This may be somewhat idealized (it is a movie, after all), but it is also the potential for transformation that an infidelity can offer a couple.

Finally, this book follows a three-step model for explaining and understanding the development of infidelity in a couple and then an explanatory model that will guide treatment and help couples and clinicians navigate the necessary steps to rebuild trust in the relationship following the disclosure of an infidelity. In the next chapter, aspects of General Systems Theory will be presented, along with some systemic conceptualizations of infidelity, as well as the three-step model.

CHAPTER 2

Historical Family Systems Review and Current State of the Art

Janet couldn't believe it. When Chuck told her that he had been having an affair for the last 3 years, her first thought was, "Oh my God, I have become my mother." She flashed back to when her mother had caught her father cheating. Janet had sworn that she would never marry a cheater. And now, here she was. She wondered if she had done something to cause it. Was this a predestined pattern that was always going to happen?

Systems are governed by rules. Whether it is a mechanical system (like an air conditioner), a natural system (like the water cycle), or a human system (like a classroom), all systems have rules that dictate how the elements within the system behave. Couples also exist in a system, and because of this, infidelity also occurs within a system. The question is, does the infidelity represent a breaking of the rules that governed the couples' system, or was it in accordance with the rules of the system? This is an important question that couples counselors must help couples determine. However, in order to be able to do this, clinicians must be able to conceptualize the relationship using systems theory.

This chapter details the basic concepts of systems theory that are important for couples counselors to understand (particularly with regards to treating infidelity). In addition, several systems theory principles specifically related to conceptualizing and treating infidelity are presented, along with a typology of affairs that is systems theory oriented. Last, a three-step explanatory and treatment model of infidelity for couples counselors will be presented that is systems based.

Basic Concepts of Systems Theory

Boundaries

According to Keim and Lappin (2002), *boundaries* are defined as "the degree of emotional connection, dependence, support, and influence between different subsystems within the family, and between these subsystems and other social systems" (p. 93). Boundaries are lines of demarcation in a relationship that may be explicitly agreed to, or implicitly agreed to, by both partners. In healthy relationships, boundaries are clear and help the couple function effectively. Boundaries can be thought of as a continuum ranging from enmeshed (extreme togetherness) to rigid (extreme separateness). Enmeshment is a state of the relationship characterized by intense dependence on the partner for emotional stability to the point where independence and autonomy are perceived as threats to the homeostasis of the couple. Change is actively resisted by the partner or the couple, and the relationship can become stifling or constricting. Boundaries also define what is and isn't allowed in the relationship. Often problems occur when a boundary is violated or ignored. In the case of infidelity, often the act of sex outside of the relationship is a significant boundary crossing or violation. Understanding the boundaries in the relationship, their origins, and how to restore them is crucial in treating infidelity.

Hierarchy

The term *hierarchy* refers to the fact that systems have several different levels. Hierarchies can be thought of as the arrangement of the boundaries within a system. For example, is the hierarchy more equal or democratic, or is it more vertical (like a command structure)? Hierarchies can influence how information flows (shared freely or tightly controlled), and how decisions are made (someone "calling the shots" or consensus being reached). However, a hierarchy can also be oppressive and dominating if it is unbalanced. Healthy couple relationships require the perception of a hierarchical balance (Keim & Lappin, 2002; Peluso & Sperry, 2018; Roberto-Forman, 2002). With infidelity, often rigid and "vertical" (one person "on top" or in charge) hierarchies play a key role (more on this will be detailed later and in Chapter 4).

Homeostasis

Homeostasis is the tendency of a system to remain constant. Systems require some semblance of order to be able to function, and a homeostatic set point is the place of optimal functioning for any given system. Even highly chaotic systems have equilibrium or balance (even if, on the outside, it doesn't appear that way). Systems regulate the status quo (or homeostasis) by resisting change. Increases in tension or anxiety within the relationship cause disequilibrium and heighten resistance to change. Even if change is good or necessary, unless the system is prepared for change (and a new homeostatic set point), it will resist the change (Roberto-Forman, 2002; Sperry & Peluso, 2018). Couples use various mechanisms, both positive and negative, to maintain balance and stability. In addition, partners may use extreme behavior in order to bring a relationship back into balance, such as having an affair if the partner is a workaholic and doesn't spend time with them. The affair can also be an extreme way to create a new homeostatic set point by changing the nature of the relationship such that it can never go back to the way it was before.

Triangles/Coalitions

When a couple gets into conflict, there is no majority rule, which often leads to a stalemate. Couples who are frequently in conflict usually develop instability in the relationship because they are caught between wanting to be close to their partner and wanting to maintain distance. Triangulation, when a third party is brought into the conflict in order to side with one of the partners, allows for the tension to be diffused and a stalemate to be broken. This is a major factor when trying to understand infidelity from a systems perspective. One partner may feel justified and vindicated, and the other may feel abandoned or unfairly ganged up on by the presence of the third party. In addition, the coalition or triangle (in the case of infidelity) allows for underlying dynamics to go unresolved (see "Typology of Affairs," following). Inevitably, triangles lead to resentment and disengagement from one another, particularly when problems need to be solved (Keim & Lappin, 2002; Sperry & Peluso, 2018).

Communication

In systems theory, the concept of communication is inclusive of all behavior. Verbal communication and nonverbal communication are equally important. Patterns of communication provide clues to the relative openness/closeness of the system, as well as help shape the behavior and functioning of family members. Communication is the feedback loop that maintains equilibrium within the system. Positive communication produces growth and development and balances the consistency of the system. Negative communication is a feedback process that is used to correct system deviations by reestablishing a previous state of equilibrium (Sperry & Peluso, 2018). This process is usually at work in couples where there is infidelity as an "acting out" usually in order to bring the other partner back.

A special pattern of communication that can often create (and maintain) problematic behavior is called a "double bind." A double bind is a type of communication where the person who has to respond can't answer in a way that is positive (i.e., "damned if you do, damned if you don't"). A double bind contains a double message (e.g., "Do what I tell you, but don't comment on any hypocrisy you notice") and some implied threat ("or else I will leave you/withdraw my love and affection for you . . ."). An example of a double bind would be one partner saying to the other: "No, go ahead, spend the weekend with you mother. I'll just stay here and work because we're in so much debt because of your spending. I just hope I don't get too lonely without you . . ." Here there is a double message (spend the weekend with your parents/I'll just keep working) and a threat (I may find someone else if you leave). The partner is unable to respond to the message without "losing" (if she goes, she'll be a jerk for leaving; if she tries to stay, she'll lose out on spending time with her family). In other words, there is no winning.

Systems theorists are also concerned with a communication process known as meta-communication, which is communication about communication. This term usually refers to the covert, nonverbal message (tone of voice, inflection, body language) that gives additional meaning to an overt, verbal message. In couples therapy, the meta-communication level is a method for understanding the subtle messages each person is conveying, as well as what that communication says about underlying system dynamics (Sperry & Peluso, 2018). Often this level of communication reveals more about the real state of affairs (pun intended!) in a relationship.

Circular Causality

This is a concept of systems theory where both parties are involved in any problem. One partner influences the other and vice versa. Does Jim have an affair because Jane nags him, or does Jane nag him because Jim is having an affair? The answer is, of course, both. Frequently this will elicit resistance from the clients as it holds both individuals responsible (at least partially), particularly when the homeostatic set point of the relationship is that one partner is the victim in the relationship and the other the perpetrator. For the clinician, the concept of circular causality means that the therapist does not have to search for a "cause" per se but can intervene from any one of several starting points and be successful. Any change in one aspect in one partner will affect the other (Sperry & Peluso, 2018). In addition, the therapist does not have to buy into the victim/perpetrator model that unproductively seeks blame and retribution (which often gets in the way of real progress in couples therapy).

Nonsummativity

Nonsummativity is the idea that the whole is greater than the sum of its parts. Any relationship is not simply the product of each individual's partner's traits or qualities, but rather is a system that is created as a result of the relationship of the two people. There are characteristics of the system and patterns of interactions that are separate and different than each individual in the system (Sperry & Peluso, 2018). For example, both partners may be great at leading other people in their work, but in the relationship they may not be able to influence the other partner. As a result, the relationship never seems to be able to make decisions or come to an agreement. Summing up the parts does not provide the whole picture. That can be done only by looking at the picture as a whole. It is the difference between a car that drives and a disassembled pile of parts that make up a car. Both are examples of complete cars, but the assembled one has a different quality about it. Same with couples' systems. It is necessary to look at the parts and understand them *as well as* pay attention to the pattern that is created by them. The clinician must similarly look for the larger pattern that encompasses the couple and the individual characteristics and behaviors that form a couple's relationship.

First- and Second-Order Change

According to Watzlawick, Weakland, and Fisch (1974), change can happen at either the first-order or second-order level. *First-order change* is a change in a system that leaves the underlying structures or organization of the system unchanged. It is relatively superficial in nature, and the change is on the behavioral level that may reduce a symptom or resolve surface issues. It does not change any of the boundaries or relationships within the system. Examples may include clarifying agreements on tasks like cooking or laundry. It can also be changing a behavior like smoking. If the relationship is relatively healthy and stable, then simple interventions or agreements will be sufficient to make meaningful change. However, if the relationship has deeper, underlying issues (as with the cases of many infidelities), then merely addressing the first-order change may temporarily halt destructive behaviors, but it will not substantially change the relationship (and often the problem behavior returns after a short while).

Second-order change refers to adjustments that change the organization of the system in very substantial and fundamental ways. Second-order change is a change in the way a couple interacts with one another and relates to themselves, the other person, and the relationship itself. There may be changes in the attitude of one or both partners, which usually results in new behaviors and a reordering of the relational dynamics. The systemic dynamic that created and maintained the problem (because it maintained the equilibrium) no longer has the power or ability to keep creating problems. For example, if alcohol use was a source of conflict in the relationship (creating bitterness and contempt from both partners), then merely giving up drinking (but not the resentment) would be first-order change. But if both partners realized the alcohol was covering up feelings of loneliness and disengagement, and instead focused on creating meaningful connection with one another, the need for problematic alcohol abuse would likely disappear. There would be other forces in the system that would be more attractive and beneficial than alcohol use. That is second-order change. It requires a good-faith commitment from both partners in the couple to change their system dynamics. While it depends on the circumstances, generally second-order change is considered better than first-order change because it changes the structures or boundaries within the system (Sperry & Peluso, 2018).

Paradoxical Interventions

Paradoxical interventions are therapeutic approaches that clinicians take in order to make systemic and second-order change. A simple definition is that a paradox contains both a statement and its opposite. So it cannot be literally true. But at the same time, it is. So there is a logical inconsistency, which can create new meanings. For example, in the famous Carly Simon song "You're So Vain" the refrain states: "You're so vain/You probably think this song is about you." This is paradoxical because if the person *wasn't* vain they *wouldn't* think the song was about them, but *because* they are vain, they think the song *is* about them (and it is!). Often (although not always) there is humor involved. An example is if you had a rock, and carved in it was the statement, "Nothing is written in stone." You would have a paradox. On the one hand, for the statement to be true, it could not be written in the stone. But if it is written in the stone, then the statement cannot be true! Both cannot simultaneously coexist, but they do! In a clinical setting, paradoxical interventions help clients change the way that they see problems (and each other). These interventions can often provide absurd, yet true, interpretations to their circumstances. They can also help clients see a different perspective to their current situations (more on this later in the book, although for a thorough treatment of this topic, see Mozdzierz, Peluso, & Lisiecki, 2014a, 2014b).

Systems Theory and Infidelity

When an infidelity happens, it seems like all the oxygen is metaphorically taken out of the room. For the couple, there is seemingly nothing else but the particulars of the infidelity, the betrayal, and the emotional aftermath. All their conversations seem to be related to it, and there is often (at least in the beginning) nothing else. However, for systemically oriented couples therapists, there is something else to the issue of infidelity. In fact, there are two important systemic principles regarding the lead-up to infidelity and the aftermath of infidelity:

1. The infidelity is *not* the central issue of concern in the relationship, it's a symptom.
2. Both partners had a contributing role in creating the conditions that led to the infidelity.

Both these systemic issues are difficult for couples to wrap their minds around. And, in truth, they are very difficult for many counselors to also conceptualize. It takes a systemic mindset and orientation to understand these two systemic principles. Therapists who embrace the systemic approach know that they will be "going against the grain" and encountering resistance in couples when they come in, especially when dealing with an infidelity. But if a couples counselor can understand these, and if a couples counselor can relate these to a couple struggling with issues of infidelity, the chances of successfully resolving infidelity (to be defined later) go up dramatically.

Systematic Principle 1: The Infidelity Is Not the Central Issue of Concern in the Relationship, It Is a Symptom

At the beginning, this may seem like a difficult concept to grasp. After all, an infidelity has occurred; isn't that the worst possible thing that could happen? And if there is an understanding that the relationship was supposed to be monogamous and lifelong, then yes, it does seem that an infidelity is the worst thing that can happen. However, the reality is that an infidelity reveals something much more problematic in the relationship. More than just the betrayal itself and the erosion of trust, an infidelity reveals that the relationship is in much more jeopardy, at a deeper level than is apparent.

So from a systemic perspective, then, the behavior of the infidelity is a symptom of the deeper issues. Just like a physical symptom, such pain, fever, or cough, is indicative of a viral syndrome or an underlying infection, so too is an infidelity. And just like a medical doctor treats the symptoms (with an analgesic for the pain and fever or a suppressant for the cough), they also treat the underlying cause (with an antibiotic or antiviral drug). Often, this treatment, along with the body's natural healing process, works well enough to take care of the problem or concern.

Sometimes the underlying cause is not treatable with minimal invasion. For example, if a patient complains of pain, but it is in the chest, the underlying cause may not be a bacterial infection but could be blocked coronary arteries. Persistent fever and cough may be an indicator of cancer. In each of these cases, the symptoms may be able to be treated effectively, but if the underlying cause is not treated, the patient could die. It is the same way with couples.

Ever since his mother died, Peter had been a different person. He was more withdrawn and morose. While he was close to his mother, her long illness had prepared them all for her passing, or so Sarah had thought. But when she died, Peter was not able to pull himself out of his grief. Now, a year later, he was not "back to normal," and she was getting impatient. His frequent trips to her graveside and talking to his mother as if she was there in the house were starting to make Janet uncomfortable. Mostly she missed how dependable Peter was. He used to make sure her car was running properly or fix broken things around the house, but now he had no interest. She would try to tell Peter how she was feeling, abandoned and alone, but all Peter would do was bring it back to his loss and emptiness. Before too long, people around her started to notice. In particular, a neighbor who had recently been divorced began to talk to her when he was walking his dog in the neighborhood. Janet had never noticed before, but he had a nice smile and was very good looking . . .

Many times, couples have issues that are like a "common cold" or generic infection. The remedy is relatively mild: learn skills to communicate, share in the chores to be done, be more collaborative with decision making. These are the couples counseling equivalent to chicken soup, a couple of aspirin, and some Penicillin. These will assist the couple to "heal" themselves in a relatively short period of time and then they can move on. But with an infidelity, the issues are much deeper, and true "healing" requires opening up individual and couple-based attitudes and feelings about being in a relationship and about each other.

Systematic Principle 2: Both Partners Had a Contributing Role in Creating the Conditions That Led to the Infidelity

This might be the hardest "sell" for a systemically oriented couples counselor. The reason is that people always want to assign blame for their pain. They want someone to bear the responsibility and often (in a childlike way) want that person to take the pain away. The reality is that if you view the couple as a system, then no one individual is to *blame*, in the traditional sense of the word. Instead, both partners created the conditions that were necessary for the one partner to stray.

Couples therapists who have a solid grounding in systems theory understand that it is the underlying dynamics of the couples system that are to "blame." They also have to be able to win the couple over to this way of conceptualizing their particular issue if they are to be successful. Returning to systemic ideas like homeostasis, nonsummativity, and circular causality, it is the system itself (which was created by the couple) that shaped the context that allowed the infidelity to occur. While both partners may have had a role to play, this is not to say that the partner who had the affair is *not* responsible for his or her individual actions and the consequences. This is a part of the "threading the needle" that systemically oriented couples counselors have to do in order to drive this principle home.

After the affair came to light, Peter was incensed. How could Janet have done that to him? He felt embarrassed and indignant. At the same time, he felt bereft. All in one year he lost his mother and now, seemingly, his wife. Janet, for her part, also felt lost. She always saw herself as a "good" person. But now she felt exposed, like everyone knew everyone judged her. Peter blamed her, and while she first accepted that blame, she now felt like Peter had abandoned her first. What was she going to do? Didn't he know it only would have been a matter of time? Now when he got angry and started to shame her, she would fight back. It would often leave them in a stalemate . . .

In the case of Peter and Janet, the "blame game" has two outcomes, neither of which are good. It is "I Win, but We Lose," where either:

1. One person can take the moral "high ground," because he or she was not the "cheater," but in doing so takes on the role of the victim (and thus "loses"); or
2. The other person claims the "right" to have cheated because he or she was abandoned by the other; in this case, the person is taking on the role of the victim (and thus "loses" as well).

By avoiding the "blame game," the couple can take their focus off themselves or their partner and instead can focus on the couple relationship itself. The benefit for the couple is that each person can be empowered to make a change to the pattern, rather than be defensive. This is the much better "We Win" scenario.

So with these two principles of systems theory application to infidelity, I want to discuss a typology of affairs that has a systems orientation to classifying different affairs according to the underlying dynamics of the couples relationship.

Typology of Affairs

Emily Brown (2001, 2007) produced a typology of affairs. What is so useful about Brown's types of affairs—although derived only by experience, and not necessarily by any empirical evidence—is that infidelity is not viewed as "one size fits all" but rather:

> The type of affair has to do with the interaction pattern between the two spouses and the issues underlying the affair . . . By identifying the message encoded in the affair, the therapist can begin to formulate a plan for treatment. The typology is based on the behavior patterns and emotional dynamics of the couple.
>
> (p. 30)

Originally the five types of affairs were the conflict-avoidance affair, the intimacy-avoidance affair, the sexual addiction affair, the split-self affair, and the exit affair. Recently, Brown has included a sixth type of affair, the entitlement affair. Each will be described in the following.

Conflict-Avoidance Affairs

The Conflict-Avoidance Affair is one in which a couple can't stand up to each other because they fear conflict. The affair screams to the spouse, "I will make you pay attention to me." Couples live with "controlled amiability," actively avoiding provoking the other. However, the straying partner is the more dissatisfied spouse, although both are participating in the "no open conflict" pact. The affair has the effect of temporarily reducing the conflicts around sex, but ultimately this is only a symptom of a deeper issue (in this case, the inability to bring up and resolve conflicts). The partner who has the affair always seems to manage to have the affair discovered, and the discovery makes clear that there are serious problems in the marriage. It usually occurs relatively early in the relationship (although it can occur much later).

Couples who try to please each other by "keeping peace" are typical of conflict-avoiding affairs. They may be perfectionistic and have an idyllic (and somewhat unrealistic) view of what a "good" relationship should be. There may be underlying depression that is masked by "peace" and pseudo-harmony in the relationship. In terms of their makeup and family of origin, Brown says "(t)hose who were taught as a child that anger was bad, who were instructed to 'look at the positive side of things,' or were punished for disagreeing, are likely to have a hard time expressing dissatisfactions" (2001, p. 33). They may view conflict as corrosive or destructive and therefore fear it. *As a result, they don't know how to ask for what they want or to have their needs met.* They often have great difficulty discussing their own personal problems and many times do not even know (or admit) how dissatisfied they are with their life.

In terms of the infidelity itself, the affair is seldom a real threat to the primary relationship, since the underlying purpose is to get the other partner to wake up to the realities of the conflict-avoidance nature of the relationship: "(t)he threat to the marriage is not the affair, but the avoidance of the conflict. The affair becomes a threat only when its message is misinterpreted or ignored" (Brown, 2001, p. 34). For example, if the affair is quickly forgiven and "swept under the rug," then it is a case of "more of the same." This will only perpetuate the underlying dynamic of conflict avoidance and set the conditions for potentially another affair. By the same token, if the relationship ends quickly after the discovery of the affair, without fully understanding the same underlying dynamics, then the same pattern of conflict avoidance will occur in the next relationship.

But this is also the type of affair that, according to Brown, has the best potential for therapeutic success. Some characteristics of this couple in treatment include extreme remorse, guilt, and responsibility on the part of the straying spouse. This can be facilitative in therapy but can also be a way to deflect the partner's anger (thus avoiding conflict). The betrayed spouse may be obsessed with the details of the affair (particularly at first) but may also wish for the therapist to do the "dirty work" of punishing and/or fixing the partner. For the therapist, the most important thing is to keep the underlying conflict and avoidance of conflict front and center in therapy and help each person see how that dynamic played into the affair, as well as the relationship. Ultimate success for this type of affair is the ability to bring up conflicts and resolve them without sweeping them under the rug.

Intimacy-Avoidance Affairs

Intimacy is the central issue in this type of affair. The affair "protects against hurt and disappointment. It is saying 'I don't want to need you so much (so I'll get some of my needs met elsewhere).' Both spouses fear letting down the barriers and becoming emotionally vulnerable" (Brown, 2001, pp. 34–35). As a result, unlike the conflict-avoiding couple, the intimacy-avoidance couple may look (on the surface) like there is more open conflict in the form of arguments and disagreements. These are all usually "smoke screens" that keep them in perpetual turmoil so they don't have to get close to one another (and possibly hurt). The affair becomes a way to find intimacy (or pseudo-intimacy) elsewhere, but when it is discovered, it can also be a source of continuing conflict (thus perpetuating the cycle of intimacy avoidance).

Typically, these affairs begin after the "honeymoon period" of the relationship is over, often a few years into a relationship. The trigger for this type of affair is the realization that there might be considerable potential for vulnerability, which triggers fear (or even panic). Thus, the affair is used to perpetuate the distracting conflict. In terms of the families of origin for these couples, they usually grew up in families where there was a lot of chaos (e.g., alcoholic or abusive households) and where conflicts and arguments were the norm (and, thus, no one demonstrated or felt any intimacy or vulnerability). Since fear of rejection is prevalent, these couples are usually very guarded and hypervigilant to the motives and behavior of the other partner. At the same time, often the only point of emotional contact is the couple's fighting, so avoiding conflict is also not a pleasant option (again, because it risks rejection).

In therapy, these couples will present with a lot of arguments and grievances. Many times they will try to triangulate the therapist and win them over to their side. Often these are "skirmishes" that are designed to bring up complaints that may be legitimate, but their purpose is not to seek resolution or understanding. Areas of conflict can include family, housework, and even sexual ability. The affair becomes a way to be pseudo-intimate with someone else and live out a temporary fantasy of intimacy (he or she "truly understands me"), which becomes leverage over his or her partner. The other partner may also have affairs as "revenge" to get even with the partner. According to Brown, there is a paradoxical nature to Intimacy-Avoidance Affairs: "they embody the pursuit of the romantic fantasy while providing the means to avoid intimacy. The paradox serves nicely to justify the affair while remaining oblivious to one's own difficulties with intimacy" (Brown, 2001, p. 36).

For the therapist, the key to treating these couples is to first get the couple to focus on their intimacy needs and see the fighting as a distraction from true intimacy. Getting the couple to express the wishes and needs underlying the conflict (and the affair) is also important for getting their "buy-in" for working on the relationship (see Chapter 7 for more on this). If the couple can learn how to open themselves up to each other, and risk vulnerability without resorting to arguments and anger to mask their loneliness, then the outlook is positive. If they cannot, and the relationship ends, the likelihood of getting involved in another high-conflict, intimacy-avoiding relationship (with the associated need for affairs) is fairly strong.

Sexual Addiction Affair

When one partner has multiple affairs with different partners that have a compulsive aspect to them, they are usually Sexual Addiction Affairs. According to Brown (2001), "these affairs are the province of those who deal with their emotional neediness by winning battles and making conquests in the hope of gaining love. Emotionally deprived, overwhelmed, or abused as children, they haven't finished growing up" (p. 37). They are often in positions of power (e.g., politics, finance), have attained some success or fame, or seek power. Whom the individual has the affair with is often inconsequential, as it is the pursuit (and inevitably succeeding) that matters. In addition, there is often the addictive nature of risk taking that is embedded in this kind of affair. The idea of breaking the rules and getting away with it is often very intoxicating.

The dynamics of the relationship that define a Sexual Addiction Affair include a spouse who may be cold and indifferent or compartmentalized and weak. So when someone gets caught, it is usually a high-drama event. Sometimes it is an "open secret" that finally gets talked about, and it brings a sense of shame and judgment from other people outside the relationship on the straying partner ("How could he do that?") and on the betrayed partner ("How could she let him do that to her?"). Often the partner doesn't want to see what is right in front of him or her.

For the person engaging in the Sexual Addiction Affair, they may have come from families of origin where they were considered to be "special" or a favorite child of one of the parents. They often come from families where there was an addiction (substances, gambling, sex) and a strong ethos of secret-keeping and "don't talk" rules. On the other hand, individuals involved in a sexual addiction may be victims of abuse themselves. In either case, the underlying dynamic is a sense of internal emptiness and pain and a need to fill the emptiness in order to avoid feeling the pain. As a result, these people go from person to person hoping to find someone to fill their needs, which ultimately fails.

For the other partner, sometimes these children were privy to their parents' affairs and had to carry the secret of them. They may have had fragile parents who could not handle the truth of a partner's affair and as children may have learned to be stronger by keeping silent. However, these individuals may also have had a sexual abuse or trauma history that predisposes them to accept this behavior from their partner because they do not believe they deserve anything better in a relationship.

Treatment for these couples often is highly specialized and focused on the addictive aspects first, before the couples issues. If the partner with the sexual addiction has sought treatment, and has adopted a recovery model, then couples-work can focus on the attachment needs and the entitlement needs that often accompany a Sexual Addiction Affair. Otherwise, the prognosis is for the relationship to continue and for continued relapses to happen as the other spouse continues to look away.

Split-Self Affair

The Split-Self Affair is centered around the idea that individuals have had (or felt they have had) to deny or repress a side to themselves for a period of years in order to keep up a façade of respectability or perceived social norms for a successful family. Often these individuals are concerned with doing the right thing, but at the expense of happiness or fulfillment. "Personal needs were sublimated as they tried to make their family be what they believed a family should be. This often meant focusing the family resources, financial and emotional, on the children" (Brown, 2001, pp. 40–41). Typically, to the outside world, these relationships look like the "perfect" family, and the partners are considered pillars of the community.

Sometimes the partners in the Split-Self Affair will say they had doubts about the marriage initially but ignored them. Maybe they felt that getting married when they did (or to whom they did) was the right thing to do or that it would be a way to gain some security. For both partners in the relationship, they "learned early in life that they were supposed to do the right thing, rather than pay attention to their own needs and feelings. They used their rational selves to survive and succeed" (p. 41). Many times, these individuals are successful personally and professionally, but not emotionally.

In their families of origin, often there may have been issues the individuals are trying to correct, or perfect, in their own families. They want to create the "perfect" family, and they invest emotional energy in attending to the children. However, when that is not satisfying enough, it can produce frustration, confusion, or loneliness. According to Brown (2001):

> In the Split-Self Affair, the marriage feels empty, as opposed to the Sexual Addiction where the individual feels empty. The partners may or may not share a bedroom, any sexual relationship is likely to be pro forma, and they lead very separate lives. Communication is limited to practical matters like taking the garbage out or social necessities.
>
> (p. 41)

In the Beatles song *She's Leaving Home*, Paul McCartney writes of a young British woman who runs away from her staid and solid, working-class family, who gave her material comforts ("We sacrificed most of our lives . . . What did we do that was wrong?"). The answer at the end of the song is because she didn't have "fun" ("Fun is the one thing that money can't buy"), and it is revealed that it was "Something inside that was always denied for so many years." This is reminiscent of the experience of individuals in the Split-Self Affair. The affair offers the opportunity for passion and fun and things that have been denied to one (or both) of the couple over the years. While it may often be seen as part of a "mid-life crisis," it is also reflective of a deeper set of issues.

Many times, the affair can go on for a number of years and may represent a significant relationship that has developed. In fact, the straying partner may be torn between the two relationships and uncertain which one to end. On the one hand, with the Split-Self Affair, the marriage is often over 10 or 20 years old (so there is a significant investment of time, resources, and emotions). But on the other hand, the relationship has become so stale that the new relationship makes the partner feel alive. Thus, the straying partner may come to therapy individually to try to sort out this issue or to come to terms with needing to tell the other partner about the relationship, and more importantly about the thoughts and feelings that were previously suppressed and now are coming to life. In general, in the case of the Split-Self Affair, the outlook is not good:

> Frequently it is too late to create a satisfying emotional partnership between the spouses. The husband may leave to marry the other woman, or may usually stay in the marriage but be emotionally committed to the affair. Women usually choose the latter option. These affairs can continue until death.
>
> (Brown, 2001, p. 45)

There are several historical examples of this (FDR and Lucy Mercer, Governor Mark Sanford) that will be presented later in the book.

Exit Affair

In the Exit Affair, one (or both) of the partners knows the relationship is over, but doesn't have the will, or courage, to end it. The affair becomes the way to get the issue of ending out in the open and force the other partner to make the final decision. Sometimes the affair is a test for one of the partners to see if they can find someone or if they are still desirable. The other person is often a friend or co-worker who has heard and seen how the relationship has deteriorated and is seen as a sympathetic or understanding person. Since the affair occurs just before the end of the relationship, it is often mistakenly thought of as the "cause" of the split. However, the relationship has often been "on life support" for a long time.

The couple may share many of the same relational dynamics as the Conflict-Avoidance Affair couples, although the desire to remain in the marriage is, obviously, gone. Many times the straying partner did not want to hurt his or her spouse but does not have the desire to work on salvaging the relationship. The betrayed spouse will typically present with anger and hurt, while the betraying spouse will typically present as remorseful but disengaged. Each will blame the other for the state of the relationship as a way to hide from the pain being felt. However, if the relationship does end, and the relational differences are not addressed, the partners will often re-create the same dynamics into the next relationship, and the cycle will continue.

Entitlement Affair

Brown recently added a new category, called Entitlement Affairs. She stated that this was a result of living so close to Washington, D.C. (she practices in Arlington, Virginia), where she has worked with successful men (in addition, she has been interviewed by the press about the affairs of John Edwards, Mark Sanford, and Nicolas Sarkozy). These men are hard-working and highly successful and as a result are used to getting what they want. The feel they have achieved a certain amount of status that entitles them to meet their emotional needs any way they want. Many times, they define themselves by their success, but because they have devoted so much of their time and energy to success, they are out of touch with the emotional self. This is when the affair occurs. Since this category of affairs is not that well-differentiated from other categories, it will be mentioned but not elaborated on here.

Overall, Brown's typology is one approach to looking at affairs (and it is by no means exhaustive!), but it fulfills the two important systemic principles for clinicians. First, it provides a good starting point for sorting out the different system dynamics of which the infidelity might be a symptom. Second, it gives both partners a way to see their participation in creating the system that allowed the affair to emerge (conflict-avoidance, intimacy-avoidance, etc.). So once you know how to classify the type of affair, the next question is if it can it be effectively treated. What kind of hope for success does the research conducted to date give clinicians and couples?

Clinical Research Findings on Infidelity: Can Treatment Really Work?

According to Kroger, Reißner, Vasterling, Schutz, and Kliem (2012), there have only been five reports of efficacy studies on the treatment of infidelity using a randomized control trial (RCT). An RCT is considered to be the "gold standard" of empirically supported treatments, as RCTs have sufficient rigor to control for extraneous variables, provide a true control group, and allow for the results to be generalizable beyond the original study sample (Castonguay, 2013). So, is couples counseling effective to treat infidelity? The short answer is yes, but there are some caveats.

In 2005, Atkins, Eldridge, Baucom, and Christensen found that couples who were in couples therapy because of an affair did have lower satisfaction scores than couples who were seeking counseling for other reasons at pre-treatment. But at post-treatment there was no significant differences in relationship satisfaction. Interestingly, couples where one partner did have an affair, but chose not to disclose it, did not seem to benefit from couples counseling. These results were replicated in a European sample seeking couples counseling, with couples maintaining satisfaction gains at 6 months post-treatment (Atkins, Marin, Lo, Klann, & Hahlweg, 2010). Greenberg, Warwar and Malcolm (2010) looked at the traumatic "injuries" following a series of events (infidelity being one of them). Not surprisingly, the "injured" (or betrayed) partner reported lower relationship satisfaction and greater personal strain at pre-treatment but showed improvement during couples therapy, at the end of treatment, and at follow-up (at 3 months). In addition, the other partner showed improvement as well.

Gordon, Baucom, and Snyder (2004) conducted a study that looked at couples who had an affair disclosed within the past 6 months and were seeking couples counseling. They investigated a specific approach that focused exclusively on infidelity and not other couples issues. Their results showed some improvement on anxiety and depression scores pre- and post-treatment for the betrayed spouse, and even higher gains for the betraying spouse on the same instruments. But at a 6-month follow-up, only the betraying partner continued to show positive effects and improved relationship satisfaction. Last, in 2012, Kroger and his associates investigated almost 90 couples in treatment (one group on a waiting list, one group in treatment). Interestingly, they found that over half (56%) of the participants dropped out before the end of treatment (underscoring the emotional volatility). Their results supported the use of couples therapy for the treatment of infidelity, particularly for the trauma and anxiety symptoms that are a part of dealing with infidelity. However, they only found mixed results in depression scores from pre- to post-treatment for the unfaithful partner, and they did not see improvements in relationship satisfaction. Again, like Gordon et al.'s study, their approach focused more on the infidelity-specific issues rather than the couples system, which could have accounted for the results.

In reviewing the research on the treatment of infidelity in couples counseling, Kessel, Moon, and Atkins (2007) found that "a hybrid approach that includes both infidelity-specific and general couple therapy strategies may provide the most realistic and flexible strategy" (p. 62). So for treatment to be successful, couples need a competent couples therapist who needs to be able to do two important things. First, the therapist needs to articulate an *explanatory* model which explains *how* the couple got into the situation they are in with the infidelity. It needs to address both the infidelity-specific aspects of what happened as well as the couple-wide issues that created the conditions where this happened. This model must contain the two systemic principles discussed prior (that the affair is a symptom and that both partners has a role in creating the conditions). Then, the couples therapist must be able to provide a *treatment* model that will: (1) guide the therapist and the therapy process through the tumultuous issues that will arise and (2) give the couple a sense of the course of treatment and that there is a "roadmap" with "light at the end of the tunnel."

I will present a simple, three-step model that I have developed after a review of most of the treatment models that have been developed (see Peluso, 2007, for many of the most common examples). A critique of previous approaches is that they are often too complicated and too full of "jargon" to be helpful to clients in the midst of the trauma that an infidelity inflicts. The three steps are simple enough to understand, and they serve as both an explanatory model and a treatment model that can be easily used by systems-based couples counselors.

The Three-Step Model for Understanding Infidelity

While infidelity is a complicated and personal issue, understanding the basic components, or "ingredients," that cause a person to stray from their partner isn't. In fact, I believe it can be explained in three easy steps, or with three simple ingredients: (1) There has to be an overall decline in satisfaction with the relationship; (2) There is unbalanced power in the relationship; and (3) There are unfulfilled fantasies, hopes, and dreams. I will discuss each of these and their contribution to infidelity (see Figure 2.1).

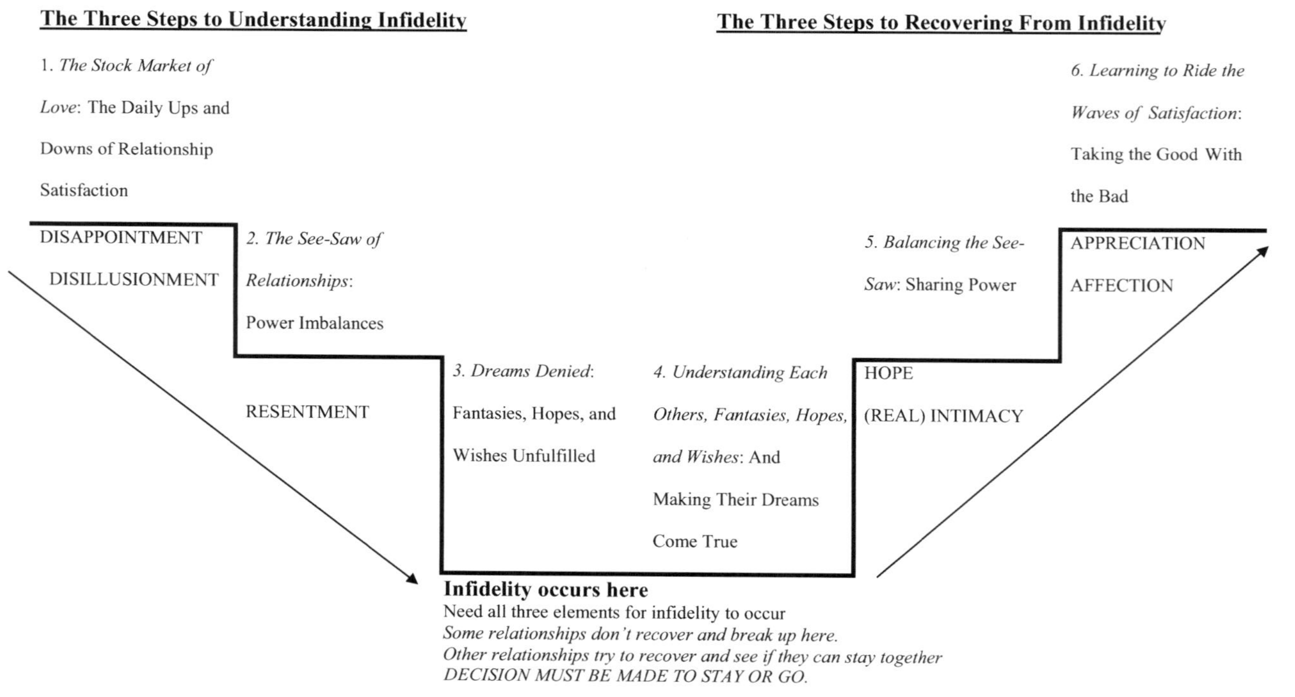

Figure 2.1.: A three-step systems model for understanding and treating infidelity

1. Perhaps, with the exception of an infidelity that results from a sexual compulsion or addiction, all infidelities are associated with a decline in *satisfaction with the relationship*. However, not all dissatisfied couples have an affair. Relationship satisfaction can bounce up and down very rapidly. This can be affected by so many factors: work, children, parents, friends, and so forth. Much like a volatile stock market, a couple's satisfaction with the relationship might be "up 25 points" some days and the next day "down 50 points." But focusing on the "day-to-day" satisfaction does not—by itself—indicate whether an infidelity will occur. The key indicator is the overall trend over time. It can tell you a lot about the "health" of the relationship: Does the relationship satisfaction over the course of the relationship trend upward or downward? Looking at the trends can tell you if there is trouble up ahead. But it is not the *only* ingredient.
2. One of the reasons for long-term dissatisfaction in a relationship is an *imbalance of power* in the relationship. It is like being on a "see-saw" when one person is bigger than the other. One person stays up all the time, and the other is down all the time. It's no fun for either. Usually, one person feels they don't have influence over the other person's actions (particularly with regard to decisions that affect the couple) or feels they sacrifice their needs and give into the other person's wants. Another way that the power balance is upset in a couple is when one partner brings in (or "triangulates") another person in the relationship (i.e., children, parents, friends), which makes the other person feel "left out" or "ganged up on" when it comes to major decisions. As a result, an infidelity is often a way of rebalancing the perception of a power imbalance (by bringing in someone else). It is a way to demonstrate to the other person that he or she has power also, although it is expressed in a negative and destructive way. Exploring issues of power imbalance within the couple, determining how it relates to dissatisfaction in the relationship, and finding ways to rebalance the power in a relationship is another important strategy for understanding infidelity. However, there are many couples who are dissatisfied with their relationship *and* feel there is an imbalance of power in their relationships *but* do not have an affair. That is because there is one final ingredient that is needed!
3. Last, the role of *unfulfilled fantasies, wishes, and dreams* in infidelity cannot be over-emphasized. When someone in a relationship gets to the point where they think, "This is never going to change, this is never going to get any better, and I am never going to get what I want out of my partner," they realize they have been deluding themselves. Everything they had hoped for, wished for, and dreamed they would get in their relationship fails to come true, and the fantasy dies. It is the critical ingredient needed, and it makes an affair so tempting. It holds the promise of fulfilling something (fantasy, wish, dream) for a person that seems to be missing in the relationship or in the person. By contrast, the *reality* of the individual's present relationship is usually fraught with struggle, negotiation, disappointment, and conflict. There is generally an imbalance in power, and there is a lot of dissatisfaction. In short, making *real* relationships work is hard *work*, while an affair (on the surface) seems to be effortless and enjoyable.

This is the point where all three ingredients are present (dissatisfaction, imbalance, and fantasy) and the infidelity occurs. The "other person" seems to make it easy and fun. They make you feel the way you always wanted to feel or how you used to feel with your partner. *Paradoxically, it almost never turns out that way!* After the fact, when the affair comes to light, the demands of the "other person" (i.e., "I never see you anymore . . ." "You promised me we would be together . . .") become the "work" while the partner becomes the *fantasy* (i.e., "I never had it so good . . ." "It was so comfortable back when . . .").

Movie: *Revolution Road*

In the 2008 movie *Revolution Road*, Kate Winslet and Leonardo DiCaprio play a couple who meet with dreams of living a bohemian life, only to marry and settle down in 1950s suburbia. In the beginning, Kate Winslet's character tries to pursue amateur acting (and fails), while DiCaprio's character is seemingly lost, having settled for a career in sales. They have two children but become aware that their life seems meaningless, monotonous, and hopeless. They hatch a plan to move to Paris to live out their dreams. However, as they are about to commit to this plan, Winslet's character gets pregnant and DiCaprio's character gets a big promotion at work. She still wants to go to Paris, while he dismisses it as a foolish dream and believes that his new salary will be able to furnish his growing family with a comfortable (if not monotonous) suburban existence. DiCaprio accepts and embraces this new reality (suggesting that his wife gets used to it too), and Winslet (powerless to stop it) becomes despondent. Inevitably, she has an affair with her neighbor.

What is interesting about this movie is that in its depiction of the couple, all three elements of the "explanatory" model are present prior to the affair. First, both members of the couple are dissatisfied with their lives and become dissatisfied with each other. Winslet begins to resent the suburban life as incongruous with her more bohemian, artistic impulses but begins to see herself becoming the "traditional" housewife, which adds to her dissatisfaction. She begins to take this out on her husband, particularly when her amateur acting fails horribly. Second, the power differentials are most strongly revealed when DiCaprio's character uses his new position (and increased salary) as more important than their aspirations to move to Paris. In addition, Winslet's character also feels like she loses her power to choose once she becomes pregnant (it was the 1950s and abortion was not an option), so there is a second power differential as well. Third, the "death of the dream" happens when the couple—who previously agreed that their life had become meandering and hopeless and that moving to Paris would be fulfilling—suddenly find themselves at odds when they realize they no longer want the same thing (he is comfortable in his new position and wealth, and she is miserable). In particular, Winslet realizes that she is trapped and will never realize her dream. This is the moment when she has an affair with her married neighbor (who professed that he loved her). However, she does not reciprocate his feelings. Instead the affair was a way of bringing the underlying frustrations and disappointment to the surface. At the same time, DiCaprio's character confesses to having an affair with a secretary at his office and wants to repair his relationship. Without giving away the ending of the movie, the result is not a pleasant one for the couple.

From a systemic point of view, *Revolution Road* also demonstrates the two systemic principles outlined prior. Clearly, the affairs that both DiCaprio's and Winslet's characters have are symptoms of larger issues, and both spouses (through their decisions about their life's circumstances) contribute to the conditions that make them possible. This is the point when an affair is disclosed. It is also a place where a major decision must be made: Do I stay or do I go? If the couple decides to stay together, then the question is: Can we save this relationship or marriage? If each person is willing to go through the process, they usually can save it. The process for exiting from an affair is the same way that you came in, except in reverse. In other words, it is the *same three steps*, only in reverse order. This means you have to explore the original wishes, dreams, and fantasies you had for each other, you have to find ways of balancing power, and then you will feel more satisfied in the relationship. Unfortunately, I believe the problem with most couples counselors is that they reverse the order and try to work on satisfaction first and dampen the emotions, which is why they are ineffective.

I think that the key to ultimately recovering intimacy following an affair is to have the excitement of the fantasy that led to the infidelity align with the fantasy about the relationship that gets created for the person who had the affair. If one partner was feeling neglected, how can they be made to feel special? If they need to feel secure, how can they be made to feel safe? At the same time, it is crucial to tap into each partner's *original* fantasies about the relationship, their feelings about relationships in general, and the expectations they had for themselves and each other ("I don't ever want to be hurt," "I want to have a happy, joyful family," etc.). Unfortunately, these will probably be tied to feelings of loss, sadness, grief, disgust, and anger initially. However, if the couple can be guided *through* those emotions (as mentioned prior), then there may be room for growth and power for deepening intimacy.

As the wishes, dreams, and fantasies are uncovered and re-negotiated, and the emotions are expressed (and tolerated), then the work through the other steps can begin. Not all couples can do this. Again, many times couples decide that too much damage has been done and that the dreams are irrevocably broken. But if a couple can take these three steps together, and if the couple has been able to tolerate the strong emotions contained as well as experienced some elements of forgiveness, the couple will have ways to discuss and rebalance the "see-saw" of power, and the "trend line" in relationship satisfaction will increase. At that point, both partners' fantasies about the relationship will begin to merge together, and each gets the best of both worlds, thus recovering and deepening intimacy.

Conclusion

The important point in this illustration is the fact that all three elements (or "steps") of the model are present. The viewer can see how each one contributes to both partners having affairs and that it is not until the final element, or step, is in place, the "death of the dream," that the affair takes place. In the next three chapters, each of these three steps will explored, and clinicians will be provided ways to help clients deconstruct the infidelity from a systemic perspective and begin to understand the dynamics within the relationship in the hopes that healing can proceed from it. Following those chapters, the next three will focus on the same three steps (in reverse) and the treatment considerations (and techniques) that couples counselors will want to use to help couples move through toward healing.

CHAPTER 3

Relationship Dissatisfaction: The Stock Market of Love

In the beginning, things were good. But after a while, they began to settle down into a pattern. Routines were good, but when the routines became ruts they couldn't break out of, the fun began to dry up in their relationship. It wasn't that the relationship was bad, far from it! It's just that the joy and delight that they once had in each other was more like a distant memory or a faded photograph than a living force in their daily lives the way it used to be.

To say that relationships have their "ups and downs" is an understatement! But the underlying sentiment that partners have about the overall relationship can have a powerful bearing on everything from interpersonal connection, to physical health, to a proclivity toward infidelity. This chapter examines the concept of relationship (or "marital") satisfaction. The research that has been conducted on this issue, and its impact on health (physical and psychological), is considered, as well as the role that it plays in creating the systemic dynamics that lead toward an infidelity. First, a review of the construct and the existing literature on relationship satisfaction.

What Is Satisfaction in Relationships and Why Is It Important?

Marital satisfaction (or relationship satisfaction) in couples is a concept that has been studied for over 5 decades. According to researchers, marital satisfaction can be defined as the attitude individuals have toward their marital relationship. Other researchers have adapted this to encompass any romantic relationships (Robles et al., 2014; Scott et al., 2017; Stone & Shackelford, 2006). There are many factors that contribute to an overall sense of satisfaction (or dissatisfaction) with a relationship. Some of these include conflict styles, experiences through the lifespan for each member of the couple, and attending to the needs of each other as well as the relationship. Inclusive of terms like *dyadic adjustment*, as well as a series of behaviors like "mate guarding," etc., marital satisfaction is a critical variable for researchers and clinicians alike. Stone and Shackelford take a more transactional approach to the construct:

> Marital satisfaction is a mental state that reflects the perceived benefits and costs of marriage to a particular person. The more costs a marriage partner

> inflicts on a person, the less satisfied one generally is with the marriage and with the marriage partner. Similarly, the greater the perceived benefits, the more satisfied one is with the marriage and with the marriage partner.
> (2006, p. 541)

They found that couples where the partners attributed negative behaviors to their spouse's character, rather than to the circumstances surrounding their behavior, tended to rate their relationship satisfaction much lower than those who attributed their partner's behavior to the circumstances surrounding them. For example, if one partner is disengaged at home, the other partner could either attribute the partner's behavior to his or her character ("Oh, he just doesn't care about me") or to the circumstances surrounding him or her ("This is tax season, and that is always a busy time for him"). These personal negative attributions not only affect relationship satisfaction, but also predict relationship dissolution as well (Stone & Shackelford, 2006).

There seems to be a reciprocal relationship between overall life satisfaction and relationship satisfaction. Researchers have found that people who have higher satisfaction with life overall (pre-marriage) have a tendency toward eventual marriage. At the same time, the relationship seems to be bi-directional, as people who are married have greater satisfaction with life than those who never marry, are separated, get divorced, or are widowed (Sperry & Peluso, 2018). In fact, using data from the General Social Survey, researchers found that of all the sources of happiness (friends, work, etc.), marital happiness had the strongest impact on *overall* happiness, and that people who stayed in unhappy marriages, in the long run, were less happy than people who got divorced or remarried (Hawkins & Booth, 2005).

Another important component of satisfaction within a marriage is the amount of social support each of the partners has for the other. Social support is highly correlated with good relationship functioning, as well as with healthful outcomes within families. Marriage partners who provide good social support for their spouse contribute to their spouse's marital satisfaction (Stone & Shackelford, 2006).

Movie: *Spanglish*

John (played by Adam Sandler) is a successful restaurateur and chef who is easy-going and enjoys cooking and spending time with his children. His wife, Deborah (played by Tea Leoni), is a former high-powered businesswoman turned stay-at-home mother. Deborah is uptight, and her neurotic and often controlling behavior often upsets the family—she mentally abuses her daughter, Bernice, by forcing her to exercise, buying her smaller-sized clothes and putting her down for certain behaviors; she frustrates John by expecting him to be submissive and accepting of her parenting style with their son, Georgie. John is more laid back and supports the mental well-being of his children, but he feels that he cannot stand up to Deborah and so usually decides to acquiesce to her wishes.

Their housekeeper, Flor, is a single mother with a daughter (Cristina) who works first as a cleaning woman for John and Deborah and soon moves in when a full-time nanny is needed. Flor is not fluent in English, and Cristina is needed to interpret for her mother. Deborah immediately becomes attached to Cristina since she is beautiful and thin, all the things that her awkward and chubby daughter, Bernice, is not, and she begins to treat Cristina more like a daughter.

John opens a new restaurant but falls into a temporary depression because of the stress of the business. However, as it becomes wildly successful (receiving four stars, and having John proclaimed as "the finest chef in America" by the *New York Times*), Deborah (who gave up her lucrative and powerful career) becomes jealous and feels that she is being left behind. She begins to spend time with a realtor who is showing her properties, and Deborah begins to have an affair with him. Deborah enrolls Cristina into a private school with Bernice, upsetting Flor, who wants Cristina to keep in touch with her Mexican roots and working-class values. Flor feels that her employer is overstepping her bounds and voices her objection to John, who tells her he is also frustrated with Deborah because Bernice has no support system from her own mother. Flor tries to encourage Bernice and build her self-confidence by showing her small acts of kindness, especially after Deborah has been hard on her.

Deborah eventually confesses that she cheated on John and begs him to forgive her and stay so that they can work things out. However, a dejected John walks out and bumps into Flor, who was about to inform him that she is quitting. He offers to give Flor a ride to the bus stop, but the pair end up going to his restaurant, where he cooks Flor a sumptuous meal. They have a genuine and deep conversation, and become closer, but Flor is afraid of the consequences of a relationship, since they both have children. Flor tells John that she has feelings for him but leaves before he can kiss her.

In the movie, there are two affairs: one that is in progress, and one that is interrupted before it can be started (although it could be argued that it is a type of emotional affair). In terms of Brown's typology, they are most likely a Conflict-Avoidance Affair, as John is desperate not to confront Deborah over her neurotic and frustratingly controlling behavior (which seems to hurt everyone in its wake). And Deborah is not willing to provoke a genuine fight with John about her unmet needs. However, what is *most* salient in this film is the lack of satisfaction that *both* partners have in the relationship, which seems to be good example of Scott et al.'s findings. Deborah's satisfaction obviously takes a spike downward as John's restaurant gets rave reviews. As she feels lonely and left out, she starts a sexual affair. Likewise, after John learns of Deborah's affair (presumably spiking his already low relationship satisfaction), he runs into Flor (whom he was already attracted to) and has an emotionally intense experience with her that flirts with becoming overtly sexual and a full-blown affair.

Relationship Satisfaction and Health

In addition to the benefits of social support that highly satisfied relationships engender, there are significant health benefits that accompany high levels of relationship satisfaction. Robles et al. (2014) reported the results of a meta-analysis summarizing the effect of marital satisfaction and health across 126 studies representing over 72,000 individuals from countries all over the world. The results were overwhelming:

> (W)e found that greater marital quality was related to better physical health, regardless of study design, marital quality measure, and publication year. Moreover, the consistent effects in longitudinal studies suggest that poor marital quality is a risk factor for poor health outcomes. In addition, we found clear evidence that greater marital quality was related to lower cardiovascular reactivity during marital conflict discussions.
>
> (p. 168)

Not surprisingly, greater relationship satisfaction effects specific medical outcomes. For example, clients with chronic illnesses, like end-stage renal disease and cardiovascular diseases, had higher levels of mortality if relationship satisfaction was low. Other objective medical outcomes were likewise negatively impacted, including development of ulcer, heart disease, and wound healing, if relationship satisfaction was low, suggesting a link between the emotional state of a relationship and physical health.

Next, there is a relationship between psychological health and relationship quality or relationship satisfaction. Again, in a meta-analysis, Robles et al. (2014) reported medium effect sizes (or magnitude of the relationship) between .42 and .37 for women and men, respectively. They noted:

> In addition, diagnosed depression was related to lower marital satisfaction, with large mean effect size *d*s ranging from 1.2 to 1.75 in cross-sectional studies . . . [and] associations between marital quality and indicators of psychological well-being (which included depressive and/or anxiety symptoms, self-esteem, life satisfaction, happiness, other psychological symptoms), greater marital quality was related to greater psychological well-being with moderate effect sizes.
>
> (Robles et al., 2014, p. 68)

Finally, they found that even when symptoms of depression and other negative affect were controlled for in their analysis, the link between relationship satisfaction and health outcomes was still strong. This finding attests to the importance of relationship satisfaction and overall health and well-being.

How Does Satisfaction Change Over Time?

While the quality of a relationship does have many benefits, it is not a static, unchanging state. It fluctuates over time, both episodically and over long periods. Previous conceptualizations of satisfaction over the lifespan of a relationship imagined a U-shaped course, with couples starting their relationships with high satisfaction (the so-called "honeymoon" phase), declining over time to a low-point (the "doldrums"), and then moving upward to high satisfaction levels comparable to levels they had in the early years. These generalizations were based on cross-sectional (and mostly survey) data with couples of varying ages. However, closer examination of couples over time revealed something different (Stanley et al., 2012).

Once researchers began to follow actual couples over the span of their relationship, the course of relationship satisfaction (its "ups and downs") was found to be much more complex. Looking at couples longitudinally, satisfaction seems to drop precipitously during the first 10 years and then gradually decreases in subsequent decades. Not all relationships decline in a predictably linear fashion, as events can cause steep drops, as well as increases. And as for relationships that are as high or higher as they were at the beginning? These make up only a minority of couples studied longitudinally (Robles et al., 2014). Given this trend, then why don't all couples head for divorce (or infidelity)? More on that later!

So what impacts these changes over time? The quality of an individual's parents' marriage seems to play a role. An interesting finding suggested that the quality of the parents' relationship, more so than whether the parents were divorced, had a greater effect on couples' relationship satisfaction. Paradoxically, shared traumatic events (from health crises to natural disasters) can *increase* relationship satisfaction. Individual differences, like attachment style, also play a role in relationship satisfaction. People with anxious or avoidant attachment styles are less satisfied than securely attached individuals. Finally, economic or work-related stressors are positively correlated with lower relationship satisfaction (Robles et al., 2014).

What About Satisfied Couples Who Divorce?

While the link between satisfaction and better outcomes, including the strength of the relationship, are obvious, there is an interesting sub-set of the population that bears reviewing: specifically, couples with marriages that have low levels of marital distress or dissatisfaction, but who still go on to divorce. Lavner and Bradbury (2012) reviewed the literature and, based on that, speculated that these couples (ones with low distress who go on to divorce) may differ from couples with low distress who do not divorce in four specific ways: "(1) lower levels of commitment, (2) poorer observed communication (higher negative and/or lower positive), (3) more maladaptive personality characteristics, and (4) higher levels of stress" (p. 2).

When they surveyed over a 10-year period, and specifically targeted these low-distressed newlyweds (who would go on to divorce), they did not find any *specific* factors that accounted for these couples getting divorced. Contrary to their speculation, they:

> found no evidence that low initial commitment characterized low-distress newlyweds who went on to dissolve their marriages, despite replicating their finding that spouses who divorced tended to be younger and had higher rates of parental divorce (among husbands). Three other factors hypothesized to

> promote relationship distress—personality traits reflecting hostility and negative affectivity, acute life events, and chronic stress—also failed to consistently distinguish between low-distress newlyweds who did and did not end their marriages at 10-year follow-up, as did self-reported relationship satisfaction over the first 4 years of marriage.
>
> (Lavner & Bradbury, 2012, p. 6)

While this finding may seem to be counter-intuitive, since low dissatisfied couples shouldn't need or want to divorce (let alone have affairs), this finding may reveal that relationship satisfaction alone is not the answer. In the three-step model presented in Chapter 2, all three factors must be present in order for an infidelity to occur. However, with that in mind, decreased relationship satisfaction may actually lead to behaviors that often are precursors to an affair.

Relationship Satisfaction and Infidelity-Related Behaviors

All this leads to the question of the impact of (low) relationship satisfaction and infidelity. While it might seem obvious, the findings are not necessarily clear-cut. It is believed that people who are more satisfied with their relationships are less likely to commit an infidelity because infidelity is equated with relationship dissolution, and people who are in a good relationship do not want to risk the relationship. In addition, researchers have investigated a number of "infidelity-related" behaviors (e.g., sexting, exchanging fantasies, or simply sharing dissatisfaction with one's spouse or partner) and their relation to satisfaction. Infidelity-related behaviors by partners have also been related to dissatisfaction with the relationship. Last, although the prevalence of infidelity is highly predicted by lower levels of relationship satisfaction, dissatisfaction in the relationship alone is not sufficient to predict the occurrence of infidelity (Starratt et al., 2017). Each of these will be considered in the following.

For decades, researchers have explored the relationship between dissatisfaction in marriage and infidelity. Relationship dissatisfaction is related to a range of infidelity-related (IR) behaviors (Shaw, Rhoades, Allen, Stanley, & Markman, 2013; Whisman, Gordon, & Chatav, 2007). Valenzuela, Halpern, and Katz (2014) found that higher overall use of online social media (like Facebook) was positively correlated with higher levels of relationship dissatisfaction, as well as a higher rate of eventual divorce. They postulated that social media likely provides a forum for social support for people in unfulfilling marriages. Additionally, social media fosters infidelity-related behaviors by providing opportunities for other infidelity-related behaviors that could cause conflict (if discovered) and erodes the quality of the relationship. According to McDaniel, Drouin, and Cravens (2017): "we suggest that this relationship is likely bi-directional; those in less satisfied relationships likely seek out these types of online interactions with others, and these interactions, in turn, may cause lower levels of satisfaction" (p. 94). All these can lead to relationship ambivalence, or "the experience of both positive and negative sentiment about the same relationship" (McDaniel et al., 2017, p. 89) which is a sentiment that is created when there have been conflicts in the past (particularly if they have not been resolved) or past betrayals and other transgressions. These often lead to suspicion of, or can be borne out of, emotional affairs, but these behaviors have been shown to be highly predictive of eventual sexual infidelity in a couple's relationship (Birditt, Miller, Fingerman, & Lefkowitz, 2009; McDaniel et al., 2017).

The Case of Tiger Woods

Eldrick "Tiger" Woods was on top of the golf world, and the world itself, in 2009. Not only was he the world's number one golfer, but he was a ubiquitous spokesperson for brands ranging from AT&T to Nike and worth billions of dollars. He had been the most dominant player in the golf world for over a decade. If he was in a tournament on Sunday and near the top, just the mere knowledge of that was likely to make his competitors melt away under the pressure and the "Tiger Roar" that crowds would cheer as he would begin to make spectacular golf shots and close in on the leader. The singular measure of success in golf is the number of "major" championships a player has won (either the Masters Tournament, the US Open, the British Open, or the PGA Championship). The person with the most was the legendary Jack Nicklaus, who had won 18. Tiger had won 14 by 2009, and it was considered to be a known fact that he would easily break the legend's record. The questions were: How much younger would Tiger be when he did it, and what would the final number of major championships be when he was done?

He also seemed to have the perfect family life. He was married to a Swedish model, and with two children they looked like the perfect family. However, a lifetime in the spotlight, and in the bubble of invulnerability that superstardom affords, Woods also had another side to his personality. According to published reports, he had seemingly voracious appetites for gambling and women. All of this came to light in November 2009 when, over the Thanksgiving holiday, the usually private Woods very publicly crashed his vehicle outside his house after being confronted by his wife over reports in the *National Enquirer* and her discovering salacious text messages on his phone to several women. Over the next few weeks and months, several dozen women came out and revealed they had had affairs with Woods over the past few years. Woods himself finally acknowledged in a February 2010 televised address: "The issue involved here was my repeated irresponsible behavior. I was unfaithful. I had affairs. I cheated. What I did is not acceptable, and I am the only person to blame."

How could this happen? In a 2010 exposé in *Vanity Fair* investigative journalist Mark Seal described the affairs thus:

> Yet something was bubbling inside him [Woods]. He had a goddess at home, but apparently she wasn't enough. He would soon lose control over his ability to say no when it came to sex. He would rely on sex for

> comfort from pain and relief from stress. Instead of love, sex would be his primary form of relationship, "for which all else may be sacrificed, including family, friends, values, health, safety, and work. As life unravels, the sex addict despairs, helplessly trapped in cycles of degradation, shame and danger." Those are the words of Patrick Carnes, Ph.D., the pioneering sex-addiction therapist, in his 1989 book, *Contrary to Love: Helping the Sexual Addict.* Woods was later reportedly treated in Carnes's clinic, in Hattiesburg, Mississippi. For, somewhere along the road to sainthood, Tiger had become a sex addict.
>
> (n.p.)

According to Brown's (2001) typology, this is indicative of the Sexual Addiction Affair, where the individual uses increasingly risky behaviors to fill a void or numb a pain that is inside. In Tiger Woods' case, several factors may explain his circumstances. First, his father, Earl Woods (whom Tiger idolized), reportedly had a history of affairs. Second, his father passed away in 2006, which may have intensified any internalized pain he already was trying to use sex to numb. Finally, Woods was also a high-dollar gambler with noted superstar athletes Charles Barkley and Michael Jordan, who introduced him to the isolating and permissive atmosphere of the VIP gambling lifestyle, where any desire can presumably be provided. In his February 2010 address, Woods may have said it best: "I felt I was entitled . . . I was wrong. I was foolish. I don't get to play by different rules. I brought this shame on myself."

Woods would be plagued by injuries to his back and knees and has not won another major tournament since 2008. There is no speculation anymore that he will ever break Jack Nicklaus's career record, and the only question that many ask is whether he will ever be able to win *another* major or if it is too late for someone who was once so dominant.

In Tiger Woods's case, while on the outside his family and circumstances were seemingly perfect, there were significant issues that impacted his marital satisfaction. And while there were clear sexual addiction factors at play (in fact, according to Brown's typology, this would certainly be an example of a Sexual Addiction Affair), the stressors of playing golf at a high level, the introduction of two young children, and the influence of his father and friends probably played a significant role in the downward, negative trajectory for their level of satisfaction in the relationship.

Lower relationship satisfaction not only affects the partner considering an affair, it can also affect a partner *fearing* their partner may stray. This can lead to the consideration of concepts like *mate value, mate guarding,* and *mate susceptibility* to infidelity. Mate value is an appraisal of the desirableness of a given partner. It can include characteristics like intelligence, personality, or physical attractiveness

(Starratt et al., 2017). Viewing a partner as having less value is associated with lower relationship satisfaction. So, if one partner no longer sees their partner as being as "valuable" as they did before, and if there is high dissatisfaction in the relationship, the probability of an infidelity goes up. At the same time, if a partner views the other partner as having a higher value, and there is a high level of dissatisfaction with the relationship, there is a greater likelihood of *mate-guarding* behaviors, which could precipitate infidelity-related behaviors (or an infidelity itself).

Mate-guarding behaviors are an attempt to prevent another person from trespassing on the relationship by having access to his or her partner. These behaviors can include monopolizing his or her partner's free time so the partner cannot form any outside interests, emotional manipulation through the use of passive-aggressive threats, to actually threatening to have an affair if the partner does not meet his or her demands. Most of this is driven from an anxious attachment style but may also be rooted in fears about his or her compatibility with a partner that is of higher "value." Mate-guarding behaviors almost exclusively occur in relationships where there is high dissatisfaction. In addition, these behaviors can have real-world consequences for the partner in the form of decreased social support or diminished opportunities in one's career. Let's take a look at an example from a couple that is clearly dissatisfied and where one partner is expressing some "mate-guarding" behaviors.

The Case of Jordan and Mike

Mike: Well, for two years, all you ever did was talk about your old boss, Jim. It was always, "Jim did this . . ." "Jim said that . . ." "Jim told me . . ." Whenever he called, you would jump to pick up the phone. You would be on the phone with him at all hours, whether late or early. Then there were the texts! We would be halfway into a conversation, and suddenly there would be that noise that he was texting, and boom! You'd go right to it!

Jordan: You're exaggerating! It wasn't like that!

Mike: Look at your texts from him! Look how *often* he would text you!

Counselor: When did you first become aware that this might be more than just a job-related issue?

Mike: I think it was when Jordan started wanting to go over to his house on the weekends. It was like you couldn't bear to be away from him for more than a day!

Counselor (to Jordan): What are your thoughts when you hear this?

Jordan: I'm upset, I think he is making it out to be something that it wasn't! It's not like I ever had *sex* with him!

Mike: I'm not saying that you did, or that you would have wanted to. I don't know. But the point is you put *him* before *me*! That's what hurt!

Jordan: It was the work! There was so much coming at us, and he needed my help to keep him on track. Sometimes all I did was go from meeting to meeting with him just to keep him focused.

Mike: Yes, but a lot of times he would talk to you about the problems that he was having with his partner and their relationship?

Jordan: Sure, but it was just as a co-worker.

Mike: Well it felt like more than that! You "lit up" every time you talked about him. Everything that he said was "so funny" or "so amazing." Hell, you even made us spend my birthday at his house with him and his partner. You didn't even plan anything for me, we just went over *there*. Didn't that say something?

Jordan: When nobody else wanted me, and after I had been demoted, he was the one who made me see that I was valuable. He made me see that I could be successful. He gave me the opportunities that no one else would or did. After all, we moved here for your career. I had to give up what I had so you could pursue your dream job. I never complained about it, but it meant that I had to scramble to get whatever I could. I never had the same feeling of security that you did. I never have.

In this case, both partners are expressing dissatisfaction with the other. Jordan harbors a long-standing dissatisfaction with Mike for moving in order to help his career (Jordan did not fare so well). And when Jordan was able to get a good position, Mike was jealous of all the time being spent away and began feeling like he was "second best" and not worth paying attention to. This led to Mike's pushing Jordan into couples counseling.

Sexual Satisfaction and Infidelity

Another area of investigation in the link between sexual satisfaction and infidelity is the role played by dissatisfaction with the sexual aspects of the relationship. According to several researchers, sexual dissatisfaction is commonly associated with couples that have a history of affairs, and, in retrospective studies, sexual dissatisfaction is viewed by the betraying partner as a precursor to having an affair (Scott et al., 2017). However, what has not been clear is how negative changes in satisfaction with the sexual relationship, over the life of the relationship, effect the proclivity to engage in an infidelity. Some theorists (espousing "perpetual problems") believe that early problems and dissatisfaction set a precedent that is carried forth into the later stages of a relationship when an infidelity occurs. Other theorists (espousing a developmental model) believe there is an accumulation of stressors and traumas that erode the relationship and produce the conditions where an infidelity can occur.

It is also noteworthy that the effects of gender on sexual dissatisfaction are also somewhat confusing. Scott et al. found their results (relating sexual dissatisfaction with instances of infidelity) were not moderated by gender. This supports several previous research findings that found some support for a stronger correlation for men with sexual dissatisfaction and infidelity, although this has not been universally found in other studies (Scott et al., 2017). At the same time, Silva, Saraiva, Albuquerque, and Arantes (2017) found that women reported strong negative evaluations of infidelity regardless of relationship quality. And while this would seemingly support a gender difference for sexual satisfaction and infidelity, this effect is not the same when compared to couples in highly satisfied relationships. In these instances, both men and women have negative attitudes toward infidelity. As a result, the traditionally observed gender differences (men are more likely to endorse infidelity) seem to apply only when relationship satisfaction is low.

At the same time, the finding is not as consistent as many believed. It does not account for those couples where sexual satisfaction in the relationship was low and an infidelity did not occur. Scott et al. (2017) report that a key difference in couples where an infidelity did not occur and one that did may be the *rate* that sexual satisfaction declined. They noted:

> Possibly, when general sexual satisfaction declines more rapidly, individuals have less hope of finding sexual satisfaction in their current relationships and are consequently more likely to look outside of their relationships for sexual satisfaction. Or conversely, the development of budding relationships and/or sexual interests in future ESI [extradyadic sexual involvement] partners may also negatively influence one's current sexual satisfaction within the primary relationship.
> (p. 403)

Thus, when individuals experience a sharp decline in sexual satisfaction (like when a baby is born), individuals with a need for excitement-seeking or novelty may then begin to be "open" to a new sexual experience. This is consistent with the three-step model proposed here.

While there is a lot of evidence that relationship dissatisfaction and sexual satisfaction are directly predictive of an infidelity, several attempts to definitively assess this and confirm it have not been successful. First, two recent longitudinal studies failed to find that sexual satisfaction significantly predicted later infidelity in either married or unmarried couples (DeMaris, 2009; Maddox Shaw, Rhoades, Allen, Stanley, & Markman, 2013). Second, Scott et al. (2017) found that by sampling a large data set of couples before and after a sexual infidelity, they were able to see trending changes in both relationship satisfaction and sexual satisfaction, but these only became significant just prior to the commencement of the affair: "The current findings suggest that both sexual satisfaction and relationship quality are most likely deteriorating together leading up to [an infidelity]" (p. 403). However, this suggests that dissatisfaction *alone* does not predict an infidelity, but that there must be other "activating agents" involved as well. This provides some *prima facie* evidence for the three-step model advocated for in this text, as there are plenty of dissatisfied relationships that do not lead to an infidelity. In fact, there must be other factors that are involved (namely, power differentials and the death of the dream, wish, or fantasy the partners had for the relationship).

A Systemic View of Relationship Satisfaction: The Stock Market Metaphor

The prior sections in this chapter have laid out a clear picture that relationship satisfaction plays a critical role in the overall health of a relationship, as well as has a bearing on a couple's susceptibility for one partner (or both) to have an affair. Indeed, if *dis*satisfaction is a "set point" in the system (equilibrium), then the relationship will tend to stay at or drift toward an overall negative emotional framework. Frustration, suspicion, and a lack of affection are characteristics of these low-satisfaction relationships. And although systems dynamics tend toward homeostasis, there is another factor that impacts the system: time. Or, more specifically, growth over time. The main concern is the overall *trend* over time. Does it trend toward growth and positive sentiment, or does it stagnate and go nowhere, or does it go down into "negative territory"? A metaphor devised by Gottman and Gottman (2017) may help illustrate this better!

The Dow Jones and Satisfaction

The Dow Jones Industrial Average (commonly referred to as "the Dow") is what most people think of when they think of the "stock market." It is a listing of 30 companies designed to give an indication of the health of the industrial portion of the American economy, but today, many of the companies in the Dow Jones do not manufacture anything. Today, the Dow Jones contains some of the most influential companies in the American economy, and its fluctuations (great and small) are seen as reflective of the overall economy (although many economists decry this tendency). However, one thing that is certain is that the Dow Jones Industrial Average does react to both events that impact the individual component companies within it and national and international events. For example, in the immediate aftermath of 9/11 the Dow Jones dropped over 600 hundred points (its third largest loss in history). And when there are large-scale international military threats, the Dow can also drop suddenly; even if the individual companies within the Dow are not directly affected, their prices can be!

For the purposes of this chapter, it is important to note that from day to day the Dow can fluctuate wildly (or at least seem to). One day it can be up 100 points, the next it can be down 250 points. And depending on your point of view, it can be good or bad, if you measure it day to day. The same can be said with relationship satisfaction. Some days the relationship can be "up" (positive) by 100, and other days it can be "down" (or negative) by 250. And people who gauge the strength of their relationship by how satisfied they are on any given day are in for quite a ride! Usually that is a strategy for dating relationships and very immature relationships but not a good strategy for building stable, long-lasting relationships over time (Gottman, 2011). Generally speaking, people who measure the strength of their relationship by "day trading" (the practice of buying and selling stock based on where the price will go in a given day) are likely to not be in the relationship for very long.

However, if couples take a "longer view" of their relationship satisfaction over time, it can say a lot about where they have been, how far they have come, and what they have experienced. To illustrate this further, let's take a look at a ten-year chart of the Dow Jones Industrial Averages from approximately April 2000 to April 2010. The interesting thing to note is that on April 3, 2000, the Dow opened at 10,863 points and closed at 11,221 points. On April 1, 10 years later, the Dow opened at 10,857 points and closed at 10,927 points. In other words, in the decade from 2000–2010, you could say that the Dow Jones went nowhere! Or you might say that it was steady and unchanging. However, looking at Figure 3.1, you can see the chart of the Dow Jones over this time period. Recall for a minute what happened in that decade. There was the dot-com bubble burst (2001–2002), the housing bubble burst, the 9/11 attacks and war in Iraq and Afghanistan, and the Great Recession of 2007–2008. There were also historic highs as the economy grew, as housing boomed, and from a government stimulus.

Metaphorically speaking, if this was your relationship chart, if you were in September 2002, you might feel "low" (7,591) compared to April 2000. But if you were to judge your relationship satisfaction going from September 2002 to October 2007 (when the Dow closed at 13,930), you would see this period of steep increase in satisfaction. You would think, "Hey, this isn't so bad!" Of course, by March 9, 2009, the financial meltdown had occurred and there was a global recession and the Dow closed at 6,547. If you were measuring your relationship satisfaction from October 2007 to March 2009, you would think the relationship was doomed.

The point here is that relationships go up and down in their satisfaction. And regardless of whether you go up, go down, or remain steady, what it depends on is your perspective. For example, if the chart in Figure 3.1 is a map of a couple's relationship, each person may have a different opinion of the chart and what it means. One may look at the tremendous highs and take pride in that or might be sad that the steady progress upward was not sustained. At the same time, the other person in the relationship might look at the lows and feel the disappointment that it wasn't better or feel pride that they were able to climb out of the "pit." And of course, one could look at the start and the close and judge that the relationship hadn't moved at all in any real way (although it does look like quite a ride!).

However, there is one more way to look at relationship satisfaction, and that is over a *longer* period of time. To illustrate this, one must look at the Dow Jones Industrial Average from almost its inception in 1896! Figure 3.2 has a chart from 1900 to 2010 (over a century). There one can see the impact of the Great Crash of 1929 and the Great Recession of the 1930s, as well as the history of the 20th and beginning of the 21st century. The point here is that the *overall* trend line is upward and positive. Sure there are rocky points, and times when there are losses or negative spikes downward, but the overall slope is positive. Now if this was a measure of the relationship over time, it would be easy to say, "This couple looks like they are, on the whole, fairly positive." Now, by contrast, couples whose overall, or global, trend line slopes downward or is negative are fairly dissatisfied in the relationship (Gottman,

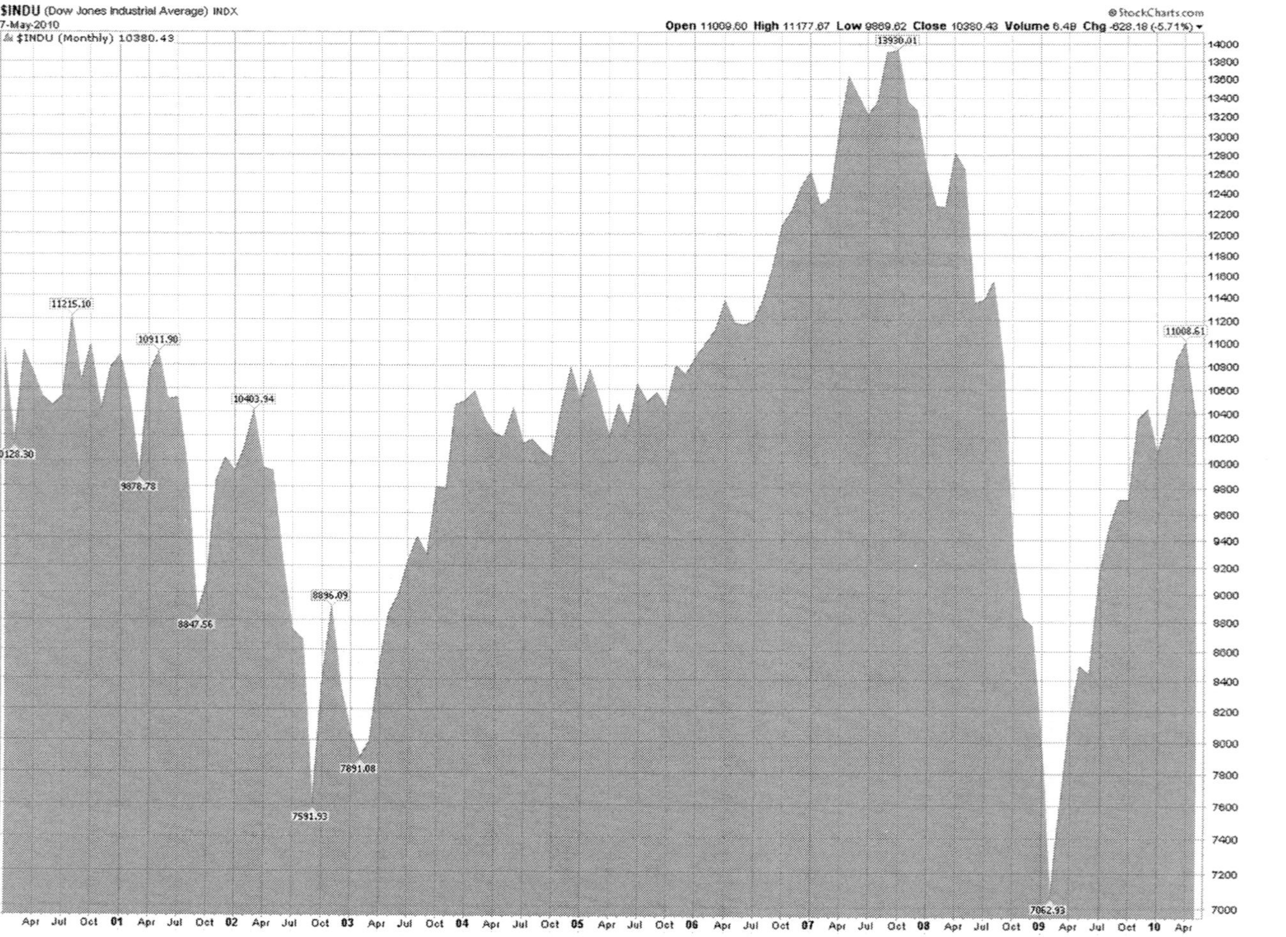

Figure 3.1.: Dow Jones Industrial Average from 2000–2010 (Chart courtesy of StockCharts.com)

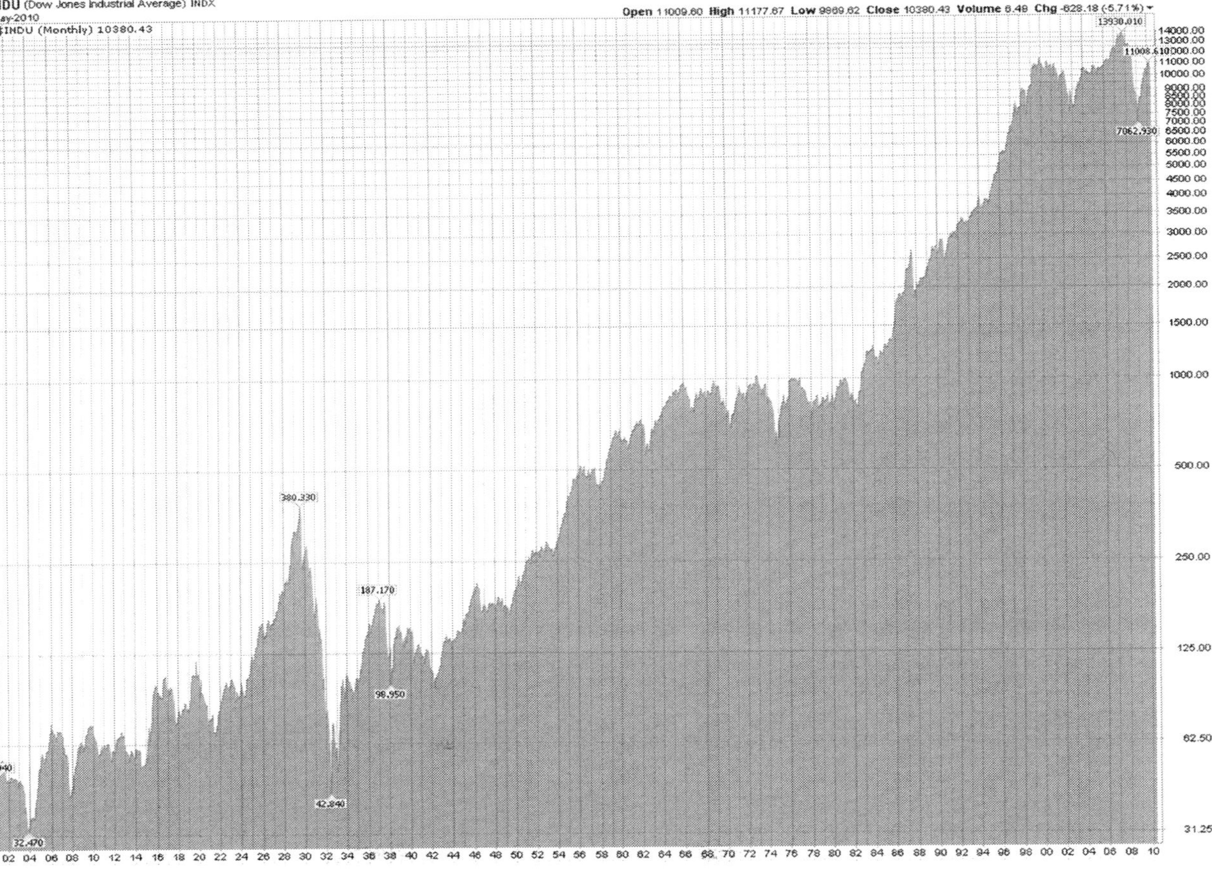

Figure 3.2.: Dow Jones Industrial Average from 1900–2010 (Chart courtesy of StockCharts.com)

2011; Gottman & Gottman, 2017). This puts them at greater risk for relationship problems, including divorce and infidelity. Thus, the idea of global satisfaction over a long period of time can be a significant factor, but it is not *the* only factor.

Now let's consider a case that had significant "ups and downs" but whose overall trend was negative, which created the conditions for an affair to occur.

Jeremy and Brittany

Jeremy initially made the appointment for couples counseling. He stated that he had "too much on his plate" and that his relationship with his wife was suffering. They were both in their late 30s, had been married for almost 15 years, and had two children. When they met, Brittany was an au pair from Ireland and was about to leave the country when Jeremy proposed. She thought that she was too young to marry but said that she was in love with Jeremy and said yes. She thought that he loved her, too, but he wound up being "manipulative and controlling, just like his father." She said that other people told her not to trust him, but she didn't listen: "I just didn't want to be without him."

Jeremy hated being compared to his father. He thought his father was abusive and had treated his mother poorly (cheating on her, leaving her financially dependent on Jeremy and his brother). He was "petty" and always "talked down to me!" He didn't see that he was acting the same way toward Brittany. Brittany's parents divorced when she was 10, and she swore that she would never do that. She saw how bitter and lonely her mother was, and she was scared that she would end up in a similar way.

Once she had children, they became the center of Brittany's life. Brittany gave up any hopes at a career, although she had begun to think about going back to school. She originally imagined a career as a nurse but was considering a medical technology degree because it would not require as much of a time commitment and because there were a number of job opportunities in the area. However, she wanted to wait until the children were older since Jeremy made enough for her to be a stay-at-home mom.

At one point Jeremy was very successful, but he had fallen on hard times. They had moved out to the West Coast and started a business which was successful. "I had a beautiful house, we had cars, furniture, whatever we wanted." But Jeremy's business partner "screwed" him, and he had to move. They moved into a modest house that was in serious need of repair, and, despite having a construction business, he never repaired the house. (This became a fitting metaphor for the relationship.) He was able to build a successful real estate business, which provided a sufficient passive income. Yet Brittany always had to ask for money. He was very controlling of the finances. He never wanted to spend it on her or the family, except when he wanted to lavish it on the children:

> He loved being "Father Christmas" though he was Scrooge to me! Even when we had money, he was always complaining about me spending it. I never spent lavishly! Just a cup of coffee with friends, and he would accuse me of bankrupting the family!

For his part, Jeremy stated that the failure of his business made him feel insecure and inadequate: "I wanted to have it all, and I was going to do that, no matter what!"

As Brittany's anxiety level rose, her OCD would also go up. She would frequently be controlling at home, constantly cleaning. Jeremy would say, "I work hard so you don't have to!" Brittany would reply: "We literally have nothing, so I work as hard as I can to keep up and clean what we have so I don't have to ask you to replace anything!" Jeremy felt like he had no hope and no freedom in the relationship. "It was more like work than work was." He confessed that over the years Brittany had given him "outs" in the relationship, but he hadn't had the courage to take them. "Now I wish I had!" At the same time, he could recall, "There was a time that I couldn't wait to get back to her." In addition, due to the condition of the house, all of the family slept in one bedroom, which meant that there was no sexual intimacy "for three or four years."

Brittany felt like she and Jeremy were "never equals" in the marriage. "I don't think he ever really committed to the marriage." For his part, Jeremy finally confessed the he was getting "tired" of being in the relationship. He was tired of Brittany's demands, and he just wanted to "withdraw" and spend more time away from home. He felt more free and easy with other people, and less so with Brittany.

At the same time, Jeremy began to work for a very wealthy family, doing remodeling for their home. The wife in that family was a lonely housewife (her husband was a banker and always gone), and she would frequently call Jeremy over to fix things or remodel rooms in the house. They would linger over coffee and found they had similar ambitions. "I could talk to her about things that I couldn't talk to Brittany about." She wanted to be noticed, and Jeremy wanted higher status and "freedom." She had bought him a phone to use to call her, and they would rendezvous at night for walks on the beach.

Brittany wanted to "fight" for the marriage. She made an effort not to confront or be "cross" with Jeremy. She desperately wanted Jeremy to notice what she was doing and fight for the marriage as well: "I want to fight for it. If it ends, I want to fight for it." Jeremy stated that he felt like he wasn't "enough" for Brittany. "I should be the one to decide if he is 'enough' for me. He is all I want!"

Ultimately Jeremy confessed to Brittany that he was having an affair and that he wanted a separation. "He said he didn't want to be married and that he didn't love me anymore." For his part, Jeremy said that he asked for a separation because, "I didn't want my life to pass me by, and I am not the person that I want to be." He expressed guilt, but not remorse. Brittany had a hard time accepting that the relationship was over.

According to Brown's typology, Jeremy's affair was most likely a Conflict-Avoidance Affair that turned into an Exit Affair. According to Jeremy, "I have always avoided 'sticky' situations." Thus when Brittany tried to fight for the relationship, Jeremy acquiesced. At the same time, Brittany gave in on things like the house and other issues when Jeremy would be insistent just to keep the peace. In the end, however, neither was very satisfied. Jeremy eventually said: "I wish I could go back to my younger self and say 'You have to stick to your guns on your core beliefs.'" Brittany, for her part, was able to see how not fighting for her relationship, in an attempt to "save" it, was only making her less and less satisfied, which then played into the infidelity occurring. If Jeremy and Brittany's relationship satisfaction over the years was charted, one would see an overall negative downward slide across the years.

Conclusion

In this chapter, the issue of relationship satisfaction and its relationship to the occurrence of infidelity has been presented. Systematically, satisfaction in any relationship goes up and down like a stock market. However, it is the perspective the couple takes on their relationship, and whether the *overall* trend is up or down, that predicts whether the global sentiment is positive or negative. While there are a myriad of ways that a relationship can become dissatisfying (work stressors, demands from children, sexual differences, other conflicts), the net result is that dissatisfaction is linked to poor health outcomes, poor psychological well-being, and divorce. And while relationship dissatisfaction is related to infidelity, it is not definitive. Relationship dissatisfaction can be thought of as a necessary, but not sufficient, condition for an infidelity to occur. This will lead to the next factor in the three-step model to be considered: power imbalances and differentials.

CHAPTER 4

Power Imbalances: The See-Saw of Love in Relationships

> *For the longest time, she felt like she was the weak one. She was the one who didn't finish her degree, and it always made her feel like she was not as smart as everyone else around her. Her partner was a genius, on the other hand. To debate was pointless because she would always lose. It was the worst when the topic was something that she wanted. She was sick and tired of being made to feel like a child just because she wanted to have things go her way for a change!*

In the last chapter, we discussed the importance of relationship satisfaction as one of the factors that contribute to the occurrence of an infidelity. Dissatisfaction is caused by the perception by one or both partners in the couple about the unfairness of the power structure of the couple dynamic and the friction that results from trying to negotiate around it. According to Gray-Little et al. (1996), power in relationships

> has typically been conceptualized as the ability to influence or to control another's behavior, and investigators have measured power in one of three ways: (a) in terms of resources, such as education or income, that form the bases of power; (b) in terms of power processes, such as the amount of talking time; or (c) in terms of who has the final say, that is, who determines the outcome in problem solving or decision making.
>
> (p. 292)

Over the past five decades, research between relationship satisfaction and power has shown several consistent findings. First, and most important, relationships with shared power (or egalitarian relationships) have the highest correlation with satisfaction. In addition, relationships where the wife or female is more dominant also seem to have greater levels of dissatisfaction than relationships where the husband or male is more dominant, although there is evidence that this is changing in later research (Baucom, Snyder, & Gordon, 2009; Gray-Little et al., 1996). There may be several reasons for the latter finding. For couples who prefer more "traditional" gender roles and divisions, wife-dominant relationships that are forced upon the couple due to financial or other circumstances (i.e., wife is primary household earner) create arrangements that are very unsatisfactory. However, if (in these relationships) the husband or male is perceived as "weak" by his partner, there may be attempts to get him to take on more of a role in the relationship and take some of the burden off of her. These may be passive aggressive (making manipulative suggestions) or merely aggressive (nagging, ridiculing, etc.), but if there is no response (or resistance), there is likely to be increased dissatisfaction and tension around power issues for both partners (Gray-Little et al., 1996).

By contrast, couples with a shared power, or egalitarian, style have two major elements in their favor: first is an orientation toward being flexible in order to accommodate shared power (and responsibility), and second, the necessary skill set for resolving conflicts when there are disagreements. In non-egalitarian (hierarchical) couples, most conflicts are resolved by deferring to the person who has more power. This leads the other partner to either have to acquiesce or try to undermine and coerce the more powerful partner if he or she wants to prevail in the conflict. Both of these results lead to increased dissatisfaction. In egalitarian couples, there is an absence of negative behaviors (whining, complaining, contempt), as well as coercive behaviors, compared to hierarchical couples, and there is an increase in consensus-building behaviors. So if this is the case, what happens in couples where there are power imbalances, and how does this contribute to an infidelity? For that, we will need to go back to childhood for a proper metaphor!

The See-Saw of Relationship: Power Imbalances

Do you remember when you were a child and you played on a see-saw (or "teeter-totter")? When was it the most fun? I'll bet it was the most fun when both you and the other person took turns going up and down. However, in order for you to do that, you both had to be (roughly) equal in size and weight. That way one person would push off the ground at the low point and could count on the other person to do the same.

Now think of a time when riding on a see-saw was *not* so fun. It was probably when it was not going anywhere and you were either stuck at the top or stuck at the bottom. Usually this happened because you were on the see-saw with someone who was bigger than you (and you were stuck at the top) or with someone smaller than you (and you were stuck at the bottom). If you were stuck at the bottom, you probably felt like the other person was getting the better end of the deal and that you had to do all the work (i.e., push hard with your legs) if you wanted to get off the ground. If you were stuck at the top you may have liked the view or were terrified at dangling so high in the air off the ground without the ability to get down. If the see-saw was going to move, it was because of the other person pushing off the ground to make it move. More importantly, you found that you were wholly dependent on the person on the bottom to eventually lower you to the ground! If that person kept sitting on his or her side, you never got down. Or if the other person just got off suddenly, you'd come crashing quickly to the ground. Either way, when you were stuck at the top, you realized (eventually) that you were at the mercy of the other person! This is not a fun way to play, can be frustratingly unfair, and may even be dangerous.

Couples relationships, when looking at issues of power, follow the same patterns as see-saws. In order to understand who has more power, we generally consider how decisions are made, who takes a "lead" role in various situations within the relationship (e.g., spending money, household chores, parenting issues), and who is responsible/takes responsibility for things in the relationship, or management of the couples lives. If the couple is more egalitarian, and power is evenly distributed, each person has a "fair share" of the responsibility for things and a fair amount of authority to make decisions. This is usually divided according to an individual's strengths. The result is a back and forth, "see-saw" dynamic in the relationship where each person (depending on the situation) is either on top ("in charge") or down below ("following along"). In egalitarian relationships, it doesn't matter where the person is, as long as they feel they can have some influence on the other person (whether they are on top or down below). It means that no one person is overburdened with making all the decisions, or having all the responsibility, and no one person is perpetually powerless and has no input.

However, when power is distributed differentially (as in hierarchical relationships), the dynamics in a relationship can begin to create tension. For example, problems can occur if one person is "on the bottom"—that is, they are *always* responsible for maintaining the relationship (like planning activities and romantic interludes) or even more mundane tasks like housework, bills, and parenting children, while the other person is "on top" and seemingly "above it all." This can build resentment quickly. For these people on the bottom, they frequently believe that "if I don't do it, it won't get done." Sometimes they may be thought of (by others) as "control freaks." For many of them, their high expectations of themselves and their lives seemingly won't let them compromise. Frequently they will say they want their partners to do some of the things they do but then will come back and criticize the efforts when they aren't done "right." The partner concludes that it is best not to even try. Nagging is almost always more preferable to criticism.

For the partner who is "on top," there may seem to be some advantages (they don't have to make the decisions, they have a greater sense of freedom), but the reality is that the cost is a loss of power in the relationship over time. The partner on top will begin to feel less and less relevant and eventually impotent or incompetent in the eyes of the partner. At the same time, the person "at the bottom" may feel pressure, or the burden to be responsible, and to always *have* to be the one to make things happen so that the relationship or family is successful. And while they can have the benefit of being able to "get their way" and shape things the way that they want, it can also become frustrating when it seems the only way to get anything accomplished is if the person on the bottom does it. This, too, builds resentment over time, and, paradoxically, the person begins to perceive that the person on top is the one with the power!

The intriguing thing is that the *reality* of whether someone is always "on top" or always "down below" is not important. Instead, it is the perception of the imbalance that is most important. It is relative. A person may feel like her or she is on the bottom (i.e., the "breadwinner" doing all the work), but the partner may perceive him or her as being "on top" (i.e., having it so easy, having the power to decide what the other person does because of their economic status). The common feeling, regardless of whether the person is on top or on bottom, is powerlessness. If people feel powerless for a long time, they will believe it is true. Both imbalances (on top and on bottom) are significant strains to the relationship.

People who feel powerless, and feel that things are out of balance in the relationship, will try to rebalance the relationship in some way. Returning to the "see-saw" picture, the sides can be balanced by adding or taking away weight. For couples, it can be the addition of *people* to the relationship quarrel (see Table 4.1 for a list of common issues or circumstances that cause or contribute to power imbalances). Family members (parents or siblings), children (a big one!), or friends are the most common people who are turned to for support (i.e., "weight"). For example, if one partner is the primary earner and makes all the financial decisions, the other partner may try to rebalance the power differential by getting emotional support for his or her plight by turning to family members or friends. The other way to balance the imbalance is to "take away" weight. This is typically done by pulling away from the relationship and turning to hobbies, work, and even alcohol or drugs. Both are done as ways to wake the other person up to what they perceive as the imbalance or unfairness in the relationship. Often, however, this brings up more resentment, and (unless there is some professional intervention) will cause the relationship to drift further or become more rigid and entrenched.

Table 4.1.: Circumstances and topics that lead to power imbalances

Things that are often causes of power imbalances:
Work
Childrearing
Money
Sex
Extended family members
Religion/Faith
Division of labor (home)
Views on genders
Substance use/abuse
Circumstances that can complicate/exacerbate power imbalances:
Economy/job loss
Children entering the family
Dual career issues
Taking care of elderly parents

Case of Kurt and Janet

Kurt (aged 40) and Janet (aged 39) had been married for 17 years. They met in their freshman year of college and married while Janet was still in college. They struggled through the "lean years" but decided that when they started having children Janet would stay at home to raise them. They both shared a deep commitment to their faith and were active in their church, eventually taking leadership positions in their congregation. Kurt became very successful managing several manufacturing factories for a large corporation and rose in the ranks of his firm quickly. As a result, he was given more responsibility for managing overseas factories, as well as domestic factories. He disliked the amount of time that he spent away from home but justified it because it afforded the family a very comfortable existence.

During this time, Janet turned a lot of her attention to her growing family. They had four children in the span of 6 years. As often happens in these cases, Kurt began to feel more and more marginalized at home and more lonely on the road. He began to drink more frequently, which upset Janet (her father was an alcoholic, and it was contrary to her religious beliefs). This created tension between the two of them, and each began to feel that the other was deliberately hurting them. After a skiing accident left him with knee problems, Kurt began to abuse prescription painkillers as well. He used his pain to justify the need for these medications, although Janet thought he was abusing them.

While on the road, Kurt began to have a series of "one-night stands." Although Janet had begun to suspect this for some time, she did not want to bring it up for fear of learning the truth, dealing with the dysfunction, and shattering her image of her family. Approximately 18 months prior, Kurt began to have a persistent low-grade fever that would spike in the evening and subside during the morning. He would frequently feel achy and sore all over his body and would take pain medication to alleviate the symptoms. Inevitably, he went to his doctor and, through a series of blood tests, confirmed that he was HIV positive. It took him about 3 months to work up the courage to tell Janet.

Initially, Janet reacted with fear. First, she was fearful of her and her children's health. She became hypervigilant about Kurt's toothbrush, silverware, plates, and glasses, putting them in a separate cupboard and admonishing the children never to use them. She refused to tell anyone in her family and became terrified that someone in her church community would find out and they would be ostracized. She felt that her position in the church, and the image everyone had of their "normal" family, was all that she had left, and to lose that would be devastating. Then, after getting tested and finding out that everyone was HIV negative, she began to react with fear and anger. At one point, she even went so far as to say, "I wish that he had told me that he had gotten the HIV as a result of doing drugs (i.e., shooting up heroin), rather than through sex with some whore."

Toward Kurt, Janet presented a cold rage. She initially refused to sleep in the same room with him (often sleeping with the children), but she feared this would "raise questions." She started to sleep in the same bed with Kurt but refused any and all intimacy with him. As a result, Kurt felt even more alone and isolated in the family. In addition, he was racked with guilt for his actions. He became depressed and contemplated suicide. He was desperate to get any affection from Janet but was often brushed aside. She would often express her fear of having to raise the children alone, even though Kurt was perfectly healthy and on medication.

From a systems perspective, the power imbalances become set points, and the dynamics of the couples system keep the couple stuck in their respective "see-saw" situations. It becomes the norm, and the forces toward equilibrium try to keep it in that configuration. In time, family, children, and other "weights" can be used to counterbalance the differential, but in the end, the system will seek to maintain homeostasis. According to Napier:

> Beneath the surface of the partners' lives, there are two people who want to live more fully, but who are trapped in a growing sense of despair and futility. Though only one partner may be intently conscious of discontent, I believe that this desperate realization grips them both: "What are we going to do? How can we ever get out of this agony?" . . . Before an affair begins, both partners have usually betrayed each other in other ways. As they begin to drift apart, she finds closeness with their daughter; he allows himself to be re-captured by his widowed mother's needs. He works late; she works out at the gym. Both partners move away from each other, hoping to be noticed and called back; they want, often poignantly, to be told that they are missed and desired. In the tumult and blaming of the affair, the bi-laterality of their "pre-affair" affairs is not noticed, and of course in the early stages of therapy the therapist doesn't point out the usually covert infidelity of the rejected partner.
>
> (2007, p. 295)

Bottom line, you are stuck, the dynamic is rigidly set, and it doesn't change without some possible discomfort. However, one of the ultimate attempts to rebalance the power is to have an affair. With Kurt and Janet, Kurt felt helpless that she had all the power. His attempt at rebalancing it by having affairs ("I'll show you!") *backfired* on him. Now he felt perpetually in a "one-down" position, and he was desperate to change it if he could.

The Case of John Edwards

"You're hot." And with those words spoken by Rielle Hunter to John Edwards in February 2006, a relationship with long-lasting consequences began. At the time, the then senator from North Carolina was in the advanced stages of contemplating a run for president of the United States during the 2008 election cycle. According to reports, she and a friend saw him in a lounge in the Regency Hotel in Manhattan, and she did not believe that the man she was eyeing across the room was the former VP candidate and senator, so she and a friend went up to the table and asked Edwards's friends if he was indeed John Edwards: "The John Edwards I saw in 2004 [when he was the Democratic vice presidential nominee] on TV I believed to be a disconnected, two-dimensional-geek kind of guy. And the man sitting across the room was not that at all" (Depaulo, 2010).

She left her business card with the words "Rielle Hunter. Being is Free." printed on it. According to her account, they arranged to meet in his room that evening, ostensibly to "help him" with his media presence. Instead, they began a sexual relationship. At the same time, his then wife of 30 years was battling breast cancer (although was in remission at the time) and was considered to be a heroic figure in the eyes of the public due to her ongoing fight against cancer. By the end of the affair, John Edwards would lose his chance for higher elected office, father a child with Hunter, and be publicly humiliated and vilified for cheating on his wife as she fought for her life. So how could this have happened?

By now, we know that even in the most public infidelities, there are multiple forces involved. The Edwards's marriage endured not just Elizabeth's cancer, but also, in 1996, the death of their eldest son in an automobile accident at age 16. Despite being an accomplished attorney, she gave up her professional life following the death of her son. In addition, Elizabeth reportedly felt that John was her intellectual inferior. She came from a military family, where her father was a Navy pilot, while John's father was a textile mill worker. They met in law school and married shortly after in 1977. However, it is reported that she would refer to him as a "hick" and would tell other people publicly that his family were "rednecks." According to other reports, while she was a devoted wife and shrewd political advisor, she also could be intimidating and angry, which she would take out on her husband. When she would get upset, he would try to pacify her or just avoid her.

Things began to change for Edwards in 2004, when he ran for president and then was picked to be John Kerry's vice president. According to many aides, he began to crave the attention and the elite circles of the "bubble" that proximity to high office afforded (security details, private jets, adulation), which fed his ego. Despite being in the US Senate for less than one term, he really felt he could be the next president of the United States. Thus, in 2006, Edwards was traveling often to secure the necessary donations and personnel for a presidential run. It was reported that he spent more time away from home to avoid Elizabeth. Hunter and Edwards continued to see each other; in April 2006 she convinced him to hire her as a videographer to produce a series of "behind the scenes" web-documentaries, which allowed them to be together without anyone questioning. On December 28, 2006, Edwards announced his candidacy for president. On December 30, 2006, Elizabeth Edwards discovered a private cell phone that Edwards used to keep in touch with Rielle, at which point he confessed to the affair. At the time he purportedly told her that it was a "one-time thing" and that the relationship was not ongoing.

However, the relationship did continue. In March 2007 John and Elizabeth Edwards announced that Elizabeth's cancer had returned and that it was "incurable." Despite this, Elizabeth insisted that John continue to campaign. At the same time, Rielle and John continued their relationship, arraigning meetings at various campaign stops. Then in May 2007, Rielle became pregnant with their daughter, Frances Quinn. Edwards denied any paternity or involvement with her, despite tabloid stories appearing. After a poor showing in the early primaries in 2008, Edwards dropped out of the presidential race. In July 2008, the *National Enquirer* broke a story with pictures that claimed to show Edwards secretly meeting Rielle and the baby in a Beverly Hills hotel. In early August, John Edwards was interviewed by ABC News, where he admitted to the affair (although he would not publicly admit paternity until 2010).

In the August 8, 2008, interview (ABC News, "Nightline"), Edwards described his thoughts on what happened and why:

> This is what happened. It's what happened with me and I think happens unfortunately more often sometimes with other people . . . Ego. Self-focus, self-importance. Now, I was slapped down to the ground when my son Wade died in 1996, in April of 1996. But then after that I ran for the senate and I got elected to the Senate and here we go again, it's the same old thing again. Adulation, respect, admiration. Then I went from being a senator, a young senator to being considered for vice president, running for president, being a vice presidential candidate and becoming a national public figure. All of which fed a self-focus, an egotism, a narcissism that leads you to believe that you can do whatever you want. You're invincible. And there will be no consequences. And nothing, nothing could be further from the truth.

The Edwardses separated in January 2010 after he admitted to fathering Rielle's daughter. In December 2010, Elizabeth Edwards died from metastatic breast cancer. She wrote two books on the subject of her husband's affair. In 2012, Rielle Hunter wrote her own account of the affair, stating at that time that she had broken up with John Edwards. In 2016, Hunter gave another interview where she revealed that she and Edwards had continued a relationship through 2015, but that they were now just co-parents, and that she still cared deeply about him, saying: "Everyone has such judgments about 'He's lost everything.' But you know, life isn't over. He's gone through an amazing transformation. And who knows what's gonna happen" (Depaulo, 2010). John Edwards has not made any additional public statements about the relationship and has returned to a law practice he established with his older daughter.

How the Affair Rebalances the See-Saw

While there are several salient elements of the Edwardses' case, the issue of perceptions of power are potentially most interesting. One the one hand, John Edwards was a senator and a vice presidential and presidential candidate, which might suggest he had considerable power. But, according to published reports, the opposite might have been true! In particular, the characterization of Edwards pacifying or avoiding his wife, as well as John Edwards' statements about needing adulation, are evidence of his perception that there was a power imbalance. Going back to Brown's typology, it would seem that this was most likely a Split-Self Affair and/or a Conflict-Avoidance Affair. According to Napier (2007):

> Most affairs seem to be the product of the partners' failure to grow and change. Before the affair occurred, there was a pervasive feeling of deadness and stasis between the couple. They went over the same ground again and again; they felt flat and tired and bored. There was a sense of disconnection and drift. Conversations seemed to go nowhere; resolutions were not acted upon. One or both may have felt progressively more hopeless, as though they might literally die from the lack of emotional oxygen in the marriage.
>
> (p. 295)

Indeed, this describes the process where a power imbalance tends to "lock" the system into a fixed interaction cycle, in which case the affair is an attempt to rebalance this, or at least get the underlying issues out in the open. In the case of John Edwards, there is evidence that John felt (or was made to feel) inferior to Elizabeth due to their respective backgrounds (her father a Naval aviator, his a textile worker) and the suggestion that she would refer to this in public. He may have originally felt that the only way to balance out their relationship was to achieve a certain level of success. He became a successful (and wealthy) trial attorney, then a senator, and then a candidate for the two highest offices, but even that might not have been enough. Instead, having an affair becomes the way to "rebalance" the see-saw, or power imbalance.

Power is the ability to have an influence over another person's actions. If one person perceives that he or she cannot influence the other person, either by "soft" influence tactics (suggestions, comments, etc.) or "hard" influence tactics, the state of the relationship will become de-stabilized and untenable (Baucom et al., 2009). If they have tried to influence one another, and failed, particularly if they perceive that the other person has utilized something outside the relationship (kids, family, job) to "weight" them down, the inclination to use an affair to rebalance the relationship becomes a strong possibility.

Recall the case of Jeremy and Brittany from Chapter 3. For them, the affair was an attempt for Jeremy to rebalance the see-saw from Brittany's attempts to get him to fix their home. At the same time, Brittany felt like she was at the mercy of Jeremy, always having to ask for money and depending on him for resources (and affection). Clearly she felt like she was the one who was stuck up in the air on the see-saw. Paradoxically, Jeremy felt that he was the same position.

Family-of-Origin Dynamics and Power Imbalances

One of the places where couples bring their conceptions of power and roles for themselves in the relationship comes from the family of origin. The influence of parental models of power sharing (or lack thereof) can be monumental in shaping how the present relationship will deal with issues of power. If the family was dominated by the mother, there may be expectations for the current relationship to be female dominated, or if it was more male dominated, there likewise may be a similar expectation. At the same time, couples may try actively to interact with each other opposite to their family of origin. One partner who grew up in a very patriarchal household may not want that in his or her relationship and may either overtly or covertly coerce the other partner to take on a more dominant role in the hopes of avoiding a relationship like his or her parents. The problems occur when these demands are unspoken and projected on to the other partner. There may be coercion and manipulation that creates other problematic dynamics, like demand/withdrawing interactions.

The demand/withdraw interaction pattern occurs when one partner approaches the other (usually in frustration) and requests change by criticizing, nagging, or complaining, while the other partner avoids the request by withdrawing altogether from the discussion in response (Christensen, 1988). Higher incidence of the demand/withdraw interaction pattern are associated with higher levels of relationship dissatisfaction (Baucom et al., 2009; Eldridge & Christensen, 2002). In his observation of this pattern, Napier (2007) has noted:

> In this kind of stereotypical dominant-submissive pattern, the one-down partner not only takes a stand to acquire more power, but is in some measure "fishing" to learn about the other partner's vulnerability. It is as if each could only see part of the other, and the affair allows both partners to reveal aspects of themselves that had been hidden. It is as if through the affair both search for being more complete people, and to see each other more clearly.
>
> (p. 296)

Consider the following case, where the couple's interactional patterns have been interwoven with their respective family-of-origin dynamics, thus causing the conditions for a non-sexual affair to occur.

Maria and Jim

Maria and Jim had been married for 30 years. Approximately 2 months prior, Maria had what she called an "epiphany" when she realized that if she stayed with Jim any longer she would be miserable for the rest of her life. She realized that her husband, Jim, who was inflexible and controlling, was "just like my mother!" She began to pursue a relationship with her dermatologist, whom she had been seeing professionally for a number of years and had a flirtatious relationship with. She went on a date with him, fully intending to have sex with him if the opportunity came around, but did not go through with it, saying: "He was a lousy kisser." However, in a heated argument, just before deciding to come to couples counseling, she confessed that she had wanted to have an affair and she no longer loved Jim. Uncharacteristically, Jim broke down and became despondent. He begged her not to leave and even threatened to commit suicide. At that point, they came for therapy.

In terms of her background, Maria was a first-generation Venezuelan whose parents had come to the United States about 10 years before she was born. They were staunchly Catholic, and while she described her father as the "head" of the family who commanded respect, the real "powerhouse" of the family was her mother. She ruled over everything that everyone did, and if you were not compliant, you would get physically disciplined. Maria tried very hard to please her mother, but she never seemed to be able to. She was a very good student, demonstrating high aptitude for science. She wanted to go to medical school, but her father actively discouraged her, and her mother would not stand up for her. Her father didn't think that women could make it through medical school and told her it would be a waste of time. When she got to college, she became rebellious and promiscuous. She felt free for the first time, and she wanted to be in control. She met Jim in college, and she fell in love with him, even though he was dismissing of her.

For his part, Jim's mother did not protect him. His father was a "big" person, powerful and intelligent. He was wealthy and had built a successful manufacturing business that was later sold, with the proceeds placed in trust for his children. This meant Jim would have a comfortable living (although not ultra-wealthy) without having to work. Jim also had a high IQ but was not connected to his emotions. His mother ordered things, and he received the message that "chaos is bad." Therefore, when Maria would become emotional, and especially when she would have outbursts of her "Latin" temper (as she would call it), Jim would try to get her to stop. Oftentimes, this meant belittling her or using his intellect to shut her down. Growing up, Jim said that he always "felt alone" and unlovable. The revelation of Maria's relationship triggered those feelings. "I'm an asshole, and I don't deserve love."

In this case, the dynamics shaping the couple are palpable. Maria, the daughter of a domineering father, married a man who had inherited money (power) from his dominant and abusive father and turned out to be controlling as well. She was a "pleaser," and he wanted control and order. Jim, for his part, was emotionally distant and became more so as they got older. Thus, the more Maria tried to please Jim, the less she was able to succeed. And like her mother, who was bitter and frustrated, she adopted a similar stance toward Jim. The affair, although non-sexual, became the vehicle for her to express these frustrations and try to balance the power. After their only son had grown up and moved out, she went back to school but was frustrated that she could not successfully enter a profession at the level she wanted to because of a lack of experience and coursework (after being advised improperly). Jim was not supportive of this and openly mocked her: "Because I was jealous, I didn't have a career (I didn't need to), but I felt useless in life. I saw that she was making something of hers and it embarrassed me." At the same time, he felt that he was nowhere near the man his father was. This produced a profoundly ambivalent reaction in him as he at the same time "did not want to be a man like my father," but also saw himself as weak and unsuccessful (which is what his father told him before he died). Again, Napier (2007) seems to understand the consequence of these families of origin:

> A pervasive aspect of many marriages is a lack of courage in dealing with emotional issues. While the partners may be courageous in other aspects of their lives, they lose their nerve in close-in encounters, usually because of long-standing fears and anxieties that both have brought from childhood. An affair "calls the question" in the marriage; it forces both partners out into the open. If one partner has been too "selfless" in trying to please the other, this strategy of compliance and accommodation eventually produces first disrespect in the other partner, then anger. "Stand up and be somebody!" the rejecting partner cries out.
>
> (p. 297)

In terms of the "see-saw" metaphor, if the relationship has deteriorated to the point where an infidelity occurs, usually both partners feel they are the one who is "on the bottom" and are somehow making a sacrifice for the other.

The Affair as Triangulation

Bowen (1978) originally defined a triangle as the unit whereby emotionality could be most easily balanced and contained. In the language of this chapter, the triangulated party is a way to rebalance the "see-saw" in the relationship. One partner may try to change the dynamics of the relationship by actively involving another generation of the family, such as a child or in-law. For example, a spouse enters a coalition with a member of another generation of the family to deal with responsibilities that were previously the responsibility of the other spouse. The left-out partner is free to under-function, and the partner in the coalition is empowered by the other generation to over-function. Of course, with an affair, the other person becomes triangulated into the dynamic of the couple as an attempt to rebalance the perceived imbalance. Like any triangle/coalition, this ultimately leads to dissatisfaction and resentment in the relationship (Sperry & Peluso, 2018).

Triangulation also occurs in the context of couples therapy. However, as Napier notes, "(p)rofessional psychotherapy has difficulty competing with the sexually charged atmosphere of the affair" (p. 298). Counselors must avoid getting coerced to align with one party or the other (siding with the "victim" of a domineering spouse or the "victim" of a philandering partner). He provides the following advice to the couples counselor to help avoid this:

> It is my sense that most partners who initiate an affair have felt rejected (or bullied, or in some way mistreated) by the very partner they are rejecting, and that their internal justification for their actions represents a kind of destructive entitlement. But of course to point this out in the beginning of therapy, when the trauma of a more literal rejection is being absorbed by the "victim," would be not only counterproductive, but injurious.
>
> (2007, p. 296)

Consider the following case.

The Case of Adam and Martina

Adam and Martina had been married for 15 years when they came for couples therapy. Adam (43 years old) initiated therapy as a result of his suspicions because his wife (age 39) was spending an inordinate amount of time at their church assisting the recently widowed pastor. Adam complained that Martina was "not spending any time with me" and that she was "ignoring her responsibilities" with their two children. Martina objected to Adam's accusations, saying that she had been complaining of Adam's aloofness throughout the marriage and that she had tried to get him to come to therapy several times, only to have him tell her that she was "the one with the problem" and not him. Martina defended herself by saying that Adam was jealous because she had found "a ministry" for herself, which meant that at least once a week Adam would have to be responsible for an evening with the kids (meal, bedtime, etc.). Adam stated that it may have started that way but had become "easily three days a week you are over there, and there is also texting and phone calls in between!"

Martina denied any adulterous relationship with her pastor but did admit that she enjoyed the fact that he "treats me like a person and not a maid." Martina elaborated that Adam recently got upset and verbally abusive because she did not have time to go to the dry cleaners and pick up his shirts, which led to a protracted fight and Adam accusing Martina of having an affair. In truth, Adam was initially attracted to Martina because she was "hot" and they had "great sex." Martina was very helpful and got Adam organized early in his career. Now Adam was very successful in his job, which allowed Martina to stay at home and primarily raise the children. Adam had expectations that Martina would always be at home taking care of the things he didn't have the time or inclination to do, which allowed him to concentrate on his career. "Now, when I need you to come to functions with me for work, you don't want to." Whereas Martina was initially attracted to Adam because he seemed so confident and self-assured, she was now resentful of his indifference to her concerns, his self-absorbed lifestyle, and his controlling behavior.

Now Let's Consider a Transcript of Their Interaction

Martina: Why is it that you don't trust me, or Pastor John for that matter?

Adam: I have a real hard time trusting anyone. I was always made to feel ridiculous whenever I showed my feelings. I would get laughed at, which hurt more, and then when I would try to get people to stop it would get worse. As I got older, I always felt that whenever I shared something deep, or something that I was thinking, I would feel nervous like, "Uh-oh, now somebody knows. Who will they tell? What do they think about me? I've said too much." I had hoped that my partner would be someone that I could be open with, and I think that in the beginning, I was. But then, over time, you would get disappointed, or would flat out tell me (or make me feel like) I was wrong. I could never get you to see that maybe I wasn't and that you were wrong. But you never back down. So I stopped. I don't know exactly when, but I did.

Martina: All I wanted was to get you to open up to me, and to talk to me.

Adam: But I don't think that you ever wanted to hear anything that I was saying. You don't agree with me on things, so I felt like, "Why bother?" It just led to more pointless conflict, and I hate that!

Martina: You can be so distant, and so cold sometimes.

Adam: I know, but I think that I am just protecting myself. I wish I was different about it, but as I have gotten older, I realize that I just don't trust people anymore. It is sad, but it is true.

Martina: And that includes me?

Adam: Yes.

Martina: What gave you the idea that you couldn't trust me?

Adam: It always seems like when you need me, and I am there for you, it is all all right. But when I need you, when I am vulnerable and need you, you get distant and cold and you blow me off.

Martina: Like when?

Adam: Okay, so let's take for example when each of us gets sick. I am always trying to take care of you. I try to keep the house quiet. I bring you up medicine, food, drinks, I come and check on you. Me? When I am sick, you look at me with disdain and almost disgust, like I am faking it, or have "man-flu." You don't treat me nicely, you don't try to make me feel better. I do it for you easily and freely, but you don't do it back for me. You make me feel like somehow I am a freeloader and should be able to shake it off. And it just makes me think: "Wow, if this is the way she treats me when I have a cold, what will it be like when I really need her?" At the same time, I see how you take off at a moment's notice whenever John needs you. How is that supposed to make me feel?

In the preceding case, the power imbalance was tilted toward Adam. He was "on the bottom" of the see-saw, and Martina felt like she was being overlooked and dismissed. There was an overall lack of satisfaction, and there seemed to be no way to break the impasse. Adam, for his part, was okay to keep the status quo, although he was dissatisfied sexually with the relationship. Of course, the imbalance became impossible for Martina to bear, and an acceptable "out" arose in her new-found religious activity. She began to develop her own interests independent of Adam, which then forced Adam to feel the burdens that she did, while she got to feel the "freedom" that Adam has (viz. power in the relationship). The complicating factor of John recently being widowed (and potentially being a more ideal replacement for Adam) suddenly made Adam more vulnerable. In this case, it is impossible to say whether or not the relationship would have turned illicit or sexual, or if Martina would have left Adam for John, but the relationship itself (and the attention that Martina was paying to John to the exclusion of Adam) was enough to get him to voice his insecurities regarding trust.

Let's consider another case from the headlines and the world of politics.

The Case of Governor Elliot Spitzer

In March 2008, a report in the *New York Times* uncovered a story that then New York governor Elliot Spitzer had engaged an exclusive escort service to arrange for sex with prostitutes. Reportedly he had several sexual encounters (up to 20) and had spent close to $100,000. When the news broke of his affairs (and infamously being anonymously known as "Client Number 9"), he was forced to resign as governor (and end a promising political career that included talk of a presidential run).

He was married to Silda Wall, a successful lawyer, for over 25 years, and they had three daughters. She told friends that her name meant "Teutonic war maiden" and was described as a person who "never made mistakes" and liked having things "perfect." She had encouraged Spitzer not to quit and to fight for his political career, and she blamed herself for the sexual affairs: "On some level, this is my fault. The wife is supposed to take care of the sex," she was quoted as saying. "This is my failing. I wasn't adequate." She had given up her career to help Spitzer with his political ambitions (first running as New York attorney general, then as governor). Other reports suggested that the stresses and demands of the governorship put a strain on their relationship that may have "tipped the scales."

Several years after the scandal, and reportedly after attempts at counseling and reconciliation, she divorced Spitzer when it was revealed that he was dating Lis Smith, who worked for his unsuccessful political campaign in 2013. Spitzer called Smith "the love of my life." However, in 2016, Spitzer and Smith split up after a Russian prostitute apparently tried to extort Spitzer for money, threatening to expose details about their relationship.

Once again, according to Brown's typology, the case of Elliot Spitzer was either a Sexual Addiction Affair or a Split-Self Affair. In terms of the power dynamics in the relationship, like John Edwards, Elliot Spitzer was married to a smart, accomplished woman who helped him in his campaign but may not have "backed down" or let him feel too powerful (despite his accomplishments as a US attorney in New York and governor of the State of New York). What is interesting is the reported comment of his wife, Silda. She blamed herself for the failing of the relationship. It was as if Emily Brown (2001) was writing with her in mind (7 years before Spitzer's affairs happened) when she wrote:

> The female spouse in the Split Self Affair believes that if there is a problem in the marriage it is due to something he has or hasn't done . . . [she is] caught up in trying to make her family fit her image of what family should be. [The wife of the sexual addict is more concerned with maintaining the public image then with her own image of the family.] She sees her role as the key one in guiding the family, and if her husband doesn't share in that endeavor, she tries to compensate for his absence. Although she would prefer that her husband be involved, her focus is on creating the right kind of family for the children. She sees herself as the primary parent and the major caretaker for family members.
>
> (p. 44)

As we consider the plight of Elliot Spitzer, and his feelings with his marriage, Napier writes as if he had Spitzer in mind (again, over a year before the details of the relationship came to light):

> Often, the person who enters an affair feels dominated and one-down in the marriage. He or she may have made tentative efforts to confront the partner, but these proved unsuccessful and were given up. The betraying spouse feels vulnerable, unappreciated, and unheard; and the affair is an angry attempt not only to hurt the other, but to gain more power in the relationship. Though an affair is carried out in stealth and deception, the eventual and anticipated revelation of the affair is effectively a fist in the face of the partner.
>
> (2007, p. 296)

Conclusion

Of course, the affair, while it can bring attention to the underlying issue of power imbalances in the relationship, often has a high cost, as Governor Spitzer and Senator Edwards learned. While there may be some ways to address the power imbalances of the primary relationship, often what happens is the that "easy-going" affair relationship becomes work, and the marriage may seem like the "ideal" (with the betraying spouse thinking: "Look what I have done!"). Remorse and guilt color the "fun" and freedom of the affair as the other person begins to make demands or intrudes on one's daily life. By contrast, the idealization of the lover may then begin to crumble: "I have wrecked my marriage and my family, and now my lover is beginning to sound like my wife (or husband)" (Napier, 2007, p. 302). While the issues of power imbalance may have been rooted in either family-of-origin dynamics or life circumstances, when they become entrenched, and limiting—when one partner winds up always stuck at the top of the see-saw or always at the bottom—something must be done to rebalance it. This can take many different forms and does not always result in an infidelity; however, when there has been sufficient inflexibility, an infidelity can become a significant method for balancing out a previously imbalanced relationship.

So while power imbalances play a powerful role, not only in relationship dissatisfaction, but also in the occurrence of infidelity, they are not enough either together with dissatisfaction or alone. Power imbalances are a necessary, but often not sufficient enough, reason for affairs to occur. They provide the fuel for an affair to occur, but often not the spark. That requires the third element: the death of the dream, the wish not coming true, and the fantasy for the relationship remaining unfulfilled. This will be covered in the next chapter.

CHAPTER 5

The Death of the Dream, the Fantasy Unfulfilled, the Wish Un-Granted, and the Opening of the Door to Infidelity

It seemed so easy when they started out their relationship. It was like one person could finish the other person's thoughts. There was never any conflict or arguments, there was only ever fun. They liked the same things and could entertain each other endlessly, whether it was talking about deep meaningful topics or frothy nonsense. They found in each other the best friend they always wanted. And it was always going to be that way. Each would be the most important person in the other one's life. There was no reason why it wasn't always going to be fun and easy.

Virtually every romantic relationship begins with the promise of finding someone to share your life with, someone who will make you feel special, important, and valued. However, each relationship also comes with a set of expectations that go deeper, which gets into a person's fantasy, or dream, of how their romantic partner should be. Most times, these expectations are unspoken (like a wish) and unexamined. That is, most people don't really, explicitly *know* what they want from a partner, they just know it when they see it. It is a tacit bargain or "deal" that is struck. It also becomes most obvious to someone when they are *not* getting it from their partner. Most importantly, it is the glue that holds the relationship together, and when it dissolves, the relationship goes with it.

What Are These Fantasies?

Some of these deals, or bargains, are around protection and safety (e.g., "If I give you what *you* want, you will protect me and keep me safe" or "If you give me what I want, I'll make you feel special"). Some deals can be playful, born out of late adolescent pleasures (e.g., sexual fulfillment), while others are serious, born out of shared childhood traumas (e.g., family substance abuse, history of sexual abuse, divorced parents, etc.). Some of the "deals" may be based on excitement and fun or not being bored. This is especially true of younger couples used to going out on the town, only to have to change that once children and work responsibilities come along. Others might have a "deal" based on "fixing" someone (i.e., "If you let me *help* you, then I will give you what you want") or healing them from some past hurt or abuse (in the family of origin or early love relationships). This is especially true of the person who says, "I always pick the *wrong* person." For the partner, he or she may make a deal such as, "I want you to take care of me or parent me." However, this gets violated when either the partner refuses to change or becomes resentful at the other partner's bossiness.

How power is shared, distributed, or used can often come from these implicit fantasies or dreams. For example, some other deals may be around "Let me be in charge/don't burden me with the details." In this instance, the power imbalance is clear. One person takes a clear "adult" role while the other person takes a clear "child" role. As mentioned in the last chapter, the problem arises when, after a while, one person doesn't want to be the person "in charge" any more, or the other person gets sick of never being able to make any decisions or have any say in determining what the couple does. When this happens, there is tension in the relationship that can either erupt into open conflict or get buried in silent resentment. Ultimately they will feel a need to try to re-distribute the balance of power, which creates *disequilibrium* (and the system reacts accordingly).

The Power of These Relationship "Deals" in the Couples System

The point is that these "deals"—these *dreams* about what one partner will do for the other—are powerful, and they are expected to last forever. This is the great myth or delusion. As life experiences change people, old assumptions must change as well. Children arrive, health issues arise, family members get sick and die, disappointments come along, and the "deal" must be re-negotiated as couples take on new responsibilities. The problem is when the deal is re-negotiated silently or covertly without much discussion. Sometimes the deal gets re-negotiated *in reaction* to changes in the partners' lives (to a new role, to accommodate health issues, due to decreased sex drive, etc.).

When these changes take place, they reverberate throughout the relationship system and get reflected in power imbalances and decreased marital satisfaction. When this happens, the disappointment and hurt are deep. It feels like a "violation" of the original terms of the deal. Even if, in their head, people can rationally acknowledge that the change "had" to happen, they will often still feel resentful because the deal, the dream, and this fantasy are so central to their identity and so important for their happiness. They may feel a sense of betrayal or being "tricked" or "cheated" out of something. Mostly, they will feel like something in the relationship has been fundamentally lost and maybe can't be brought back. It doesn't have to be that way, but it often is. When one person—consciously or not—believes that it can't be brought back, this is where all the things that were once tolerated (decreased satisfaction, perceived power imbalance) become intolerable. This is "the last straw." This is the spark that ignites the infidelity. Like any fire, it consumes itself and leaves behind destruction.

Infidelity—or more specifically the "other person"—holds the promise of the deal fulfilled or makes the "dream" come true (or an even a "better dream" come true). In someone's mind, this person is now the one who *really* "gets" them and deeply understands them (see "The Case of Governor Mark Sanford," following). This is what makes an "emotional infidelity" or "cyber-affair" or other non-sexual infidelity just as much of a betrayal as a sexual one. It is a connectedness at the level of the *self* of the person. In many cases, that place was occupied by the primary partner or spouse (or at least he or she had access to it). It is the intimacies and private thoughts and feelings that, because of the agreed upon "deal," they were able to share in.

But once the perception of the deal or fantasy or dream is lost and won't be fulfilled, the partner begins to shut down and close down emotionally. Unfortunately, the other person may not be aware of it. Often, these subtle changes occur over time and are too subtle to be noticed. People become too preoccupied in themselves to notice the other person's change. It might be because of work pressures, or child demands, or responsibilities to parents or other family members, or it might be that the partner is too self-absorbed to care to notice. Until it is too late . . . !

Fulfilling the Lost Dream Through Infidelity

For many people, the affair—whether it is emotional, cyber, or physical—fulfills something they feel is lacking in their primary relationship on two levels, the external and the internal. Externally, they may feel they are not valued or seen as worthy, heroic, or essential. The affair then becomes a way a person can act out their fantasized role as they cannot do in their primary relationship. They play the role of a lifetime, the role they always dreamed of playing. This is *role fulfillment*. It could be: "I am a good lover (who is not rejected)." "I am valued." "I am competent." "I can make someone feel good." In other words, the person feels like they can define themselves—they can be—the way they always imagined themselves.

However, that isn't the end of it. The power of the affair is in the fulfillment of fantasy that goes *internally* to the core of someone's being. This may make them feel free of the burdens of their current relationship, their obligations to work or family that—for reasons of dissatisfaction or a perception of an imbalance of power in the relationship—feel like a crushing weight. They may feel like they are trapped by the life choices made long ago that simply are not working out the way they had planned or hoped for. They may feel like their life is passing them by and that opportunities for happiness are slipping by them. They may think they are getting the "short end of the stick" in the relationship (e.g., power differential) and that if they don't do something about it, their soul will slowly die. For the individual, the affair becomes a way to reconnect with a sense of one's self that has been (or feels like it is) lost. The sense of fulfillment goes right to the core of the person: it is a *soul fulfillment*. And even though it might be fleeting, it is often *very* powerful.

The Case of Governor Mark Sanford

On June 18, 2009, South Carolina governor Mark Sanford seemingly disappeared from the state, and his whereabouts were unknown to his staff, his security detail, and even his wife. As word of this got out to the media, the governor's staff put out a story that the governor was "hiking the Appalachian Trail" and would be difficult to reach. On June 24, 2009, Governor Sanford was discovered retuning to the United States from a trip to Argentina. In the following few days, it would be revealed that he had been pursuing a relationship with Maria Belen Chapur, a former journalist, who had met Governor Sanford in 2001, at which point they had struck up a friendship. In 2008, the relationship turned sexual, and in January 2009, Governor Sanford's wife, Jenny, discovered a letter that he had written to Maria. The Sanfords had been married for 20 years at the time, and the couple had four sons. He had been a rising star in the Republican Party and was chairman of the Republican Governors Association, which put him on many people's "short list" for potential vice presidential or presidential candidacy. While the scandal that followed created a buzz about the affair, it was not until later details came out that the exact nature of the relationship, and the *type* of infidelity, would be revealed.

When Governor Sanford admitted to the relationship with Chapur, in published reports, he stated that he had "met my soul mate." From the beginning, Sanford said that "there was some kind of connection" with Chapur. This is in stark contrast to how Jenny Sanford described the beginning of her relationship with Sanford to the *Washington Post*: "It wasn't exactly love at first sight. It was more like friendship at first sight" (Marcus, 2009). After the revelation of the affair, published reports about Mark and Jenny Sanford's relationship provided additional information that further bolstered this assertion. She was a very successful woman in her own right, came from a prominent Chicago family, and had a successful career in an investment firm before meeting Sanford. In 1994, after the birth of their second son (and while she was in the hospital), Mark Sanford told her that he wanted to run for Congress. She managed his successful campaign and his subsequent campaigns for governor, acting as his political advisor. During their marriage, Mark acknowledged that there had been "a handful of instances wherein I crossed the lines I shouldn't have crossed as a married man, but never crossed the ultimate line" until his relationship with Chapur deepened in 2008.

Several email exchanges between Chapur and Sanford were released (and, although not explicitly authenticated, they were not denied) by the South Carolina newspaper *The State* and shed additional light on the dynamics of the "split-self" nature of the affair. In an email dated July 10, 2008, Governor Sanford presumably wrote:

> The rarest of all commodities in this world is love. It is that thing that we all yearn for at some level—to be simply loved unconditionally for

> nothing more than who we are—not what we can get, give or become . . . I wish I could wish it away, but this soul-mate feel I alluded to is real . . . please sleep soundly knowing that despite the best efforts of my head my heart cries out for you, your voice, your body, the touch of your lips, the touch of your finger tips and an even deeper connection to your soul. I love you.

Here, Sanford expresses the split within himself about the feelings he had being with Chapur and the sense of obligation that he felt living up to the "code" he had for himself in his life. While he did try to reconcile with Jenny following the discovery of the affair, ultimately the Sanfords divorced in 2010.

Although in 2012 Mark Sanford and Maria Belen Chapur were reported to be engaged, in 2014 he announced that they had broken off the engagement due to legal proceedings following Sanford's divorce. In 2013, Sanford returned to the US House of Representatives following a special election to fill a vacant seat. He was re-elected in 2014 and 2016.

In this case, there are several issues to point out. First, in terms of Brown's typology, this clearly seems like a Split-Self Affair, where one (or both) of the partners feels like a part of them has been suppressed while trying to "keep up appearances" of the marriage. What is also noteworthy is that Sanford acknowledged that he had "crossed lines" previously before meeting Maria, although never the "ultimate line." This is indicative of many infidelities that don't "just happen" out of the blue. To put it in the context of a systems dynamic, this is evidence that there were issues in the marriage that created the conditions where the infidelity could occur. In other words, Sanford likely did not feel like he was getting his needs met with his wife (possibly because of time apart due to work or the fact that they had four sons). Thus, his boundary "crossings" could have been a way to express some feeling, or have some experience that he longed for, but because of his "values" he could not *violate* that boundary. In fact, Sanford even said that he was a person of values and that what he had done violated a personal code. But like many people who commit an infidelity, even though they say they try to live by a "code," or a set of morals and values, there is something so powerful about the "dream" or "fantasy," coupled with a yearning for emotional connection, that allows people to abandon it in the hopes of finding fulfillment.

So what was so powerful for Sanford? What made him (and so many others) risk so much? The most honest statements about this from Sanford may be contained in his emails. There he acknowledges that his relationship with Maria awoke something that was "dead" in him or not there in his marriage. There is a sense of freedom and fulfillment: "The rarest of all commodities in this world is love. It is that thing that we all yearn for at some level—to be simply loved unconditionally for nothing more than who we are." In this, he confesses that he has *not* been feeling this in his marriage. As a politician, it is easy to see how one may feel a great deal of judgment and acceptance based on what one can *do* or *accomplish* for other people. As with many other accomplished individuals, they may feel like the only way they are cared for is by doing something for someone else. This becomes the cornerstone of the "bargain" they strike with their spouse or partner initially: "Let me do for you and don't reject me!" However, invariably there are disappointments, and these can lead to a withdrawal of affection. A cycle of over-achieving to earn back affection can be built in, but eventually it is a diminishing return ("No matter what I do, I can't please him/her!"), and that is when the idea is born that "I will never be able to fulfill my partner and get the love *I* want and need in return." This is when the door opens and the infidelity (the promise of a new partner who can understand me) arrives. As Sanford pointed out in his email, Maria aroused a feeling that she was his "soul mate."

But to get to this point is not easy. In fact, sometimes it is painful to the point of anguish. In the press conference where he admitted to the affair, Sanford said: "I spent the last five days of my life crying in Argentina. I'm committed to trying to get my heart right." Again, this is a further example of the Split-Self Affair. There is considerable confusion and sadness that accompanies the infidelity because there are two relationships that are impacted: the original relationship (where a dream has died), and the new relationship (that has the hope of fulfillment, but often not the freedom to pursue it). In Mark Sanford's case (as with many others), the Split-Self Affair portends the end of the original marriage and the pursuit of a new relationship. But with other types of affairs (Intimacy-Avoidance, Conflict-Avoidance), the work must begin to find a way to mourn the deal that has died, repair the damage in the relationship, and begin to forge a new dream (more on each of these in Chapters 6 and 7).

So taken together, the affair represents an external *role fulfillment* and an internal *soul fulfillment* that tap into people's dreams and fantasies about how life *should* be (to them). This does not mean there isn't a cost or consequences for these actions. Nor does it mean the feelings will last (they seldom ever do). But this is the reason why—when satisfaction is low in a relationship, and power is perceived to be imbalanced—the temptation is *so* great and why it gets acted on. But before discussing this further, it is important to know where these dreams come from, how they develop, and how they get negotiated by couples.

Where Do These Fantasies, Wishes, or Dreams Come From?

In order to more fully understand the fantasies, wishes, or dreams that power the relationship (and their importance when they go unfulfilled or the partners decide they won't come true), it is important to uncover the underlying purposes of them, as well as the systemic forces within the family of origin that created them.

The Need to Belong

Inherent in all human beings is the need to belong. Baumeister and Leary (1995) conducted an exhaustive review of the literature in social and developmental psychology on the need to belong and concluded that the need to belong is a critical element for individuals to join with others in a social context for personal well-being (i.e., survival). It is important for the creation of secure attachments, which are maintained by relationships with other people, as well as the development of schema dynamics like the view of self and view of others (Mozdzierz et al., 2014a). Interestingly, they found that a person's perceptions of his or her self-esteem differentially impacts his or her behaviors in social groups. Thus, individuals who have a high level of self-esteem do not join social groups (or relationships) just to meet the need to belong but do so willingly and deliberately out of a desire to contribute to a social group, whereas people with low self-esteem tend to join groups (or relationships) primarily to meet the need to belong (Sperry & Peluso, 2018).

In fact, Baumeister and Leary found that not only is the need to belong sufficient to explain why people form social bonds, but it is also sufficient to explain why they avoid rupturing existing bonds. These social bonds shape the way a person thinks about situations and are crucial for the experience of positive emotions (by meeting the need to belong) as well as the opposite case. They also found that the need to belong can be satisfied by maintaining a few close relationships (not just large social groups) and that, when individuals are deprived of these relationships, or when the quality of the relationship is poor, individuals report diminished satisfaction. They concluded that there is overwhelming evidence to conclude that the need to belong is a basic, pervasive, and powerful motivator for humans. In fact, they grasped the psychological implications of failing to meet the need to belong on the self:

> A great deal of people's psychological difficulties reflect emotional and behavioral reactions to perceived threats to social bonds . . . many of the emotional problems for which people seek professional help (anxiety, depression, grief, loneliness, relationship problems and the like) result from people's failure to meet their belongingness needs. Furthermore, a great deal of neurotic, maladaptive and destructive behavior seems to reflect either desperate attempts to establish or maintain relationships with other people or sheer frustration and purposelessness when one's own need to belong goes unmet.
>
> (p. 521)

So when it comes to romantic relationships, they are borne out of a need to belong, and they are the mechanism for people to meet this need to belong to a couple or system. The dreams, wishes, or fantasies—on which these relationships are the vehicle—fulfill this need to belong. And, as Baumeister and Leary point out, when people *don't* or *can't* meet this need, psychological problems can occur (depression, anxiety, etc.), including relationship problems. This is why the need to belong is crucial to understanding the "bargain" the couple strikes to fulfill each other's dreams, wishes, and fantasies. At the same time, it helps explain *why*, when the bargain is broken and one or both partners feel like they won't get their dreams, wishes, or fantasies fulfilled, an infidelity is likely to occur. It is because the need to belong is so important and the lack of belonging can be so painful.

Family Systems Dynamic That Created Them

So, if the need to belong is so important, and is the reason why relationships are formed, where do the specific needs that create the unique dynamics of the "bargain" for meeting each person's emotional needs come from? What drives the *where* of each person's fantasy, dream, or wish? These are usually rooted in experiences from early childhood in the family of origin. Sometimes these are messages that are received from one's parents. For example, some parents may pamper or spoil their child, and they may give them a sense that they are special or that the rules don't apply to them. These people may feel entitled to have their every need met, immediately. This may become an expectation they carry forward into adulthood and have for their partner when they get into a relationship. If their partner has a *complimentary* wish, dream, or fantasy ("If I care and nurture my partner, they will do the same for me!"), they will work very hard to please their partner with the entitlement wish. And that partner may make good on the bargain and reciprocate (i.e., do the same), but only when it suits them and only if it does not conflict with their needs or wants (which will take priority in their mind).

For the partner who was hoping for reciprocity, this might be okay in the beginning, but usually resentment will build up, and before too long they may not want to give in to every whim from their partner. At this point, if the system has created the "meet my needs any time and place" as part of its homeostatic set point (and the "reciprocal" has not), when the other partner wants to revisit or change this, it will provoke the system to provide feedback (in the form of resistance) to change. The homeostasis may feel constricting or unsatisfying and may lead the other partner to stop meeting the partner's entitled expectations. Again, this will perturb the system, and the system will provide resistance to keep equilibrium. If this becomes intolerable (because the "reciprocal" needs are not being met *or* because the entitled expectations are not being met), one or both individuals may feel that the "bargain" has been broken and may look elsewhere for comfort or belonging.

Other times, these dreams, wishes, and fantasies come from unmet needs in the family of origin. As a result, the relationship becomes a way to get the other partner to give a person some of the nurturing or parenting always wanted. People idealize what they will get or accept in a partner and in a relationship. For example, parents might be demanding and bossy, withdrawing their love and affection if their children are not compliant or cooperative. As those children grow up, they may want a partner who will *always* love them unconditionally. They may not want someone who puts a lot of demands on them. Again, if they find a partner with reciprocal needs (i.e., keep me safe, don't abandon me), the bargain may work well. However, if the partner with the "safety" and "abandonment" concerns gets worried that the partner will not meet his or her needs, the individual may criticize the other partner. This will violate the "unconditional" part of the bargain (as it feels demanding, just like the parents were). In turn, this dynamic can, over time, lead to one or both people feeling hopeless that they will ever get their needs met by the other person. And, as with the prior scenario, this break is when an infidelity is likely to happen.

Table 5.1.: A partial list of common themes contained in wishes, dreams, and fantasies for relationships

Please keep me safe/Don't hurt me
Play with me/Have fun
Make me feel special
Make me feel powerful
Take care of me
Make me feel sexually fulfilled
Don't hassle me/Don't boss me around
Don't make me take responsibility/Don't make me make decisions
Don't make me feel lonely
Don't abandon me
Cater to my needs
Comfort me/Don't make me scared
Don't make me grow up!

By now it should be clear that there is a relationship between the need to belong, family-of-origin dynamics, and the development of these wishes, dreams, and fantasies about the relationship. It should also be clear how these wishes, dreams, and fantasies affect a person's choice of partner and what they negotiate in the deal/hope for in the marriage. Still not sure about what these dreams, wishes, or fantasies are? A partial list is contained in Table 5.1.

How Do the Dreams Die?

Every relationship is based on an often unspoken agreement. It is a deal that is made between the two people to fulfill their unmet needs and unfulfilled dreams, wishes, or frustrations that originate in the family of origin and help people meet the need to belong. As a result, these dreams don't die easily once a person has committed to them. However, at some point, one person in a relationship has felt *so* dissatisfied for *so* long, and has felt the power imbalance so severely, but has held on for *so* long. These people hope that at some point their partner will come around, see what they have been doing, feel bad about it, and hold up their end of the bargain. But then, an *awful* realization comes and a dark thought enters their mind: that they will never get their deepest needs met, their wish granted, their fantasy fulfilled, or their dream to come true with *this person*. No matter what. They believe they will wait forever and still it won't be done. Sometimes these deals start off promising but get re-negotiated to conform to old models (family of origin) of relationships, which maybe a person *didn't* want to re-create, in order to cope with changes and disappointment. This is when the door opens. This is when one or both partners seek out a way to feel satisfied, rebalance the "see-saw," and feel powerful (instead of power*less*). They seek to have their wish granted, their dream come true, and their fantasies fulfilled by turning to someone else. This is the context in which *all* infidelities occur (physical and non-physical), regardless of the underlying cause (Intimacy-Avoidance Affair, Split-Self Affair, etc.).

The Case of Bill and Jane

Bill was 43 years old when he came to counseling complaining of marital difficulties with his 38-year-old wife, Jane. The couple had been married for 8 years and had a 3-year-old son. Bill described the early parts of his relationship with Jane as "fun and exciting." Jane had been an executive at an insurance company, and Bill worked in an investment brokerage. They had met socially through co-workers and had an immediate chemistry. "She always wanted to *do* things. We would go out to dinners or drinks with friends. On weekends we would just pack up and go to the mountains, or sometime just overnights to places we hadn't been." Bill stated that he had waited until he was "good and ready" to get married. "I waited until I had lived a single life, and then settled down. I wasn't in a rush." When he met Jane, he felt great compatibility with her: "She was focused on her work, and she was good. She and I lived by the motto 'Work Hard, Play Hard.'"

When it came to having children, Bill also felt that he and Jane didn't rush into that either.

> We knew we wanted to spend time as a couple and do the things we wanted to do first, before having children. We knew that our lives would change, and so we spent the first five years of our marriage on us and then decided to start a family. It is what we talked about.

Bill said that they were good at communicating their needs to one another: "We were usually on the same page, and even if we disagreed, I knew where she was coming from."

Things began to change about 7 months into Jane's pregnancy. She developed preeclampsia and was required to be on bed rest for the last 6 weeks of her pregnancy. After a normal delivery, however, Jane experienced extreme post-partum depression that required hospitalization. "I was really scared," said Bill. "She was unable to get out of bed or care for herself, let alone our son." After a brief stay, she was prescribed medication and seemed to be doing better. "But then she changed." According to Bill, Jane's original plan was to take 3 months off and then return to work: "She definitely did not want to give up her career. Being a 'stay-at-home' mom was never in her plan at all." Then, when their son was about 2 months old, Jane announced that she had changed her mind and was going to quit her job. "I was surprised, to say the least, but I wanted to be supportive, so I agreed to it." When asked if she offered any explanation, Bill said, "She never wanted to discuss it. It was a closed subject."

Bill had received promotions at work and was a senior executive, which afforded them the ability to live on one income. "I didn't resent that. In fact, that was how my parents lived, so I didn't think anything of it one way or another." Bill also reported that for the first year or so, he understood that Jane would be primarily focused on their son, and he admitted feeling like "a third-wheel" when he was at home. "I would try to help and pitch in, but all I would get was grief. Nothing ever seemed good enough for Jane!" Bill said she was especially critical when it came to their son. "That might have been the worst part! A couple of times she would accuse me of putting him at risk! That was crazy, just because I didn't do things exactly the way that she did or thought they should be. I really felt like that got in the way of me and my son bonding!"

As time went on, however, Bill stated that his relationship with his son got better, while his relationship with Jane got worse. "He's now at the age where he wants 'Daddy! Daddy! Daddy!' And to be a 'little man' which I think drives Jane crazy." Bill stated that he tries to give Jane a break and take his son out for a day, but "she won't even call her friends or go out for lunch or coffee!" When asked about time for he and Jane as a couple, he responded, "Forget that! She won't even *think* about going out or doing anything with me!" Bill also described that Jane's parents live approximately 20 minutes away and, despite that, have never had a "sleep-over" with their grandson. "They have begged her several times, but at first he was too young, then it was because he was sick, but I think they are all excuses."

Matters came to a head about 8 months ago when Bill had an important business meeting at a resort, with all expenses paid and spouses invited to come. Jane had agreed to go, albeit reluctantly, and let their son stay with her parents. A few days before, their son seemed to have a cold, and Jane got concerned. Her parents agreed to stay at Bill and Jane's house (rather than take their grandson out of his "familiar settings" to their house, which concerned Jane). But once that was resolved, Bill began to get excited. Perhaps this trip was a way to shake Jane out of her "funk" and maybe re-kindle the old spark within her. However, as the day came, Jane refused to go, saying that their son was too sick for her to be away from him. "That was the last straw!" according to Bill. He left after a big argument. "It was mortifying for me! Everyone was asking where Jane was and I had to make up some BS excuse." He said that it was not the first time, either, and that he was frequently making excuses for Jane's absence at business functions.

> I just don't get it. I mean we have a lot of friends who have children, and sure, in the first few months they don't go out much, but after three years? I finally began to think, "Maybe it's me she doesn't want to be with?" and that hit me like a tremendous weight.

Bill started to think that maybe they were heading for a divorce, which brought on feelings of depression. "I never wanted to be one of 'those guys' who were single dads and divorced." Bill revealed that his mother and father were married for over 40 years, until his dad's sudden death 5 years ago. Bill described himself as very close to his father ("He was my idol!"). His father coached his little league team, and Bill saw himself and his marriage as being modeled after his parents. "I guess they had their problems, but I never saw it. They were partners, and they were in love right up to the end." When asked what he thought about when he thought about he and Jane getting a divorce, he said: "failure."

Bill discussed that his career usually requires him to go out with clients and entertain them.

> I used to only go once in a while, but as I got promoted, I felt that I had to go out more and more. In the beginning, I would ask Jane to come along, but then I just stopped because I knew she wouldn't say yes.

This also became an area of tension between him and Jane. One night, approximately 6 months ago, he was out with a group of co-workers at a bar and was sitting at a table. "I always felt that I had a good 'poker face' and could hide my feelings." But this one night, Amanda, an attractive friend of another co-worker that Bill had known for a while, came up to him and asked how he was doing. "I smiled and said 'Fine,' and she said, 'You know I can tell that you are hurting,' and she stroked my arm. Man, that was it!" At that moment, Bill suddenly felt there was someone who truly understood him and saw through the mask he was using to hide his pain. For the next few weeks, they began meeting for drinks and occasional dinners. He really enjoyed her company and how he felt when he was with her. Then, about 4 months ago, they began a physical relationship.

> Now, I have become one of "those guys" that I swore that I would never become. I didn't plan for things to happen this way, but I really enjoy *feeling* something again. But I dread if Jane ever finds out, I don't know if she could handle it mentally and emotionally.

In this case, Bill's fantasy about the marriage was that if he waited long enough and found the right person, everything would work out fine. His parents had a good relationship, and he also felt that if he and Jane could work together, they would be able to be successful. Deeply, though, he wanted someone to notice and care for him, rather than abandon him. He wanted a "partner" and a "playmate." He was not unreasonable in his demands of Jane (he tried to understand her needs post-partum), but he slowly realized that she was changing the conditions of the "bargain" they had initially struck. It is also clear that Bill had hope that Jane would "snap out of it" or "come around" and be some semblance of her old self. However, Bill's hopes were dashed when she refused to come to the resort meeting with him.

That was the point that he decided he was not going to get his partner back and was not going to get his needs met. It also became the opportunity to allow other people to come in and fill that void.

How the Death of the Dream, the Fantasy Unfulfilled, and the Wish Un-Granted "Open the Door" to Infidelity

The philosopher Fredric Nietzsche famously said: "He who has a 'why' can endure any 'how.'" For couples, this means enduring many trials, disappointments, and hurts in the hopes that they *might* get their needs met. Many would say that this is the state of marriage—enduring all sorts of difficulties in order to get your deepest wishes fulfilled. But once the "why" (in this case the dream, wish, or fantasy) goes away, the desire and ability to endure rapidly diminish. Sadly, this would be a great opportunity for the couple to make genuine changes if they were working in therapy. Instead, the infidelity becomes the force for change. More specifically, the disillusionment comes swiftly (although there may have been a long buildup to it). The "last straw," or "breaking point," or "point of no return" happens, and suddenly a relationship with a person that may have been platonic (a co-worker, neighbor, or friend) begins to take on a new significance. An innocent flirtation that may have been dismissed in the past, or that may have been denied due to a sense of commitment or morality, suddenly shifts and is accepted. Thus begins (or completes) the journey toward an infidelity (note that this can also can exist with a complete stranger as well). The point is that there seems to be an invitation that is accepted, a willingness that was not acknowledged, and a permission given that would not have been given if there hadn't been a steady decrease in satisfaction, a chronic imbalance of power, and the realization that the dream would not come to pass, the wish would not come true, and the fantasy—indeed, the foundation of the bargain for the primary relationship—would not be fulfilled.

Fantasy and Play (and the Affair)

Part of fantasy that is so attractive or enticing is the sense of fun and play that comes with it. It is why, I think, we are so obsessed with happiness, and why so many people feel miserable! They pursue happiness, but not fun or play (remember the Beatles' *She's Leaving Home*?). In other words, they do it too seriously and usually fail miserably (sadly, therapy may play a part in this). More often than not, because of responsibilities or obligations (to work, kids, etc.), adults give up on things that are fun or enjoyable. In short, they give up on the fantasy because they are too busy trying to manage their lives. The problem is that the desire or the dream/fantasy never really dies or goes away. Instead it hides and waits for an opportunity to spring out, or it becomes a zombified, nightmarish version of the dream it once was (i.e., you dream of the big house but then you have to spend all of your time working to pay for it).

Most people know that their life is not a constant parade of joy, fun, and play. It is not an endless trip to Disney World, but when people—especially couples—no longer make the time for fun or play, part of the original "magic," part of the negotiated "deal" they made, indeed part of the fantasy, begins to die. As that happens the couple begins to lose touch with one another. This makes room in the relationship for other people to fill the spaces that open up. It is often intoxicating when someone who is in a relationship where there is no fun or play, or the fantasy is downplayed or not being met, finds themselves in a situation where an affair can happen, and that sense of fun and play—often in the form of excitement, flirtation, arousal, and so on—begins to or offers to re-awaken or reconnect with something lost. This is why affairs often start as "fantasies" (ironically enough) in someone's head. *This* is part of the beginning phase of the affair where the person begins to not only fantasize about the possibilities of the affair, but begins to take some playful actions (contacting by emails, phone calls, Facebook, MySpace, etc.). These actions give a sense of excitement or thrill indicative of the early stages of the relationship and at the same time are the things that are missing from the primary relationship.

So when someone comes along who captures the attention of the person committing the infidelity, and holds the promise of fun and fulfillment, the draw is compelling. In the early parts of these relationships, there is always some form of deep, intimate sharing. It touches on the level of fantasy. Somewhere along the line, in the primary relationship, that level of sharing doesn't happen. This is usually because of power imbalances in the relationship and dissatisfaction with the relationship. But in the infidelity relationship, satisfaction is usually artificially high, and power is equally shared. The other person becomes idealized and imbued with great power to fulfill fantasies. Gus Napier, a pioneer of systemic family therapy, along with his mentor, Carl Whitaker, said of affairs:

> As Whitaker has said . . . it is possible to see the lover as a kind of psychotherapist: someone who, famously, listens and understands. The stereotype of the spouse who "doesn't understand me" is of course a convenient excuse for the affair, but it can also be true. The betraying partner may operate out of "destructive entitlement" . . . and may justify the affair as a rightful response to rejection, abandonment, or abuse. As therapists we should not be too sympathetic with the rejecting partner, at least initially, as victim of his or her spouse; but it is wise to remember that underneath the decision to have an affair lies a considerable amount of pain and desperation.
>
> (Napier, 2007, p. 298)

Movie: *Little Children*

Living in an upper-middle-class New England suburb, Sarah and Richard Pierce have a dysfunctional marriage. Sarah's marriage to Richard is sexless because he is addicted to Internet pornography. One day she catches him masturbating in his office, and they begin to sleep separately. They have an infant daughter, Lucy, whom Sarah regularly brings to a local park with other parents and children. Brad Adamson is a househusband who brings his infant son, Aaron. Brad has yet to pass the Massachusetts state bar exam and doesn't even want to be a lawyer. He continually is looking for connections to his youth, when his life held so much promise. As such, he too is in an unsatisfying marriage to his beautiful and driven wife, Kathy, the household breadwinner. Kathy pushes him to succeed. She makes documentaries for public television for a living. They live a bit beyond their means, forcing them to accept financial support from Kathy's mother. Their sex life is nonexistent because Kathy is too self-involved in her career and being a mother. When he is supposed to be studying for the bar exam, Brad instead plays on a local football team or sits and watches teenagers skateboard outside his house, fantasizing about being young and carefree again.

By chance, Sarah and Brad get to know each other at the park and are attracted to each other if only in their search for that something missing in their lives. The question becomes what they are to do with their feelings. Both Brad and Sarah have unhappy home lives. She buys a flattering swimsuit and begins to attend the public pool because she knows she will see Brad there. They begin a deep if platonic relationship, and their children become friends as well. Sarah craves being sexually desired by someone as conventionally handsome and masculine as Brad.

One day in the park with the children, it begins to rain, and Sarah and Brad take Lucy and Aaron back to her house and put the kids to bed. Brad looks at one of Sarah's books and finds a photo of him in a collection of Shakespearean sonnets. While Sarah is drying towels in her basement, Brad kisses her, and they are unable to contain their desire for each other. They have passionate sex in the basement while their children sleep upstairs. Later, when Brad skips taking the bar exam again, Kathy grows suspicious and tells Brad to invite Sarah, Richard, and Lucy over for dinner. The intimacy evident between Brad and Sarah confirms her suspicions, and Kathy arranges for her mother to come for an extended visit so Brad and Sarah can't see one another anymore. When Brad's football team plays its final game, Sarah attends (while Kathy does not) and cheers as Brad scores the winning touchdown.

Afterwards, Brad and Sarah make out on the field. He admits that this is the happiest moment of his life and convinces Sarah to run away with him. That same night, Sarah and Brad agree to meet in the park to run away together. Brad tells Aaron he loves him before putting him to bed, writes Kathy a note explaining why he is leaving her, and then sneaks out while she and her mother finish the dishes. Before he can get to the park, he is distracted by skateboarding teenagers, who convince him to try a jump himself. Brad does so but falls and knocks himself out. When he regains consciousness, he asks the paramedics to call his wife and tell her to meet him at the hospital. It turns out that he never left the note for her, and he tells one of the skateboarders to dispose of it for him. Meanwhile, Sarah takes Lucy to the park to rendezvous with Brad, but when Lucy disappears, Sarah panics and rushes to find her, forgetting about Brad. After Sarah finds Lucy and puts her in the car, Sarah starts crying, realizing her getaway with Brad is just a fantasy. So while they spend a lot of time fantasizing about the future they could have together, in the end they realize their relationship is just an escape from their marital problems, which they ultimately have to face.

Much like other affairs, in the movie Brad and Sarah are both dissatisfied in their marriages, and there is a power imbalance in their relationship. However, it is not until they both realize that their partners will not be able to fulfill their dreams for the relationship (Sarah because her husband prefers Internet porn, Brad because his wife is more focused on her work) that the infidelity occurs. Moreover, there is the shared realization that each is not only attracted to each other, but that each can fulfill the other. Thus the fantasy begins of running away, of being the idealized person the other one wants (who will make them feel wanted and desirable and give them the satisfaction that they crave). However, before it can be realized, reality sets in. This happens a lot in affairs. Before and during the affair, the real relationship seems to be all work and no fun. The fantasized relationship seems so easy and not much work. The paradoxical thing is that many times after the affair is revealed, the real relationship becomes fantasized in hindsight ("Oh, I blew it, I never knew how good I had it; I wish I could just turn back the clock") and the relationship with the "other person" becomes *work* as that person begins to put demands on the cheater ("You promised me you would leave"). In the movie *Little Children*, it is the *real* relationships, the marriages that Sarah and Brad have, that are more real and therefore are the ones they choose. Often, but not always, this is the case for couples, where the infidelity is a symptom and an impetus for change in the primary relationship, not a reason to abandon it.

Conclusion

In a lot of instances, the experience of infidelity may be a combination of accomplishment and shame, fulfillment and embarrassment, and relief and anxiety. It is the experience of relief after a period of self-denial, but the cost is usually the violation of one's values. At the same time, it can be the fuel for real change to occur (and in fact, because of the way the couple has structured the relationship, it becomes the only way to do so). The irony is that with the infidelity, one usually gets the fantasy without the work, which can feel good, but also empty (because it is not real). At the same time, the reality of the primary relationship may be work, but it holds the promise of getting the fantasy in a more real and substantial way. Most times, in the end, this is more real and fulfilling (except in cases of Split-Self Affairs).

While the infidelity might be the fuel for change, it does come at a cost. Often the disclosure phase, where the infidelity is discovered by the partner, is fraught with pain and trauma. It is one of the most tumultuous and emotional periods for couples. It is where the relationship will either survive or not, and it is where most couples counselors are introduced into the couples' system. It is also the place where well-trained couples counselors can be the most effective and have the greatest impact in people's lives. This important phase will be discussed in the next chapter.

CHAPTER 6

Detonation of the Bomb: Infidelity Discovered, the Partner's Perspective, and the Decision to Pick Up the Pieces or Pack It In

I almost didn't believe it when I heard it. I felt like the floor underneath me dropped out, and I started to fall. I also had this sense of calm, and in my head I felt like I was thinking about this very rationally. It was only after a few minutes that I was aware that someone was screaming, and that person was me!

Up to this point, the last four chapters of this book have been focused on the factors that *explain* infidelity from a systems-oriented viewpoint. Much of that takes place before a couple ever sees a counselor. However, it is often at the point of discovering that an infidelity has occurred, or if a couple has been in counseling for a relatively short period of time when an infidelity is admitted to, that the issue must be attended. However, before any treatment can occur, the couple must go through the initial stage of absorbing the reality of the infidelity. This is often the beginning of treatment, and the point where competent, systemic couples therapists can make the most difference or where poorly trained clinicians stumble blindly in the dark. Why? Because the hardest thing to do (for a clinician) takes place here. As mentioned in Chapter 2, the systemic couples counselor has to convince both partners that the infidelity is a symptom of something more fundamentally wrong in the relationship and that each partner had a role to play in creating the conditions that created the opportunity for the infidelity to occur (and therefore both have a role to play in recovering from it). Of course, this flies in the face of the idea of a "victim" and a "cheater" that most clinicians tacitly accept. The problem is that this is a trap that usually leads to failed counseling and failed relationships. Instead, a truly systemic approach is needed. This chapter is devoted solely to understanding this initial phase and the important clinical considerations that need to be made.

Disclosure Versus Discovery

Infidelity is exposed by one of two pathways: disclosure or discovery. There are separate reasons for each of these, but the manner in which an infidelity is uncovered can have an impact on treatment initially. Each is unique and requires some exploration and consideration.

Disclosure

Disclosure is the decision of the partner who has committed the affair to tell his or her partner about his or her relationship with someone else. This decision usually arouses tremendous anxiety, but it proceeds either from a sense of guilt or responsibility (as in the case of Conflict-Avoidance or Intimacy-Avoidance Affairs) or a desire to leave (as in the case of Split-Self or Exit Affairs). The person who committed the infidelity may have originally thought it could be kept a secret or hoped the affair would never come to light. What the person could not count on was the internal struggle between his or her view of self ("I am a good person") or his or her values ("I believe in honesty and integrity") and the reality of the situation ("I did something shameful and have not been able to be true to myself"). Pioneering Systemic Family Therapy therapist and writer Gus Napier (2007) summed up the experience of the person wrestling with these feelings thus:

> While Dostoyevsky's portrait of the "compulsion to confess" lays guilt at the heart of this impulse to come clean, we can surmise that the adulterous lover may have a more growthful impulse: to connect the two separated and antagonistic parts of the self. How does one make oneself face up to having lived a duplicitous life? To having two split-off selves? Confess, or get discovered, in an affair. Here are the two realities, out in the open, compelling us to face who we are. And by the way, the person victimized by this process is really furious. When the adulterous spouse is discovered or confesses, he or she often experiences some relief. While the affair has been mythologized in our culture as a romantic experience, in reality most affairs are rushed and guilty, and they have a quality of grimy, cheap desperation. Sneaking around and stealing pleasure isn't convenient or easy; and then there is the guilt. When the betrayed spouse finally knows the truth, his or her anger may be easier to deal with than the betraying partner's self-blame.
>
> (pp. 301–302)

In other words, the desire to escape the pain and embarrassment of being found out is outweighed by the relief at not having to keep a secret anymore. While it takes courage for the person to disclose to his or her actions to the partner, he or she is not likely to get "credit" for courage, as the partner's shock, trauma, and pain can become overwhelming and equally guilt inducing. In fact, relief is quickly replaced with other negative feelings:

> The betraying spouse is also flooded with shame and embarrassment; and as the damage caused in the spouse becomes more visible, the adulterer must register the impact of his or her actions. While the vulnerability of the rejected spouse is often palpable and poignant, the therapist must also deal with the vulnerability of the adulterous spouse, who is often a seriously unhappy, or seriously troubled, individual. The affair may have temporarily ameliorated this person's sense of self-doubt, or isolation, or underlying depression; but

> the progression of events may put this person at risk. If the affair ends, the marriage is usually unrepaired at that point; and the spouse is hardly ready to console the erring spouse around the sense of loss which he or she experiences.
> (Napier, 2007, p. 302)

Thus it falls to the therapist to be able to work with both the betrayed partner's anger and pain, but also the disclosing partner's sensitivity and need for some validation for trying to "make things right." This is where the systems perspective can come in (more about that in the following). However, if an infidelity is not disclosed by the betraying partner, it is often revealed in a more dramatic and potentially devastating way: discovery.

Discovery

It can happen in a myriad of ways, whether it is a receipt for an expensive gift or an explicit letter (Oh, who am I kidding? It would be an email or text today!), voicemail, or some other sign, a discovery of an affair is usually an accident and unplanned. As a result, it comes with a shock to both the betrayed spouse and the cheating spouse. It means there is no real warning and no real preparation. Many times, the timing can downright awful (in public, at family functions, etc.) compared to planned disclosures, where one person can be prepared (and may even have a counselor ready or actually disclose in the session).

The other method for unplanned discovery is when the "other person" (or his or her significant other) chooses to unveil the infidelity to the unknowing partner. If it is the other person, it is usually because that person feels he or she has not been treated fairly (i.e., promises made to leave the spouse have gone unfulfilled, etc.), and so the discovery is often done with malice or spite. And if it is the other person's partner who discovered the affair, he or she is often unveiling the infidelity to cause maximum damage and hurt in retaliation.

Regardless of how the discovery takes place, the reaction is usually shock and denial. Sometimes the betrayed partner feels that either "I should have known" or "I knew (suspected) all along and I didn't do anything about it." In both cases, there is usually some self-blame which may not necessarily be expressed, but it is important for the clinician to be aware of this. Napier (2007) put it thus:

> One partner has lived in an illusion of normalcy, trusting, at least consciously, in the surface that he or she can see. The couple has shared daily routines, had intimate conversations, managed child care together, even had sex. While the rejected partner can usually look back and see "signs" that he or she ignored or minimized, the trauma of a shattered sense of what is real and true is tremendous. It is as if the fabric of perceived reality is ripped asunder; what had seemed so is not. The experience is comparable to a death—in this instance, of trust. And for people who bring from childhood a formative experience of rejection and betrayal (and who doesn't?), the discovery of a partner's affair confirms deeply held fears and unconscious predictions: "What was I

> thinking? How could I ever have trusted you?" And perhaps covertly: "I knew it would happen, sometime." Just as a deeply bonded marriage can ameliorate childhood traumas in the individuals, betrayal in marriage exacerbates the earlier injuries: "I thought I could trust you; now I know I can't trust anybody, ever again."
>
> (p. 299)

Once an affair is discovered (or disclosed), the partner will feel a sense of dis-reality, where nothing makes sense. The partner may find that little things don't add up and may even feel some cognitive disturbances as he or she ruminates over the information about the infidelity (or begins to obsess over the information not disclosed or discovered about the infidelity). As a result, her or she may feel an emotional disequilibrium, where their reactions may not be proportional (i.e., small slights spark feelings of rage). Again, Napier provides guidance for the clinician:

> Re-working the sense of reality, and of self-perception, is a profoundly important and difficult process for the rejected partner. In addition to increasing the self-blame and self-doubt in the "victim" of the affair, the adulterous partner's rejection may also cause the spouse to make a more accurate appraisal of his or her faults and weaknesses. While the rejected partner may be overtly blaming, he or she is also actively engaged with the question: "What did I do wrong?" This self-search, mixed as it is with rage and hurt, is an effort to attempt to make changes that may salvage the relationship. A partner who has been sexually "cool," may, for example, alternate being enraged with being sexually provocative; and the couple in the midst of tremendous emotional upheaval may have passionate sexual encounters, which may then degenerate into further rage and blaming. While the rejected partner's anger, if it is openly expressed, may be self-affirming, it may also be a way of concealing hurt, which may feel much too vulnerable an emotion to reveal to a partner whom he or she does not trust.
>
> (2007, p. 300)

The bottom line is that once the affair has been revealed, whether by disclosure or by discovery, the next immediate phase, the reaction to the news, is one that is generally heavily influenced by trauma, and understanding the traumatic nature of the infidelity (and its impact) is the first task for the couples counselor.

The Trauma of Infidelity and Its Immediate Impact

Once the infidelity has been revealed, and if the couple is in counseling at the time of the disclosure/discovery of it (or as a result of it), dealing with the trauma issues will set the stage for effectively treating the couple (Snyder, Baucom, & Gordon, 2007). Partners who have been betrayed will report wildly vacillating feelings of rage, powerlessness, abandonment, and shock (Abrahms Spring, 1996; Kessel et al., 2007; Snyder et al., 2007). According to Snyder et al.: "Similar to reactions observed in post-traumatic stress disorder . . . they report violation of fundamental assumptions regarding their participating partner, themselves, and their relationship . . . shattering core beliefs essential to emotional security" (2007, p. 102). So the traumatic aspect of the early disclosure of infidelity is highly salient. In fact, these partners, when they learn the truth:

> can suddenly develop full-blown obsessional neuroses. In fact, the severity of the reaction may seem at the edge of psychosis. The need to know the identity of the co-conspirator is of course immediate, and important; but in an effort to re-construct a sense of reality, a great many details are brought up, often repeatedly: When did it begin? What did you do? Where did you go? The level of questioning can feel abusive to the rejecting partner, and this defensive response in the adulterer can add to the sense of outrage and injury in the rejected spouse. Against the replies, which may not be truthful, but which often reveal more and more as the rejected partner pursues each detail, the rejected partner measures himself or herself, feeling alternately inferior, wanting, ashamed, stupid, gullible; and, of course, angry.
>
> (Napier, 2007, p. 300)

All these are classic signs of traumatic reactions. With the rupture in trust that occurs when an infidelity is revealed, and given the often "out of the blue" shock that the news presents (regardless of whether it was disclosed or discovered), couples may feel a sense of paralysis and that they cannot (or do not know how to) move forward. Even if the infidelity relationship is over, without an understanding about why and how the infidelity happened, there cannot be any forward movement. At the same time, the partner may have opposing feelings playing a "tug of war" internally. On the one hand, the partner wants the information (indeed, the truth), but on the other hand, the partner may recoil at the thought of learning details that are painful from a person once thought to be trustworthy, but no longer (Snyder et al., 2007). All these conflicting emotions can produce a series of experiences and behaviors that are confusing, contradictory, and seemingly unreal. As a result, it may be helpful to review some of the diagnostic criteria relevant to acute stress disorder as reported in the *DSM-V* (APA, 2013) in the box following.

DSM-V Diagnostic Criteria: Traumatic Stress Disorder

Note that some of the diagnostic criteria not relevant to infidelity have been redacted, so this should not serve as an inclusive resource to diagnose acute stress disorder.

A. Exposure to actual or threatened death, serious injury, or sexual violation in one (or more) of the following ways:
   - Directly experiencing the traumatic event(s).
   - Witnessing, in person, the events(s) as it occurred to others.

- Learning that the traumatic events(s) occurred to a close family member or close friend.
- Experiencing repeated or extreme exposure to aversive details of the traumatic event(s) (e.g., first responders collecting human remains; police officers repeatedly exposed to details of child abuse). Note: This does not apply to exposure through electronic media, television, movies, or pictures unless this exposure is work related.

B. Presence of nine (or more) of the following symptoms from any of the five categories of intrusion, negative mood, dissociation, avoidance, and arousal, beginning or worsening after the traumatic event(s) occurred:

Intrusion Symptoms

- Recurrent, involuntary, and intrusive distressing memories of the traumatic event(s).
- Recurrent distressing dreams in which the content and/or affect of the dream are related to the events(s).
- Dissociative reactions (e.g., flashbacks) in which the individual feels or acts as if the traumatic event(s) were recurring.
- Intense or prolonged psychological distress or marked physiological reactions in response to internal or external cues that symbolize or resemble an aspect of the traumatic events.

Negative Mood

- Persistent inability to experience positive emotions (e.g., inability to experience happiness, satisfaction, or loving feelings).

Dissociative Symptoms

- An altered sense of the reality of one's surroundings or oneself (e.g., seeing oneself from another's perspective, being in a daze, time slowing).
- Inability to remember an important aspect of the traumatic events(s).

Avoidance Symptoms

- Efforts to avoid distressing memories, thoughts, or feelings about or closely associated with the traumatic event(s).
- Efforts to avoid external reminders (people, places, conversations, activities, objects, situations) that arouse distressing memories, thoughts, or feelings about or closely associated with the traumatic event(s).

Arousal Symptoms

- Sleep disturbance (e.g., difficulty falling or staying asleep, restless sleep).

- Irritable behavior and angry outbursts typically expressed as verbal or physical aggression toward people or objects.
- Hypervigilance.
- Problems with concentration.
- Exaggerated startle response.

C. The duration of the disturbance (symptoms in Criterion B) is 3 days to 1 month after trauma exposure. Note: Symptoms typically begin immediately after the trauma, but persistence for at least 3 days and up to a month is needed to meet disorder criteria.

D. The disturbance causes clinically significant distress or impairment in social, occupational, or other important areas of functioning.

Source: American Psychiatric Association, 2013, *Diagnostic and statistical manual of mental disorders: DSM-V. (5th ed.)*, Washington, D.C.: American Psychiatric Association. ISBN 0890425558.

As noted in the criteria, onset of acute stress disorder can be immediately after the traumatic event, and the acute phase can last from 3 days to approximately 1 month. If the traumatic symptoms last more than 1 month, then consideration of a diagnosis of post-traumatic stress disorder may be appropriate. Regardless of whether the diagnostic threshold is reached for acute stress disorder or post-traumatic stress disorder, once the revelation of an infidelity occurs, there will likely be some traumatic response. For example, the betrayed partner may present with feeling intrusive thoughts, ruminating about the "other person" (their looks, the nature of the sex, the quality of the sex), inability to sleep, sleeping too much, not wanting to talk to his or her partner, excessively questioning his or her partner, inability to concentrate at work or at home. Accurately assessing for these symptoms, as well as providing a normalizing context for these responses, is crucial for couples to begin to process and absorb the information and the implications of it for themselves.

It is important to remember that not only the betrayed partner, but the straying partner, may exhibit some of these traumatic symptoms. For example, in the case of someone planning to disclose an affair, one can imagine that the feelings of guilt and "need to confess" bring about acute anticipatory anxiety, negative mood, and intrusive thoughts. This may also occur in the example of a discovery, where there has been no "lead time" for the partner committing the infidelity to prepare to have this secret "outed." Often it is easy (and maybe tempting) to feel less sympathy or pity for this partner, but Pittman (2007) reminds us:

> The person who has screwed around has kept it secret, has lived behind enemy lines for fear of discovery and has finally had to face his or her own loneliness. The one who has been screwing around shamefully has had less fun and more pain than the one who has been bopping around life as usual.

> You don't have to punish the person who's been having the affair—the affair is its own punishment. To get into a relationship with someone who followed you home is a terrible embarrassment and keeps you frightened most of the time. The fact that you're behind enemy lines with that person, means that you feel less intimacy with the real people in your life and more with the enemy, because that person who shares your secret knows something about you that no one would accept or tolerate. You have to see the person who has been working through this affair in secrecy, in silence, as having already been punished sufficiently. Toleration of imperfections and personal failures is one of the bases for intimacy.
>
> (p. 288)

According to Snyder et al. (2007), acute symptoms of depression, including suicidality, are likely to be present with the straying partner as well. The level of conflict, distress, and dissatisfaction may lead to verbal (or even physical) aggression and violence. As a result, the couples counselor should develop a treatment plan to work with the immediate trauma of the revelation and then move quickly into a treatment model to help the couple address the underlying issues (should they decide to stay together; more on that later in this chapter).

Treatment Strategies for Trauma

Broadly speaking, there are two approaches that can inform approaches in the immediate aftermath of the revelation of infidelity: traumatic responsiveness and interpersonal forgiveness. Treatments that focus on *traumatic responsiveness* help clients focus "more clearly on the trauma, expose them to the memories of the trauma, and help them to reconstruct their basic schemas about how the world operates and regain a new sense of control over their outcomes" (Snyder et al., 2007, p. 103). In fact, Glass (2003) listed four critical elements for healing the trauma of infidelity: (1) Reverse the "walls" (and "windows" in the extramarital triangle to place the betrayed partner inside (i.e., windows = transparency) and the affair partner outside (i.e., walls = barriers and privacy); (2) Establish safety by stopping contact with the "other person"; (3) Rebuild trust by being completely honest about the affair; and (4) Help understand the meaning of the affair by discussing the story of the affair (not just the sexual or romantic encounter).

The second approach, *interpersonal forgiveness*, is more difficult to manage in the early phase, but the elements of it are worth noting. In forgiveness-based approaches, the process is primarily focused on developing a different understanding of why the infidelity occurred and creating a new meaning for the affair (Gordon & Baucom, 1998; Rowe et al., 1989; Snyder et al., 2007). These approaches have three common elements: "(a) gaining a more balanced view of the offender and the event, (b) decreasing negative affect toward the offender, potentially along with increased compassion, and (c) giving up the right to punish the offender further" (Snyder et al., 2007, p. 103). So while the idea of "forgiveness" may seem like it is about the straying partner, it is about the betrayed partner and managing the traumatic experiences as well.

Many times the betrayed partner will say: "What if I can't forgive my partner?" It may mean that a person is not ready yet to begin to work on the relationship issues; on the other hand, it may mean that the partner will *never* be ready (or able) to take this step. If that is the case, and forgiveness is impossible, the relationship is likely over. However, rushing through this process can often do more harm than good. Decisions made in the heat of the moment can have the advantage of the perception of clarity, but they can also have the disadvantage of being ill-timed or even wrong. Regardless of the underlying approach that a counselor takes in the disclosure/discovery phase, there are some guidelines for "the session after" the affair is revealed. Two of these approaches will be discussed next.

The Session After: Modified Infidelity Debriefing Process

Juhnke and his colleagues (Juhnke et al., 2008) adapted a critical incident debriefing approach that they called the "Modified Infidelity Debriefing Process" (Juhnke et al., 2008) to help guide clinicians during an initial debriefing session after an infidelity has been revealed. Their approach has seven steps. They are: Introduction, Fact Finding, Thoughts and Cognitions, Reactions to Infidelity, Meaning, Immediate Needs, and Commitment. According to Juhnke et al., the initial session may take up to 2 hours, and it is highly recommended that the couple go through all of the steps (or as many as feasible). Going through these stages

> provides partners the opportunity to discuss their infidelity experiences and associated feelings. In both overt and perceived infidelity cases the victims often require greater discussion time by describing their reactions to the perceived cheating or betrayal. It is imperative that couples' counselors allow victims to describe their feelings. However, counselors must maintain administrative control and insure sessions don't drift into fruitless, verbal or emotional bashing.
>
> (Juhnke et al., 2008, p. 311)

In addition, the authors recommend that sessions that go more than 2 1/2 hours have a tendency toward unproductive expressions of emotion and will be less effective, therapeutically. However, if they are able to work through each of the interconnected debriefing steps, this is preferable. Each stage is designed to "move clients from their cognitive thoughts regarding the infidelity experience, into their feelings associated to the infidelity, and finally back to cognitions regarding how the couple wishes the relationship to either change or end" (Juhnke et al., 2008, p. 311). As they complete each stage, and once they have completed all the stages, the goal is to allow the couple to experience a sense of control and empowerment. For the betrayed spouse, especially as he or she is coming to terms with the revealing of the infidelity, this is particularly important. Likewise, for the partner who has committed the infidelity, seeing the potential to genuinely rebuild trust and possibly rebuild the relationship can offer much needed relief and encouragement.

If, however, they cannot work through all the stages, Juhnke et al. recommend that couples write letters that allow them the time to reflect and describe the experiences they were not able to get out initially. If necessary, couples should return at the next possible opportunity (even the next day) to complete these steps. Now, let's look at each of the steps in some detail.

1. **Introduction:** This phase is important for orienting the couple to what the Modified Infidelity Debriefing Process will accomplish. Couples at this phase are often *dis*oriented, and anyone who can offer them a process that is clearly laid out and can provide some semblance of stability (even if just for the initial debriefing session) is greatly appreciated. In addition, this phase includes developing the basic counseling relationship and building rapport. The other major task at this stage is to help victims describe their experience of the disclosure of their partner's infidelity, experienced both during and immediately after the disclosure, in order to begin to process it and put it in some type of context. It is also important to discuss what topics will be discussed (the couple's definition of infidelity, boundary setting, and rules needed to continue the relationship) (Juhnke et al., 2008). It is also an opportunity for the counselor to assess the level of functioning of the couple and to provide encouragement to the couple for coming to counseling.

   Juhnke et al. (2008) write that the final step in the introduction process is to have each person commit to a minimum of four sessions of follow-up. This ties back into the final step of this debriefing process (commitment). While the majority of couples who come for couples counseling after an affair has been discovered are willing to make this agreement, there are a number of others that are not able to make this commitment. It is often because they have either decided to end the relationship or are dubious about the counseling process and its ability to truly help the situation. In that case, helping clients give voice to that concern can help increase their willingness to continue with the debriefing session. Asking clarifying questions of the partners about their goals is sometimes warranted at this point ("Perhaps you are not prepared to forgive your partner, and you are not sure if you ever will, but if you are not yet ready to work on the relationship, are you interested in getting help to understand your reactions right now?") in order for couples to "buy in" to the debriefing process.
2. **Fact Finding:** "The primary goal within the client couples' fact finding stage is to help the identified victim discuss the non-emotional facts leading to the infidelity disclosure" (Juhnke et al., 2008, p. 311). This is a particularly important "entry point" into the story of the infidelity for the counselor. It begins the narrative in a nonjudgmental way. It also helps based on whether the uncovering of the infidelity was due to disclosure (the betraying partner chose to tell their partner about the infidelity) or if it was discovered (by the betrayed partner). Information about the circumstances of how the disclosure

or discovery occurred can also be useful in getting factual, non-emotional details out about the events surrounding the revelation of the infidelity. However, it is important that the couple understand that getting "just the facts" does not mean that their emotions will not be discussed and explored, but that this will come at the "reactions" phase. Instead, this phase begins to lay out the "facts" of the infidelity as they appear on the surface to each person. This also allows for the couples counselor to ask about whether victims ever *suspected* that their partners were engaging in an outside relationship or prior disclosed (or undisclosed) infidelities. Last, this can serve as an opportunity to ask the betraying partner about the circumstances that led to choosing to disclose or the events that preceded a discovery. In addition, at this point, the three-step model for *understanding* infidelity can be introduced to the couple, which can often structure their conversation in the following stages.

3. **Thoughts and Cognitions:** "The goal within the thoughts and cognitions stage is to gently encourage partners to move from discussing external, relatively safe, non-emotional facts regarding the infidelity, to their personal thoughts surrounding overt or perceived infidelity. Thus, this is a transitional stage between cognitions and emotions" (Juhnke et al., 2008, p. 312). The first goal in this stage is to begin to bring the conversation into the mind of each of the partners and to get more of their subjective perceptions of the events they discussed. This also begins to get to the thoughts and cognitions each person had, which "sets the stage" to discuss their emotions. It also gets each person to begin to take a reflective approach to the circumstances they are describing (an important part of "perspective taking" that they will need for later elements of treatment). The couple can take an external view of themselves and the relationship. This will also help them see their couple relationship as a system and begin to see the two systemic principles from Chapter 2 (that the infidelity is a symptom and that each person had a role in creating the conditions). Thoughts and cognitions can be automatic or deliberate, and they can be narrative and textual (i.e., "I can't believe she did that!") or more visual ("I just keep seeing her with another man!"). This is important to help the couple label these and categorize them appropriately (which gives them a sense of control over them).

   Prompting questions like: "What was your first thought when . . . ?" can help each person begin to get into their individual mindsets when they first began to discuss the infidelity. In addition, asking about thoughts in the subsequent time following the first revelation can also be helpful: "And in the last few (days, weeks), how has your thinking changed about . . . ?" This can bring about reassurance.
4. **Reactions to Infidelity:** "In this stage the goal is to help overt victims move into the affective reactions they may have regarding the disclosed infidelity. The focus should be kept upon the victim's discussion of the infidelity" (Juhnke et al., 2008, p. 312). This can be one of the more difficult stages to process, but it is also one of the most important. First, the counselor needs to be prepared to have each client express very strong emotions. Next, the counselor needs to be prepared to give each partner enough time to be able to fully express their

emotional reactions. Finally, the counselor must be ready to keep the focus on each person's reaction to the infidelity (especially the betrayed partner), and not necessarily focus on the straying partner. For example:

> When I heard what he was telling me, I was so hurt and I was so angry that I didn't want to be near him. I just felt this hot rage come over me, and you know how they say that "people who are angry see red?" Well, I literally "saw red" that is how angry I was.

Contrast this to an unproductive venting or personal attack, such as:

> You stupid, selfish jerk! You are worthless like your father was! You said you would never become someone like him, but you are worse! I should have listened to my friends when they said that you were no good, but I was an idiot and I believed you when you said that you loved me!

Re-directing clients' focus back to themselves can help them get back on track, but it is important to balance this without making clients feel like you are stifling their expression of emotion. Ask questions like, "What has been the hardest part for you during this?" or "Can you describe what was the 'lowest point' for you emotionally during this process?" Again, the goal is to get the couple to hear the other's feelings without being overwhelmed or flooded by them. This provides a structure for later processing of these feelings.

5. **Meaning:** "The goal within this stage is to help the victim transition from the often acutely affective domain back toward the cognitive domain. As the emotionally charged reactions begin to wane, the couples' counselor asks questions that promote cognitive vis-à-vis emotionally based responses" (Juhnke et al., 2008, p. 312). This is a process where the counselor helps the couple put their experiences, thoughts, and feelings into a framework that allows them to *begin* (and it is only a beginning) to understand what is happening to them (both the infidelity and the systemic elements of the relationship). For example, "This fear that you have about Jane leaving you after hearing of your affair is a reflection of how much you realize that you do need her." Or, "You say, 'I was suspicious but I didn't listen to my gut,' but it seems like you are outwardly punishing her. However, based on your reactions and thoughts, you are also punishing yourself in ways that others may not see." Creating meaning-based statements requires a balance of both cognitive and emotional elements. Last, empathizing statements that take the expressed emotions and put them in the context of the cognitions and thoughts (earlier step) can help make the feelings seem less random and out of control as well as provide a deeper meaning for them. It is this deeper meaning expressed in the emotion that can provide clues about the wish, dream, or fantasy for the relationship that was violated by the infidelity. In the next chapter, this information is crucial to help the couple take the next step in healing the relationship by re-defining a new dream, wish, or fantasy for the relationship (Snyder, Baucom, & Gordon, 2008).

6. **Immediate Needs:** The goal at this stage is to help the couple (particularly the betrayed partner) identify the most immediate needs. This is an important step as it gets each member of the couple to reflect on what they need to do immediately. Sometimes, the clients will express unrealistic wishes ("I wish that this had never happened," "I wish I could turn back time and undo the last few days/months/years," etc.). However, the goal is to get the couple to focus on the immediate reality of the situation. It gives the betrayed spouse the first real opportunity to ask something tangible of the betraying partner, and it likewise gives the straying partner a chance to show his or her true remorse by submitting to and fulfilling these requests. Sometimes there is a tangible task that can be performed ("I don't have the energy to deal with the kids in the mornings right now" or "I need to know that you have ended the affair"), while other times there may be an expression of something more ethereal (i.e., "I just need space"). The request in this step "buys time" for the couple to get prepared to do the work in the next few chapters to truly rebuild the relationship. Prompts like "What do you need the most from your partner right now?" can open up a myriad of possibilities. It is the couples counselor's job to make sure that these requests are focused, are realistic, and will potentially have a beneficial effect on stabilizing the relationship. Ask "circular questions" like, "And if he does that, how are you likely to respond? And if you respond like that, what is he likely to do . . . ?" The couple's ability (or inability) to answer these questions can give the counselor an idea about whether the couple has moved too quickly through the Modified Infidelity Debriefing Process. In this phase, some of the considerations that will be presented in Snyder et al.'s model of immediate trauma can also be inserted (i.e., boundaries, who to talk to about infidelity, etc.). It will also portend what the likely responses will be in the next and final step, commitment.
7. **Commitment:** "At this point the couple has progressed from cognitive discussions of the infidelity experience, through an emotional debriefing of their feelings and experiences, and back to the cognitive focused stages that allow discussion of their immediate needs" (Juhnke et al., 2008, p. 313). The goal of this last stage is to ascertain, after going through the Modified Infidelity Debriefing Process, whether the couple is ready to take on the challenges of treating the infidelity. If neither partner is committed, the relationship may be over (i.e., an Exit Affair). At this point, individual counseling to be able to deal with the aftermath of the ending of the relationship can be negotiated, as well as divorce counseling (particularly if there are children). If, however, both partners are committed, then outlining the steps of treatment (see Chapters 2–5) will be important at this point. Last, if one member is able to make a commitment, and the other member is not, there may have been a step that was missed or rushed in the Modified Infidelity Debriefing Process. At the end of the chapter, a framework for assessing the couple's readiness to commit will be discussed.

According to Juhnke et al. (2008), successfully completing the Modified Infidelity Debriefing Process accomplishes three things: (1) commitment to each other and overcoming the past infidelity obstacle, (2) being able to successfully negotiate the infidelity challenge, and (3) willingness to engage in continued counseling. Success at this phase is indicative of eventual success in treatment. And while the Modified Infidelity Debriefing Process is useful in helping a client work through many of the difficult issues of the immediate aftermath following a revelation of an infidelity, there are several other considerations that must be taken into account. These will be discussed next.

Additional Tasks to Accomplish During the Disclosure or Discovery Phase

While the steps of the Modified Infidelity Debriefing Process can help clients deal with the immediate aftermath of the revealing of the affair, and prepare the couple to make the decision to work on their relationship, there are several common areas that many couples need guidance in navigating (Snyder et al., 2008). Specifically, these are: (1) boundary setting, (2) self-care techniques, (3) time-out and "venting" techniques, (4) emotional expressiveness skills and discussion of the impact of the affair, and (5) coping with flashbacks.

Boundary Setting

The first area that needs to be discussed early on in the therapeutic endeavor is boundaries. Because of the traumatic nature of the disclosure or discovery of infidelity, all previous relationship "norms" (at least in the initial phase) tend to go out the window. As a result, the partners (and generally the betrayed spouse) may not know what the proper boundaries are. Prior to the revelation of the infidelity, the partners may have felt that the other person was the first one they could turn to for support (although the betraying partner has already chosen to turn toward the "other person"). As a result, the immediate response is to talk to people outside the relationship about things they would never previously talk about. So in the initial phase, it is important to have the couple work through several areas of boundaries. The main three areas of boundaries are: (1) how to relate to each other, (2) how to deal with the "other person," and (3) who to talk to for support and what to share about the infidelity with them.

First, boundaries within the couple's relationship must be addressed in order to create a sense of safety in the relationship following the exposure of an infidelity. One of the first areas to cover is the boundaries around negative feelings (e.g., Glass's "walls" and "windows"). A balance must be struck between the genuine expression of feelings (especially when they are negative) and overwhelming the relationship with negativity (which could lead to withdrawal). Thus, setting limits on these negative interactions will create safety. For example, if one partner is feeling insecure about the other partner's whereabouts, a creative solution is for the other partner to take the responsibility of telling that person where he or she is (or texting, "sharing their location" on their phone, etc.). The goal will be for the partner to say, "Enough, I don't need to know *every* store you stop at." In addition, negotiating times for discussion, questions, and so forth can be helpful in decreasing the pressure to ask questions and express frustrations or upset (see Box 6.1 following). Initially, some couples may not be ready to talk about relationship boundary issues concerning physical contact (including sex), but issues of seeking comfort from the other person (asking for a hug, kissing, physical proximity) will need to be discussed at some point when the couple is ready.

A second aspect of boundaries is what to do if the couple has to meet or interact with the "other person." What if they *know* the other person (a friend, neighbor, or relative)? What if they have to see the other person at work? What if they have to see the other person in town? Opinions of what to do with this range from one espoused by Esther Perel, a relationship counselor who has written on the subject, who recommends bringing in the "other person" and either working with him or her in session or at least bringing his or her voice in the session (i.e., "Consider how the other person might feel"), to one that says that all contact must be immediately and permanently cut off. However, the more appropriate question is: "Do you really want to save your relationship?" If yes, then the couple needs to find a way to negotiate what level of contact is allowable. If it is at all possible, contact should be cut off, as this provides the cleanest and clearest boundary. However, if it is not possible, there has to be an agreed-upon set of conditions for contact with the other person. If the betraying partner says, "But you don't understand . . ." it may mean that he or she may not be willing to work on the relationship and may be trying to keep a tie to the other person. What it may also mean is that there is some fear (or despair) that the primary relationship will not ever change. It also depends on what type of affair has occurred. For example, if it is a Conflict-Avoidance or Intimacy-Avoidance Affair, it might not be a problem. However, for a Split-Self Affair, there might be a significant tie to the other person. At the same time, this is a desperate time for the couple, and it calls for desperate measures. Each person has to be "all in" or must "get out." This may be harsh, but it is often necessary. Therefore, discussing the boundary issues related to the other person is vital. This might include discussing how and whether to tell the other person that the partner has been told about the infidelity. It may also include having the couple agree that any contact with the other person will be immediately disclosed to the partner, and the couple should set time aside to process it.

Finally, discussing who to talk to outside the couple about the infidelity (if anyone) is also an important boundary to set. Why is this important? It is important because in the beginning, in order to either get support, or because they are so traumatized (and it may be evident on their face), betrayed spouses will be asked by friends, family members, and even mild acquaintances: "What's wrong?" If they share details about the infidelity, including that an infidelity has occurred, it may cause long-term damage to the relationship in the eyes of friends, family, or the community. The problem is that once that information is out, it is impossible to take it back. There are a few reasons why this is potentially important. There is almost a fear of contagion when someone learns a friend has been unfaithful to his or her spouse or partner. Other people will distance themselves. They change their opinion of that person. This is why public disclosure must be considered carefully. At the same time, families and friends may feel empowered to come in and, in an effort to support the betrayed partner, may try to convince him or her to leave when he or she is not ready to. Last, if the family and friends have given advice to "kick 'em to the curb" and the couple decides to remain together and work it out, there may be some embarrassment and strain in that relationship. At the same time, these concerns must be balanced with the idea of helping the partners get and use social supports. Neither person should feel isolated and unable to get support. So discussing who to talk to, and what will be discussed, is important for each person to feel safe, as well as to preserve the relationship for future functioning. Therefore, the couple may agree to turn to a couple they can trust or to one friend (or relative) each they know will support them. It is crucial that each person tell the other who they have chosen to tell and to discuss any concerns they may have about that person knowing. In this way, each person can get additional support without the other person feeling too vulnerable about it.

Self-Care Guidelines

The disclosure or discovery of an affair can take a significant emotional, cognitive, and physical toll on both partners. Unfortunately, during this time, due to the traumatic nature of the revelation, couples often fail to take care of themselves. Sometimes it is because of the aforementioned traumatic reaction and symptoms, while other times it may be due to feelings of unworthiness or thinking one is unlovable. As a result, basic needs for one's self or family (particularly if there are children) may be neglected. It is important for the couples counselor to be able to assess this level of functioning. It is also important for the couples counselor to remind each person about taking care of themselves and not giving into notions of self-punishment or self-denial. Clients may need to be given permission to do basic (and maybe even additional) self-care. According to Snyder et al. (2007), three broad domains of self-care to consider are: (1) physical care (which includes eating properly; sleeping well; paying attention to increases in caffeine, alcohol, or other drugs; and physical exercise); (2) social support (following from the discussion on "boundaries" and agreements about what is appropriate to discuss and whom to discuss things in a way that will be helpful, not hurtful); and (3) spiritual support (which can include formal and informal religious practices like prayer, meditation, and talking with clergy, consistent with the person's belief system). Clients may need "permission" from a professional to take the time and effort to do these things. It may need to be conveyed that this is important in order to have the resources—cognitively and emotionally—to tackle the demanding therapeutic tasks in the next phases of treatment.

Time-Out and Venting Techniques

As discussed prior, being able to discuss the negative emotions is important, but this can also degenerate into non-productive blaming or hurtful exchanges, which only damages things further. At the same time (as will be discussed in Chapter 7), the couple (and the couples counselor) does not want to diffuse the emotion or signal that it is not welcome or helpful. However, educating the couple on some of the physiological changes that occur with intense emotions, and instituting a technique for dealing with it, can often be useful. In terms of the physiological aspects of intense negative emotion, Gottman and Gottman (2017) noted that physiological arousal, particularly over 100 beats per minute during a conflict discussion, leads to increases in stress hormones (cortisol) and the experience of emotional flooding. People who are flooded "have trouble remembering what they ever liked about their partners . . . give or receive affection, [is] empathetic, and [even] polite and courteous. Positive social skills such as shared humor seem to be inaccessible" (p. 13). As a result, when couples dealing with the trauma of infidelity get flooded, the conversations generally go from bad to worse. The important thing is to de-escalate the conflict by walking away. However, if this is not previously agreed to, it may look like one partner is withdrawing or running away from the discussion, which could escalate the other partner even more. Instead, it is important to have a "time-out" procedure where couples agree that when they feel they are flooded they agree to stop talking, disengage from each other for an agreed-upon period of time, and then come back and discuss the issue again. Gottman and Gottman reported that, in their laboratory experiments, after interrupting a couple having a fight, and then instructing them to quietly read something for 20 minutes, when they went back to discussing the conflict, they found:

> When we compared the last 5 minutes of the first conversation to the first 5 minutes of the second conversation, it was like these people had a brain transplant. Suddenly in the second conversation, they were reasonable, rational, had their sense of humor back, could listen, and could be affectionate and empathetic one again.
>
> (2017, p. 13)

As a result, time-out exercises, coupled with providing knowledge about the couple's physiological responses, are a powerful tool in helping the clients discuss their conflicts in a productive way without sacrificing the powerful emotions that come with conflict.

Discussing the Impact of the Affair

Of course, one of the most important elements of the early stage of learning about infidelity is the partner discussing the impact of the affair on him or her. This must take place in the context of a safe space (boundary) where (1) the other partner will hear and support the betrayed partner, (2) there is no fear of the other person being used to ameliorate the betraying partner's feelings, and (3) other people (not involved in the infidelity) will not be inappropriately roped into the conflict. There must also be an ability to tolerate the emotions that will come with this (venting and time-out) in order for this to be successful. However, there is often a need for "justice" or revenge on the part of the betrayed partner, which can render these conversations ineffective, since the betraying partner will either meekly accept the blame and absorb the negativity from the betrayed partner or will run away from the negativity. In either case, the betrayed spouse may not feel he or she has been sufficiently heard (which continues a cycle of frustration and felt injustice). From a systemic perspective, this can often trigger past relationship hurts and bitterness felt by the betraying partner, which may have been used as justification for the infidelity. As a result, neither person is in a position to feel sympathy for the other, and the conversation ceases being productive. A final unproductive element is the betrayed partner's incessant questions. In the beginning, the betraying partner may feel obligated to answer as many questions as possible, but if the betrayed partner feels like the same questions are coming again and again, or if the questions are non-stop, he or she is likely going to become frustrated and shut down. This will only perpetuate frustration on the part of the other partner, and thus a cycle of negative interactions will emerge, further dividing the couple. Box 6.1 has a clinical exercise that can help with this negative interaction.

Box 6.1 Clinical Exercise: The Need for Questions and Information Versus Protecting the Relationship From Attack

This is a question that gets asked a lot, particularly in the beginning phases of disclosure of an infidelity. Often times, the betrayed partner has questions or wants details and information. This need is based on anxiety or anger, but as time goes on it can be based on curiosity and genuine inquiry. And while the other partner (usually) wants to be forthcoming, there are often feelings of embarrassment or pain that come up. As a result, the partner may not want to re-live or re-experience the events and details and will withdraw. The betraying partner may feel like he or she is being "attacked" or "grilled." This withdrawal only feeds into the anxiety and anger of the betrayed spouse and, if he or she pursues the other partner, likewise feeds into the feelings of shame and perceptions of attack. This leads to a stalemate that neither likes or wants. Or it leads to each person feeling like there is little hope for the relationship.

One of the biggest issues for these couples is the fear of being blindsided by the other person and being put on the defensive. There are two problems with this: (1) it is likely to cause a person to react poorly and say things that are in-artful or destructive, and (2) it is likely to have the opposite effect of what the person wants (i.e., instead of getting information, he or she will feel frustrated if/when the other partner withdraws or stonewalls). Therefore, a negotiated exercise is helpful in order to balance the needs of each partner.

First, the couple must agree on the period of time that they will allow to go by in between meetings to discuss questions that the other person may have about the infidelity. This could range from days to a week (though it probably shouldn't be longer than a week in the beginning). The counselor should refrain from being involved in the decision and let the couple negotiate the appropriate time frame. The counselor may need to facilitate this, however. During these times, they will both agree to discuss the questions and issues that they have for one another surrounding the affair and the relationship in general.

Next, the couple must agree that in between those discussion times, they will refrain from asking questions of each other. This reduces the fears of being blindsided. However, during these times, if one or the other have questions, thoughts, concerns, and so on, they should write them down in some fashion (on paper, in a computer file, etc.). Then, at some negotiated point *before* their meeting (again, they should decide if it is 24 hours or 48 hours before), they give the other person their written-down thoughts and questions so the couple is prepared to discuss them at the appointed time. Again, this reduces the anxiety of being blindsided, and it also gives each person time to be prepared for what topics will be discussed or what questions will be asked. It also allows the other partner to thoughtfully prepare his or her answers. Too often, couples will seize on the *way* someone inartfully phrased something instead of the spirit in which they wanted to say something (but did not).

Couples may choose to use the therapy time as a time to bring in these questions and topics. Also, couples may want to bring in their written notes to show the therapist. Frequently, these can be a good indicator of whether the pace of therapy is correct. Also, how the questions and topics change (or don't change) can be an indicator of progress.

This process allows partners to explore their reactions in a calmer fashion and express their feelings in ways that are not abusive or attacking and that will not lead to the partner being ignored. In helping structure the couple having this discussion, Pittman (2007) suggests that couples avoid merely asking the question "why." He says:

> "Why" questions are notoriously difficult to answer because there is always so many factors. What I am looking for is "how" did you make the decision . . . "What" and "how" questions are far more important than "why" questions, but they are not popular.
>
> (p. 284)

Thus, the betraying partner needs to understand that his or her own perspective of the infidelity will not be truly understood by the betrayed partner unless the betrayed partner believes that the betraying partner understands *his or her* perspective and shows remorse. This is accomplished by having discussions about the affair in a way that is ultimately satisfactory for the betrayed partner (Snyder et al., 2007).

Coping With Flashbacks

Another aspect of dealing with the trauma of disclosure or discovery of infidelity is the concept of flashbacks. Flashbacks are the experience of sudden and intense emotional and cognitive "re-experiencing" of a traumatic event that feels real (or is indistinguishable from reality). Often the betrayed partner will experience a flood of intense feelings and may even have physiological responses (increased heart rate, uncontrolled crying, etc.), which could lead the person to experience panic-like symptoms. Usually, there is an identifiable triggering event that sets off the "flashback." For example, a husband may discover a text on his wife's phone from a telephone number that he does not recognize. This may remind him of unexplained texts and phone calls that were made during the affair that she denied at the time. When he presents the current text to her, she assures him that it is a mis-dialed text and that she is not re-engaging with her former lover. The denial triggers a flood of affect related to his wife's affair. If she is not cognizant of what her husband is experiencing, her husband's behavior may look irrational, and she may feel like he is not "moving on" or truly forgiving her. It is important for the couples counselor to be able to explain that flashbacks are a natural part of the healing process and may even signal *positive* progress by the couple if they are able to effectively manage the flashback. By using the "time-out" process, expression and venting, and understanding physiological responses, as well as reflective question writing, couples are taught to differentiate between the behavior in the past compared to the feelings that stem from the flashback trigger. However, if the couple is not oriented about the concepts of flashbacks, they may not be able to effectively cope with them.

Box 6.2 Clinical Exercise: THE Question!

Last, I want to close with an exercise I do early in treatment with couples coping with an infidelity. It is something I call "THE Question," and it elicits each partner's sense of readiness to commit/re-commit to the relationship. In setting this up, it is important to remind the couple that they can always make decisions later, but they can't undo decisions that they make now. Fast decisions may feel good in the short-term. But fast poor decisions can have long-term repercussions. For example, telling extended family members may bring about a wave of support, but later on it may bring about fears of being judged (especially if the couple stays together and works through the issues).

Therefore, in order to assess the couple's readiness to move into the next phase of the treatment, the question that I ask is:

"Have you decided whether or not to stay in the relationship?"

Now, before the couple has a chance to answer, I go over what the potential responses *are* and what they potentially *mean*.

First, I tell them what this question is *not* asking. It is *not* asking if you intend to stay or go. It is asking if you have made the decision whether to stay or go, which is vastly different. In other words, is your mind clear on this yet, or are you still in a fog about this (i.e., too traumatized to focus)?

Then, I tell them what this question *is* asking. It *is* putting the decision to move forward, or maybe to say "Hold on just a second," in *both* partners' hands. Again, the goal is not to rush into a treatment that one or both people are not ready to begin.

Then, I tell them what the answers *mean*.

> "Yes" simply means that "I've made a decision that I am comfortable with" (we don't know what that means yet).
>
> "No" simply means that "I have not yet made a decision that I am certain of or comfortable with."
>
> Try not to accept "I don't know" for an answer, as "No" is a sufficient answer for people who don't know, but it is more certain and definitive than "I don't know."

Then comes the "moment of truth" where the couple reveals their individual answers. If both answer "yes," that they have made a decision, ask if they are willing to share what that answer is (usually they are). If both say that they have decided to stay in the relationship, you can proceed to the treatment steps (in the next chapter). If either of the partners say they do *not* want to stay in the relationship, the focus shifts to working with the couple to understand the meaning of the dissolution of the relationship. Finally, if either person answers "no" that they have not made a decision, that is a "red light" that they are not ready to make a decision. At this point, moving forward may not be possible or prudent, or it may have to proceed slowly. Sometimes, answering "no" to deciding whether or not to stay in the relationship is an indicator for couples that they need an individual session with the couples counselor to explore their feelings or just need more time to let the immediate aftermath of the infidelity set in. The key elements at this stage are patience (and not rushing the couple) and power (ensuring that both partners know they can control the path forward).

The End of the Beginning, and the Beginning of the End . . .

If a couple has known about an affair or infidelity for some time (a few months or even years), the processes described in this chapter may not be necessary. After completing this phase, the therapist should have a good understanding of how committed the couple is for treatment and what the prognosis is. This is where the couple can be introduced to the three-step model for *treating* the infidelity (which is a recapitulation, in reverse, of the three-step model for understanding infidelity). Then you can go right into "the biggest sales job a therapist will ever have to do!"

CHAPTER 7

Exploring the Wishes, Dreams, and Fantasies Unfulfilled and/or Developing New Ones to Pursue Together

The challenge of whether the couple can break out of their compromised "identities" in the marriage is of course subject to the same fears and insecurities, and the same failures of nerve, that led them to their impasse. The decision by one partner to have an affair is an enormous gamble, and it may be a failure. One or both may lose their nerve in confronting their problems; they may break up unnecessarily, or they may paper over their anguish and decide to behave themselves. Periodic affairs may become the norm in the relationship. But it is also possible that both can take courage from having their difficulties squarely in their faces, and they may achieve greater levels of honesty and intimacy.

(Napier, 2007, p. 297)

A Treatment Model for Working With Infidelity

In Chapter 2, I presented a three-step *explanatory* model for understanding infidelity (how and why it occurs). Specifically, it is these three factors: (1) global dissatisfaction with the relationship over a period of time, (2) a perceived power imbalance, and (3) the death of the dream, wish, or fantasy for the relationship and a person's realization that he or she would never get his or her needs met by the other partner. In Figure 7.1, on the left side, these factors are three descending steps down to where the door is open to the infidelity, and one partner walks through it. Chapters 3, 4, and 5 explored each of these three descending steps. And after helping a couple through the immediate aftermath of the discovery or disclosure of an affair, it is time to work on the systems dynamics of the couple's relationship.

This is where the *treatment* model for helping a couple recover from infidelity begins. On the right side of Figure 7.1, the same three factors are displayed as three ascending steps that must be worked on to help the couple. These steps are the reverse of the explanatory model, with rebuilding a shared dream coming first, balancing the power differentials, and then learning how to ride the ups and downs of satisfaction in the relationship. This model gives the couple a roadmap for how treatment will go and explains what they can expect from each phase. It helps give hope to the couple, as well, that there is the possibility of an end point or recovery (although things will be different in the relationship).

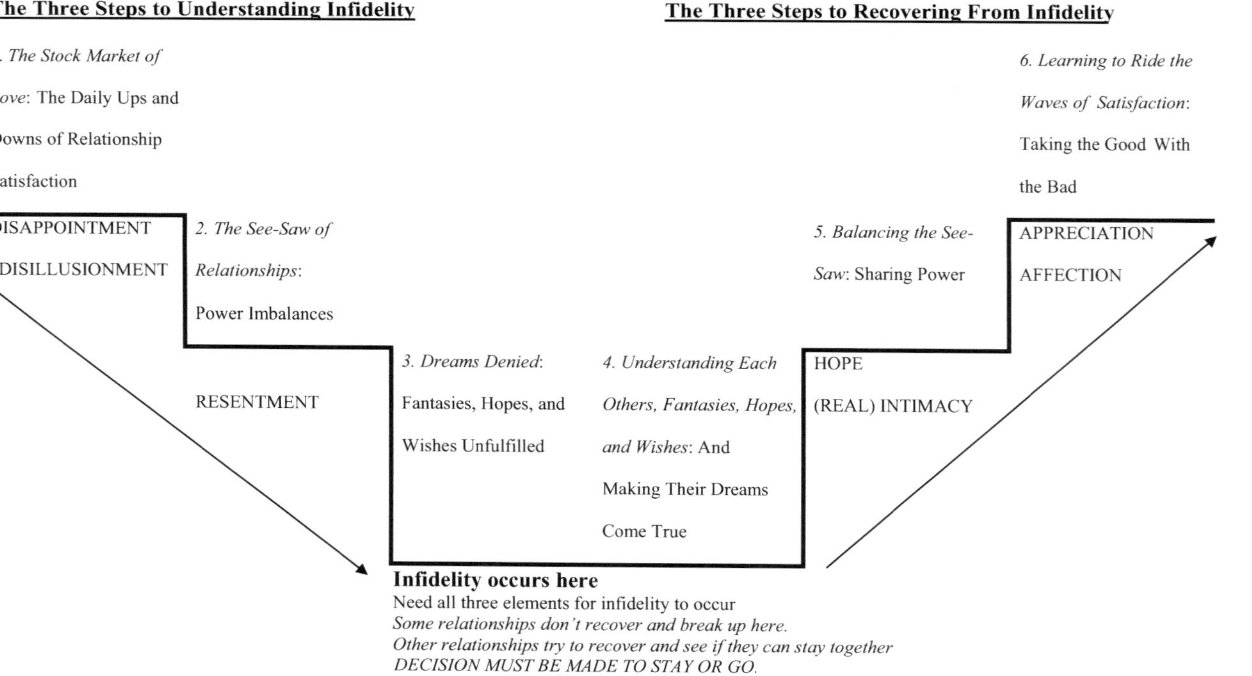

Figure 7.1.: The three-step model for understanding infidelity

This chapter discusses the process and techniques of exploring the original dreams/wishes/fantasies each partner brought into the relationship. It explores the "bargain" that was struck and why/how the infidelity broke that agreement. Techniques for exploring the emotions that result from this broken trust are discussed. Finally, the chapter provides a discussion of methods to guide a couple toward creating new, shared dreams and a "new deal" for the relationship.

Here Is Where the Real Work Begins

Once a couple has decided they do want to work on their relationship, and after the initial shock of the revelation of the infidelity has passed, the real work of couples counseling begins. However, this does not mean the couple will not experience any flashbacks or other significant negative emotions. In fact, there will be many emotional oscillations for the couple, between feeling like they are doing well and have "gotten past the worst of it" and being emotionally triggered and feeling despair for the relationship because it feels like they haven't made any significant progress. And while the emotions that come up may seem to jeopardize the therapy, it is *crucial* that the couples counselor doesn't diffuse the emotion (especially in the face of the despair the clients may feel). Too often, couples counselors don't know how to work with strong emotions and see them as harmful or unproductive. While, yes, there are times when emotional reactions can create further damage to a relationship, the answer is not diffusing emotions, making them inert, forcing them "underground," or discharging them. This does one of two things: either causes the couple to miss out on an important opportunity for real connection with one another or causes one (or both) of the partners to hide their emotions. This will simply re-create (or reinforce) the systems dynamics that created the conditions for the infidelity in the first place (i.e., conflict-avoidance, intimacy-avoidance, etc.).

Instead, couples counseling (and couples counselors) have to start with the strong emotions. Exploring the dreams, wishes, and fantasies that were part of the "bargain" for the relationship (see Chapter 5), and how the infidelity violated these, is the way to understand the source of these emotions. Understanding these dreams, wishes, and fantasies provides the framework to cope with all the difficult emotions. If the couples counseling doesn't do this, those emotions are likely to leak out and destroy whatever progress could be made. The tactical mistake many couples counselors make is to save the work on the emotional and shared dreams level until later in the therapy, when things are "calmer." Usually, the first task many couples counselors have a couple work on is having a "date night" or working on basic communication skills. And although there is an important time and place for that, in the case of working with couples to recover from an infidelity, it should not be the first area of intervention. Again, this is a mistake. The goal here is to work with the couple to explore their deepest wishes and their deepest hurts (particularly in regards to how the relationship dynamics have failed to make those wishes come true) and, finally, to create a new, shared dream that is explicit, rather than implicit. This will provide the fuel to effect real change in the systemic dynamics of the relationship.

However, this process won't happen without some pain as well. Grief may be evident here as both partners "say goodbye" to old ways of believing and behaving. There may also be some systemic "pull back" or "change-back" at this point. Each of these will be discussed briefly next.

Grief

Grief is the process of experiencing loss and coming to an understanding of the meaning of the loss, as well as being able to move forward with one's life. Many clinicians and lay people are familiar with Kübler-Ross's (1969) stages of grief: shock/denial, anger, bargaining, sadness/depression, acceptance, and hope. These are emotional states people tend to move through, although not necessarily in a linear or exclusive format. In other words, some may be experienced together, others may be experienced in a different order, and some may not be experienced at all. Educating clients about grief is important in helping them understand the emotions they are experiencing and accurately labeling them. Worden (2009) stated that in addition to the experience of grief there were four *tasks* of grief one must work through. The first is to acknowledge the grief (or "tell the story"), the second is to experience the emotions of the grief, the third is to make meaning of the loss, and the last is to change the nature of the relationship with the person (or relationship) that is lost.

While grief is usually discussed in the context of the death of a loved one, when an infidelity is revealed, there is an experience of grief for both partners. They must grieve the loss of the relationship they once had or *thought* they had. And they must grieve the loss of the dream, wish, or fantasy they had for the relationship. Also, as mentioned in the last chapter, because of the traumatic nature of the infidelity, they may have to grieve the loss of identity they had for themselves in the relationship. As Napier (2007) wrote:

> Victims of affairs usually realize that they have participated, at least unconsciously, in the setup and enactment of the spouse's affair. They didn't *make* the decision to have the affair, but they may experience considerable shame as they look at the signs they ignored. It is later work in therapy for the rejected spouse to examine and to learn from the unconscious prediction of betrayal in the marriage; but it is important that this individual grapple with the childhood underpinnings of that predicted rejection.
>
> (p. 300)

In other words, they must grieve the loss of the relationship and come to terms with the part they played in creating the conditions that led to the affair. This often requires them to reconsider some of the assumptions they had about the relationship, as well as some of the ideals they carried forward from their own family of origin (more on that later in this chapter).

One other aspect of grief enters the picture at this stage as well—the person who strayed may have to "grieve" the old relationship with the "other person."

Real feelings for the other person might have been created, and this will be tough to give up, particularly in the case of the Split-Self Affair. Some people may say they cannot make a choice. Not choosing is a choice. Make no mistake. It means *not* choosing the primary relationship. However, if they have made the commitment to stay with their partner, this type of grief will have to be explored and incorporated. This is over and above the work on the primary relationship. The partner may feel threatened, but this is an opportunity to return to the needs that were ignored and the dreams/fantasies that caused the infidelity in the first place!

"Change-Back" in the System

Recalling from Chapter 2 the discussion about systems theory, all systems seek to maintain homeostasis and equilibrium. As a result, discussing these topics, which can invariably change the system, will provoke an emotional reaction that may seem counter-intuitive: the desire to maintain (or go back to) the status quo. It is a tempting "pull" for the couple to "sweep" the infidelity "under the rug," offer some forgiveness to the person who cheated, and "move forward." In systems theory, these are "change-back" messages that the system imposes on the individuals when they attempt to make changes. When one person makes a change, the other members of the system must also adapt and change. When they resist this change, the person who was trying to make a (positive) change may feel like "no one cares" and like he or she shouldn't even bother making a change. As a result, the person will give up the new behavior. The paradoxical thing is that the family may even have been asking for or wanting the change (like dieting, giving up smoking, quitting drinking), but the system-level behaviors have been designed to deal with the problem behavior, and in order to accommodate the new behavior, the system has to change. Recall from Chapter 2 that systems tend to resist change; therefore, any systemic change must be deliberate and conscious.

With infidelity and couples, the couples system needs to change, and this begins at the level of the wishes, dreams, or fantasies for the relationship. It means the couple has to begin to work together to structure their conversations to work on this level of change. At the same time, discussing these topics is not easy, but at this point, the couple has to be willing to do so. One of the things they have to do, according to Esther Perel (2017) is to move from accusation to investigation when talking about the infidelity. Some ways to discuss feelings and deeper meaning to effect systematic change may include:

> "Thank you for trusting me with your feelings." (show gratitude for the trust)
> "Please tell me what your needs are."
> "Please tell me what you are feeling insecure about."
> "What am I missing (in the relationship) and not doing successfully?"
> "Do we talk less than we used to?"
> "Do we argue more than we used to?"
> "What old patterns do you see us falling into that are concerning?"

"How can we interrupt that and do something different in the relationship that doesn't raise alarming feelings?"
"What was the thing that hurt you the most about the betrayal?"
"What was the thing that led you to think the betrayal was okay in the first place?"
"I am not asking you to accept what I have done, I want you to accept me. I want to earn that."
"How can I support your dreams?"

These questions or prompts don't "shy away" from the difficult topics the couple must discuss in order to avoid the "change-back" dynamic at the system level. The couple that can reach this point deserve a lot of credit. They have decided to come to terms with what was not working in their relationship. They have also decided to be willing to be vulnerable with each other again.

A lot of times couples will ask: "Can people change? Can relationships that have been damaged be repaired?" As couples counselors, we usually tell them: "Yes, but usually they have to be something that they really want. Something they really want to fight for, or something that really makes them afraid to lose." This can seem counter-intuitive. You might think, "Shouldn't people stay together out of love?" And the answer is, "*Sure!*" But when relationships get to a point of deterioration (due to neglect, poor behavior, etc.), and at least one person is thinking of ending the relationship or connecting with someone else, there needs to be something more desperate. There needs to be something to fight for or a fear of loss as well. The funny thing is that it is the same thing with very satisfied relationships. If they need to make some correction, they need to have something to "fight for" (usually some shared vision or goal) or need to be afraid of something bad happening. Actually, all relationships have an element of fear in them that keeps them together. Table 7.1 provides a list of some of these common fears that are embedded in relationships.

The work of beginning to help a couple work through the issues of an infidelity begins with creating new dreams, wishes, or fantasies about the relationship. Understanding the emotional aspect of grief, and the systemic dynamics that may impede this work, is important. However, there are a number of clinical tools, from a variety of theoretical perspectives, and techniques that can help couples counselors facilitate exploration of the old relationship's dreams, wishes, and fantasies and

Table 7.1.: Common fears embedded in relationships

Negative Fear (Self-Focused)	*Positive Fear (Other Focused)*
Fear of failure	Fear of losing connection with loved one
Fear of loneliness	Fear of losing intimacy
Fear of abandonment	Fear of causing loved one pain
Fear of financial loss/loss of status	Fear of failing to live up to others' expectations
Fear of embarrassment	Fear of not keeping promises

provide a bridge to creating new, explicit ones together. These include earliest recollections, Most Memorable Observations, imago exercise, and the dreams within conflict exercise. These techniques will be explored in detail next.

Techniques to Help Build New Shared Dreams, Wishes, or Fantasies for the Relationship

Early Recollections

Early recollections (ERs) is a technique that was created by Alfred Adler in the early 20th century and utilized by Adlerian counselors. ERs can be an especially rich source of clinical understanding about client schemas/personality and thinking. ERs proceed from the concept that memory and memories are not cast in stone, but are a reconstruction, and that asking individuals to recollect something from a very early period of their life will by-pass any defensiveness about themselves or attitudes in the present day ("After all, I was only a child then!"). In addition, the recollections selected will be emotionally and thematically congruent with the person's experiences in the present day (rather than in the past) (Clark, 2002). As Garry and Polaschek (2000) noted:

> The "autobiographical memories" that tell the story of our lives are always undergoing revision precisely because our sense of self is too. We are continually extracting new information from old experiences and filling in gaps in ways that serve some current demand. Consciously or not, we use imagination to reinvent our past, and with it, our present and future.
>
> (p. 6)

As a result, in the context of couples counseling for the treatment of infidelity, collecting early recollections can be a rich source of information about each partner's wishes, dreams, or fantasies about the relationship, and their role in it, as well as the impact of the experience of the affair on them. Last, the information in the ERs can be helpful in creating a new, shared dream, wish, or fantasy for the couple.

The process of collecting early recollections begins with the prompt, "Think back a long time ago to when you were little, and try to recall one of your earliest memories, one of the first things that you can remember" (Clark, 2002, p. 92). Each early recollection should be a single, specific incident generally before the age of 8, and the counselor should follow up with three additional questions (see Table 7.2):

1. "Is there anything else you can recall in the memory?"
2. "What is the most vivid part of the memory that stands out for you?"
3. "What feelings or emotions did you have at that time?"

(Carlson, Watts, & Maniacci, 2006; Clark, 2002)

Table 7.2.: The early recollection interview process

The following is a suggested approach to gathering early recollections in couple therapy, used in teaching graduate students and mental health practitioners (adapted from Kern, Belangee, & Eckstein, 2004).

1 Inform the partner that the therapist will be recording information that might, at first, seem irrelevant to the counseling process.
   "I would like you to go back as far as you can—preferably before the age of seven—and tell me what is the first thing in your life that you can remember? Perhaps it was something you saw, something you did, or something that happened. It should be somewhat like a snippet of video tape—with a beginning, a middle and an end. For example, 'I can remember one time when . . .'"
2 Take one recollection at a time, and process it immediately with the couple.
3 As the client provides the early recollection, it is important to write it down verbatim and to refrain from asking clarification questions that may lead the client. The therapist wants as much unedited information as possible. Any attempt by the therapist to ask for clarifying information may interfere with the process. After the verbatim scribing of the memories, the client is asked, "What happened then?"
4 When the client has finished recalling the memory, the therapist asks, "What is the clearest detail?' or "If you were able to take a picture or snapshot of the most vivid part of that memory, what would it be?"
5 Then the therapist asks, "As you zero in on that detail, what is the feeling that comes up for you?"

Note: This description provides an overview of the early recollection technique. A complete examination of the interpretive process of early recollections is beyond the scope of this book. The interested reader is referred to several excellent resources for how to utilize and interpret early recollections (please see Carlson et al., 2006; Clark, 2002).

Generally speaking, three ERs are collected, although more could be collected. Some clients may be able to easily offer several recollections, while others might struggle to come up with one. Clark noted that three early recollections usually provides sufficient interpretive data and does not take an overwhelming amount of time. Next, the thematic elements of the recollections are considered. If the client includes individuals in the early recollection, they should not be interpreted as *specific people* but as *prototypes*. For example, adults or parents might represent authority figures or guardians. Themes related to social relationships may also give clues about some of the clients' feelings about the current relationship, as well as the impact of the infidelity. Last, the counselor may notice that some early recollections may show the client as an observer, watching "the action" or others as life goes by, rather than as a participant in relationships and life. As Adler (1931/1998) stated:

> The first memory will show the individual's fundamental view of life, her first satisfactory expression of her attitude. It allows us to see at one glance what she has taken as the starting point for her development. I would never investigate a personality without asking for the first memory.
>
> (p. 60)

In processing the recollection, the person telling the memory gains quick insight into his or her own behavior. At the same time, the partner who is listening develops rapport with the partner and a new understanding of the belief system that is the foundation for current behavior. Such early recollections can help a couple have insight to the impasse they have established. It is not unusual for clients to suddenly gain their own insight into issues in their lives as they relate their early recollections. Let's take a look at an example from a couple:

Early Recollections Example

Hers

1. I was 4 years old and was having Christmas at my grandmother's. I got one of those big kitchen sets that you stand in, pretend to cook, and "play house." I remember being in the dining room, playing with it. I was exciting and I was so happy.
2. I remember I was living up north with my mother. My grandfather was visiting us, and we were going to go out to dinner to a Chinese restaurant. I was so excited. It was my first time, and it felt so special. I was excited and happy.
3. I remember I was 3 or 4 years old. I was with my father's side of the family. They were all wise-asses, and I remember making up stories about Jacques Cousteau and that he had died because of an electric eel. My uncle believed me. I couldn't believe how gullible he was! I thought it was the funniest thing that I fooled him!

His

1. When I was 5 or 6 mom and dad got a divorce. I remember being 5 years old and my mother going to work. She got a job as a waitress at night. I remember her coming home and her counting the change that she got in tips on the dining room table. She was so tired. It made me feel sad, she was tired and worked so hard.
2. I remember that first Christmas after Mom threw my father out of the house. We made lists of what we wanted and my father got us everything that we put down on the list. We got everything that we asked for. I was so excited and happy.
3. I remember one time when I was about 4 years old, my father and grandmother got into a really heated argument. I don't remember what it was about. Mom got upset, and Dad had gotten way out of line. My grandmother beat him up, smacking at him and telling him he was awful. All of us were sitting in the living room with our eyes popping out of our head. She was short, but she was cool about everything. Dad was embarrassed. I just remember that she put him back in line and thinking that he deserved it. "You get what you deserve." It made me feel happy.

Can you guess who had the affair and who didn't? In this couple, the wife had the affair with a friend whom she had a close platonic relationship with for some time. The husband worked as a firefighter and was away from the home several nights a week. At first, she would say how much she missed him the nights that he wasn't there but that she was proud of what he did for the community. But as the years went by, and he spent off nights either playing cards, playing softball (in the spring and summer), or bowling in the winter, she began to feel that he was taking her for granted and that she was less and less special. These themes are reflected in her early recollections ("playing house," then being excited about going for Chinese with her grandfather, and finally getting the attention from her male relative). For the husband's part, he felt he worked hard and deserved his time off. He felt he was a good father to the children because he provided for them, but he never felt "comfortable" at home. However, upon learning about the affair, he resisted the temptation to tell all of their friends and family, but his anger and betrayal frequently overwhelmed him.

In this example, it is easy to see where not only the themes that went into the initial "bargain" for the relationship (both had a need to feel special and attended to), but their life circumstances and choices (indeed the couples system that they created), did not allow them to get what they needed from each other. At the same time, the ERs provide a potential avenue for the couple to begin to explore creating a new, shared dream for the relationship that is explicit and that both agree to work on together (see Table 7.3 for a list of common themes).

Table 7.3.: Common themes or what people want out of a relationship

To feel special or important	To not be rejected
To have fun	To be protected and safe
To be pampered	To not be neglected
To feel powerful	To belong
To be wanted	To not be abandoned
To feel desirable	To be heroic

Most Memorable Observation (MMO) Technique

Walton (1998) outlined a technique that uses many of the autobiographical techniques related to early recollections. He developed this technique to help parents who were experiencing conflicts with their children to recognize how some of their reactions (or *over*-reactions) to their children's behaviors were based on their beliefs about parenting that were carried forward from their family of origin. The original prompt for the Most Memorable Observation technique, according to Walton (1998), would be to ask a client:

> Sometime in our early teenage years, or even in late preteen years, it seems very common for each of us to look around our family life and draw a

> conclusion about some aspect of life that appears to be important. Sometimes it is positive, "I really like this aspect of life in our family. When I get to be an adult I'd like it to be just this way in my own family." Often it is negative, "I don't like this at all. This is really distasteful. When I get to be an adult I am going to do everything I can to keep this from occurring in my family." What was it for you? As you think of life in your family about age 11, 12, 13 or so, what conclusion do you think you drew? It may have been positive, it may have been negative, or it may have been both.
>
> (p. 488)

I have modified the prompt to ask couples about their Most Memorable Observation about their *parents'* relationship and any "conclusions" they may have adopted based on that. Often, this can help the couples counselor help the couple understand the nature of the "bargain" they made in the relationship and how that may have helped create the systemic dynamic that led to the infidelity. It can also help in creating a new, shared dream for the couple. So, for example, the prompt may start: "Think back to your parents' relationship. If they were divorced by this time, think about their relationship to each other post-divorce, as well as their relationship to any new partners/step-parents."

Now let's take a look at an example from Bill and Jane in Chapter 5. They were asked about their most memorable observations about their parents' relationship. Here is Bill's:

> I remember my mom and dad would spend every Friday and Saturday night going out. They would either be going out to dinner, or parties or something. They always seemed to have a good time. When I was young, we always had a babysitter, which I loved because they were fun. But I guess around age 14, my sister and I were allowed to be by ourselves at home. I remember thinking that I would want to make sure that I had fun and do exciting things when I got married.

So for him, the problem was an absence of "fun" with his wife. The original fantasy he had bargained for in the relationship had a theme of: "I will try to make your dreams/wishes/fantasies for this relationship come true if you will be my playmate and friend." However, after their child was born, his wife wanted to stay at home and not join him on trips or dinners out with friends, so he found ways to have fun all by himself (which led to an affair). But it wasn't what he really wanted. Next is Jane's Most Memorable Observation of her parents:

> Because Dad was in the Air Force, we had to move around *a lot*! I remember hating that feeling when Dad would come home and nonchalantly say we were going to have to leave in a month or so. Then he would be gone and Mom would have to do all the packing, organizing, and comforting. I remember being 13 years old and we were going to have to move across the country again. It was a nightmare! I thought to myself: I am never going to marry

> someone who would leave me behind to do all the work and make decisions that would hurt me without thinking about how it was going to affect me!

For her, the problem was an absence of partnership with her husband. The original fantasy she had for the relationship had a theme of: "I will try to make your dreams/wishes/fantasies for this relationship come true if you promise that you won't abandon me or make me feel alone." But when the baby came and Bill was traveling or out of town, she began to feel abandoned. She poured all her focus on organizing everything and making all the decisions, since it seemed Bill was never around. She felt like someone had to be the one to do it (like her mom did), so she just did it. When she learned of Bill's affair, she felt so alone and betrayed because she had figured this was a "phase" they would go through and he'd eventually keep his end of the bargain. But he didn't.

The next part of the discussion is to help each person see where their old dream, wish, or fantasy came from for some of these observations and why they fueled such deep pain. Then, when the couple are ready, help them create a new, shared dream or fantasy, one that is explicit and incorporates some (if not all) of their old dreams. For Bill and Jane, they agreed that their new dream would be: "We will try to make each other feel a sense of partnership and fun together. We want to share good times and decisions together."

Imago Technique

Sigmund Freud originally used the term *imago* (Latin for image) to describe a person's unconscious (and idealized) mental representation of a parent, which is formed early in life and retained in adulthood (Love & Shulkin, 2001). Harville Hendrix extended Freud's idea of the imago and made it a central feature of relationship function (and dysfunction). He created Imago Relationship Therapy (IRT), a psychodynamic approach that begins with the basic premise that each partner in the relationship comes with certain frustrations and wounds that are incorporated into the person's imago. The relationship has the power to heal these wounds by understanding the needs that were not met in childhood and providing the support and affection that were missing without being coerced into it (Hendrix, 1996; Luquet, 1998; Sperry & Peluso, 2018). They created an easy-to-use exercise that couples counselors can use with couples to help them uncover their imagos and share them with each other (see Table 7.4).

Much like early recollections or Most Memorable Observations, the imago exercise is a way to tap into the underlying needs or wants of the couple and how these tie into the dreams, wishes, and fantasies they have for the relationship. When couples come to counseling, they are each trying to get their needs met by the other person but have not been successful. Often this is because they were not consciously aware of these needs. As a result, the couple becomes confused and frustrated when their partners violate these expectations (particularly when an infidelity happens). It is at this point that painful feelings of disappointment from one's childhood experiences come to the surface. These usually must be dealt with

Table 7.4.: Imago exercise

Take a sheet of paper and divide it into five sections labeled A, B, C, D, and E. Answer the following questions in the designated areas of the paper:

A. Think about yourself as a young child (from birth to 18 years old), and list at least three outstanding negative traits of the people who raised you or had an influence on your life (e.g., angry, mean, disinterested, sad, depressed, etc.).
B. Now list three positive characteristics of these people (e.g., caring, giving, jovial, smart, funny, etc.).
C. Thinking back to your family growing up, what did you need or want the most from the people around you—what was your heart's desire (e.g., I needed to feel safe, I needed to feel important, etc.)?
D. Now recall the happiest memories of childhood. These can be with your family, with friends, in school, out of school, etc. Then list how you felt during these times (e.g., happy, secure, loved, etc.).
E. Last, think back on the frustrations you had as a child, not just with your family but with anybody (friends, etc.), and describe how you responded to these frustrations (e.g., getting angry, yelling, working harder, keeping to myself, blaming others, etc.).

Once these are all completed, go back and write in the following statements before each of the responses:

1. "I am attracted to a person who is . . ."
2. "and I expect him or her to be . . ."
3. "so that I can get . . ."
4. "and feel . . ."
5. "but I stop myself from getting this by . . ."

Once all of these are filled out, you have a picture of each partner's imago.

Note: Adapted from *Getting the love you want: A guide for couples*, by H. Hendrix, 1988, New York: Henry Holt; Imago theory and the psychology of attraction, by P. Love and S. Shulkin, 2001, *The Family Journal: Counseling and Psychotherapy for Couples and Families*, 9(3), 246–249; and The relational paradigm, by W. Luquet, 1998, in W. Luquet and M. T. Hannah (Eds.), *Healing in the relational paradigm: The imago relationship casebook* (pp. 1–18), New York: Brunner/Mazel.

before they cause more damage to the relationship (Luquet, 1998). However, it is also an opportunity to be able to show how each person (regardless of whether or not they were the one who committed the infidelity) brings in their unspoken dynamics and expectations from childhood. Table 7.5 has examples of responses from a couple using the imago exercise.

While the couple may not always agree with the responses (generally the answers to the question of *who* they are attracted to), often the responses startle each person with their accuracy. The exercise is most effective if done with both partners together. In the aforementioned example, each person is able to take a step back and see the part each plays in not getting their needs met or not making their dreams and fantasies (". . . so that I can get . . . and feel . . .") come true (". . . but I stop myself from getting this by . . ."). They can also uncover the hidden expectations they have for the other person (". . . and I expect him or her to be . . ."), which can often be an unfairly high standard to achieve if the other person is not aware of it.

Table 7.5.: Imago exercise responses from a couple

	Her Responses	*His Responses*
1 I am attracted to a person who is . . .	angry, cold, stubborn, critical	temperamental, stern, aggressive
2 and I expect him or her to be . . .	giving, happy, childish	caring, supportive, easy-going
3 so that I can get . . .	to be held, safe, childlike	friendship, attraction, love
4 and feel . . .	amazing, fun	secure, happy, joyful
5 but I stop myself from getting this by . . .	hiding embarrassment, yelling	fighting back, acting spoiled, getting defensive, acting out

However, it is from this exercise that the shared dream can begin to take shape. By taking each person's positive expectations of the other, the feelings that they want to feel, and the goals they have, they can create an explicit set of expectations, fantasies, wishes, or dreams that both can agree on. In addition, they can use the final responses to be "warning signs" that one or the other person is feeling insecure about the relationship or fearful they are not getting their needs met. When these are noticed, then the couple can remind each other of the shared dream and what they are trying to work toward. This can help them step back from whatever the immediate conflict is (as well as the old, ineffective systemic responses) and consider the larger explicit goals (and, thus, a new equilibrium point).

Dreams Within Conflict

Drs. John and Julie Gottman have taken the over 45 years of their research and clinical experience with couples and developed a system of couples therapy (Gottman Method Couples Therapy). In their observations of couples (those who were highly successful and those that were not), they discovered that *all* relationships had conflicts. Most conflicts (approximately 69%) were about "perpetual issues"—or issues that did not have a solution. These include personal preferences or differences in personality that are not likely to change in a person. Some couples just seemed to be forever "deadlocked" by the conflicts, while others found a way to move past them (although not necessarily solve them). So what made the "masters" of marriage better than the "disasters" of marriage? Their answer:

> Our conclusion is that the masters of relationship (couples who stay together and are not unhappy) know how to move from gridlock to dialogue on their perpetual problems because they are able to both (a) express a fundamental acceptance of their partners' personality and (b) discuss and understand the existential hidden agendas, the dreams in their partner's position on the issue.
> (Gottman & Gottman, 2017, p. 18)

In their approach, they employ a graphic called the "Sound Relationship House" to depict all the factors they have discovered go into a functioning and satisfying relationship. One of the top "floors" in the house is "Managing Conflict" (particularly the unresolvable conflict), followed by the top levels of the house ("Making Life Dreams Come True" and "Creating Shared Meaning"). All three of these elements are crucial for successful relationships. But if couples are perpetually getting stuck (gridlocked) in conflicts that have no resolution, there is no way either to make dreams come true or create shared meaning. One way to help couples who seem to always get stuck in gridlock is to use a technique called the "Dreams Within Conflict" intervention. It is designed to get couples to examine "the *meaning* of each person's position and [find] ways to honor each person's dreams and core needs with respect to his or her position on the issue" (p. 18). It also is a useful method for helping couples explore those unexpressed wishes, dreams, and fantasies about the relationship and begin to forge new ones together. Table 7.6 outlines the exercise.

Many times, couples are not comfortable or skilled in asking questions that encourage a response from their partner without sounding like they are criticizing

Table 7.6.: "Dreams Within Conflict" exercise

Remember that beneath every gridlock problem there is something each of you wishes for, a story, a life dream. In this exercise, ***do not try to solve the problem at all.*** The idea is to talk about what your position *means* to you, to share your various thoughts and feelings behind it. The intent is to get to the symbolic meaning behind your position rather than to argue for your position.

You will take turns—one of you will be the Speaker and the other Listener.

The Speaker

As the Speaker you will speak about the dream, the meaning, behind your position. Your job is to pull back layers. Like brainstorming, there are no silly ideas, and nothing is written in stone. It's a time to explore out loud.

The Listener

The other person will play the role of Listener.

As the Listener you will ask questions or offer statements which aid your partner in revealing his/her dream.

No defending; no judging; no criticism;

No arguing for your position. No giving of opinions.

Some sample questions:

What's behind your position?	Is there some history to it?
What does it symbolize?	Why is this so important to you?
What's the story?	What does the issue mean to you?

After the Speaker has spoken for a while, the couples counselor may want to pull out the list of possible dreams and see if any are pertinent.

Then reverse roles.

Note: Gottman (2011). Clinicians interested in learning more about the certification process are encouraged to go to www.gottman.com for more details about training.

or probing. Gottman Method Therapists regularly provide handouts with some sample questions (see Table 7.7).

Finally, many of the dreams that underlie the conflicts have some common themes across couples. Gottman (2011) provides a list of these for clinicians to more easily categorize them for couples (see Table 7.8). Of course, these must be tailored for each couple, and this is not an exhaustive list.

Now let's take a look at a case study and employ the "Dreams Within Conflict" exercise to look at how the technique can be used to help couples create a new shared dream, wish, or fantasy for the relationship.

Table 7.7.: Sample questions for the dream listener

Use these questions to elicit more information from one partner about his or her dreams. This will allow him or her to describe the dreams in better detail, and the listener will gain a sense of the importance of these dreams to the dreamer.
What do you believe about this issue?
What do you feel about it?
What does that mean to you?
Tell me the meaning of these things to you.
Is there a story behind this for you?
Does this relate to your history in some way?
What do you want? What do you need?
Tell me why is this important to you?
What is the meaning of your position on this issue?
What are all your feelings about this?
Are there any feelings you have left out here?
What do you wish for here?
What would be your ideal dream here?
What do you imagine things would be like if you got what you wanted?
Is there a deeper purpose or goal in this for you?
In what way is it central to who you are as a person, to your core identity?
Does this relate to some belief or value for you?
Is there a fear or disaster scenario in not having this dream honored?

Note: Adapted from *The Science of Trust* (Gottman, 2011)

Table 7.8.: Sample thematic classifications of dreams

A sense of freedom	The experience of peace
Exploring who I am	Adventure
A spiritual journey	Justice
Honor	Unity with my past
Healing	Knowing my family
Becoming all I can be	Having a sense of power
Exploring a creative side of myself	Becoming more powerful

Getting over past hurts	Becoming more competent
Asking God for forgiveness	Exploring an old part of myself I have lost
Getting over a personal hang-up	Having a sense of order
Being able to be productive	A place and a time to just "be"
Being able to truly relax	Reflecting on my life
Getting my priorities in order	Finishing something important
Exploring the physical side of myself	Being able to compete and win
Travel	Quietness
Atonement	Building something important
Saying goodbye to something	The ideal of love

Note: Adapted from *The Science of Trust* (Gottman, 2011).

Analeese and Derek

Analeese (aged 42) and Derek (aged 45) had been married for 21 years. They had two children, a 15-year-old daughter named Jill and a 10-year-old son named Alex. They came in for couples counseling after it was revealed that Analeese had an affair with a co-worker. An additional complicating factor was that Analeese and Derek both work at the same law firm (she as a paralegal, he as an attorney) and that Analeese's lover, Phil, also worked at the same firm as a partner.

Analeese and Derek reported that the quality of their relationship had been suffering over the last few years. Derek stated that he felt that this was due to their increased involvement with the children's lives (coaching teams, etc.) and admitted that he had become over-committed at work but justified it by saying that his success had provided a very comfortable lifestyle for his family. Analeese angrily stated that she had spent almost two decades sacrificing her ambitions (to go back to law school, etc.) in order to support Derek's career and that, in return, he was often cold and uncommunicative. She reflected that she had married Derek because she saw herself as a "good girl" and that "it was the thing you were supposed to do." However, she recently had begun to wonder if she had ever loved Derek at all. On the other hand, being with Phil made her feel "alive."

In the midst of the marital chaos, there were problems with the children. Jill was acting out primarily against her mother by arguing, running away for several days at a time, experimenting with drugs, and eventually becoming pregnant. The younger son, Alex, began to flunk classes in school and dropped his sports activities, when previously he was an "A" student and enjoyed playing several sports. It was later revealed that Jill had discovered her mother's affair long before Derek had. She saw a text on her mother's phone with a photo of her mother and Phil kissing. She never told her dad, which made her feel like a "traitor" for keeping the secret, but she did not know how to tell her father (whom Jill loved but saw as "lazy"). For his part, Alex just felt neglected by his mother and sensed the family drifting apart. While his sports were a point of connection for him and his father, he began to withdraw and spend his time playing online games in his room for hours and hours with no one coming to check on him.

The affair was discovered only after Phil's wife filed for divorce. She had discovered that he and Analeese were having a sexual relationship and used the evidence she had found in the divorce proceedings. As a result, other people in the firm heard the story (or rumors), and Derek was mortified. "I felt like everyone knew that I had been played for a fool!" Analeese felt there was no reason to change her job and that the "office gossip" would go away ("We weren't the first co-workers there to get caught fooling around, and we won't be the last!"). Derek thought of leaving, but he couldn't have the same level of success that he had where he was, so he felt trapped. At the same time, Phil agreed to break off the relationship with Analeese, although she was having difficulty separating her feelings for Phil.

In terms of Brown's (2001) typology, this was a Split-Self Affair. Analeese felt like she had suppressed her feelings (as well as her career) for Derek and the family, and she felt like she was "owed" a chance to do something for herself and to "live a little." When looking at the "dream within the conflict," it is important to look at the conflicts.

Derek: My wife is never there for me. I am always doing something, and when I have some "down time," I just want to relax with her. But instead, she gets cranky and I wind up alone. She is constantly trying to persuade me to accompany her to parties, to go out dancing, try new restaurants and bars, but I don't want to. So she dumps the kids with me and goes for a "girls night out" almost every week. I just don't get it!

Analeese: My husband's ways are stifling me. He's out of the house doing things with the kids or work and when it is time for just us, all he wants is to stay in and watch Netflix. I can barely get him off the couch. He doesn't understand what I want in life. I want to live a little while we are still young. I just want to feel free and have a chance to do what *I* want. With or without him!

Now, let's take a look at the possible dreams within the conflict:

Derek: My parents were poor and had to work all the time to make ends meet. I always wore hand-me-downs or thrift store clothes. And when my parents were around, all they would do is argue over money. I would go outside and play in the woods until after dark just so I didn't have to hear them. I would go over to friends' houses and dream that I could live in a home like theirs. I was always embarrassed to have anyone come over to my house because it was so shabby. I've never been able to have any sense of stability. I've never been able to relax, living in what I guess must have been a permanent state of anxiety. Now that we have a really good life and have "made it" all I want to do in my free time is cuddle up on the couch with a good book, or watch a movie together, or make meals together, take walks around our beautiful neighborhood, talk about anything and everything deep into the night with the woman I adore.

Analeese: I was always the good girl. I did everything I was told, and I thought that would make me happy. It never made my mom happy, but I thought I could do better than her. I thought that if I married a better man than she did and we were able to have good careers we would be happy. I was raised in an unhappy home. My mom was always sad, and my dad was always gone. He seemed to be having fun, but I felt that I never got to share in any of it. When I got into high school, I could finally escape. I got a car, had a boyfriend, we would go out to movies and dances. It was all so exciting. I never wanted to lose that feeling.

Once these dreams underlying the conflict are revealed (for him success means the freedom to enjoy life, and for her success means being able to experience the excitement of life), each can begin to move forward from the gridlocked conflict (you just want to stay home vs. you just want to escape) and begin to create a shared dream around the idea of "what does it mean to be able to enjoy life now that you have earned success?" Therefore, this has to be done consciously, thoughtfully, and together. The couple gets to decide what they want to include and what they want to exclude. Maybe they even get to have conversations they never had before or never dreamed of having before.

When couples can do this, it is helpful to create a joint statement and put it in writing. It is also helpful to include the word "we" in it as often as possible. For example:

> *We want to always keep each other's hearts safe. We want to minimize hurt and maximize fun and joy. We will do this by working together, sharing together, and playing together every opportunity we can.*

Throughout the rest of treatment, this joint statement can be a touchstone for helping the couple gain the courage to have the difficult conversations to come and shape a new future together.

Conclusion: Furthering the Creation of New Dreams, Wishes, and Fantasies

And while this is the *beginning* of treatment for infidelity, it is also an important end point as well. It is the renewed dream, wish, or fantasy that the couple decides to work toward together that will allow them ultimately to be successful. And although there is still a lot of work to do, successfully achieving this goal can dramatically increase the chances for success for the couple. The next chapter discusses the issue of power imbalances and sharing power.

CHAPTER **8**

Rebalancing the See-Saw: Sharing Power and Working Together

She hated always having to ask him for money to buy necessities. He was afraid of what he thought was her "reckless" spending. At the same time, when they were at home, he resented how she made him feel like he couldn't do anything right with the kids or the house. She felt like he would never pitch in or help her with any of the household chores. "We both work, and yet I am the one who is in charge of the laundry?" They remembered a time when it didn't use be this way and when they worked together . . .

The previous chapter discussed the concept of creating a new dream, wish, or fantasy for the relationship. And contrary to the original dream, wish, or fantasy that each partner came into the relationship with, the new one is explicit and shared. But it doesn't end there. In fact, the power imbalances that helped create the conditions where the infidelity occurred don't magically disappear just because there is a shared vision for the relationship. However, it does begin to make discussing the power differentials much easier.

In this chapter, issues of power and fairness will be discussed. This will require the couple to understand their relationship as a separate system they co-create, rather than simply two people's needs coming together. From a systemic viewpoint, techniques to rebalance power differentials will require negotiation skills as well as communication skills. This chapter discusses techniques for accomplishing these tasks.

Wishes, Fantasies, Dreams, and Power

As mentioned in Chapter 4, power is the ability to influence another person to do something or having one's wishes followed by another person. Struggles over power are at the heart of all conflicts for couples. Gottman and Gottman (2017) have discussed the concept of "perpetually gridlocked issues" for couples. In fact, they say that the majority of conflicts couples face are perpetual and unsolvable. These are conflicts that, at their heart, are about power. They come from individual wants and needs, and, depending on whether or not the couple want to compromise, there may not be a solution. The ability to arrive at an amicable agreement when a problem cannot be solved—when there is a conflict about values or deeply held beliefs—is one of the most important balances a couple can achieve. If they can, there is a true commitment to sharing power: to allow another person's position or will to coexist with yours, even if it is diametrically opposed to yours. And make no mistake! The conflicts don't end just because there is a new dream or fantasy or bargain. In fact, sometimes they can be more pointed and uncomfortable.

While these conflicts and power imbalances can be long-standing and entrenched, recovering from an affair requires a shift in these old ways of operating. These must be examined and changed. Two of the most common root causes of power imbalance are sex and money. The issues of sexual satisfaction and financial decision making in couples are closely linked to issues of intimacy, boundaries, and power (see the genogram section that follows for a more in-depth discussion). Decisions about money, how it is spent, and who spends it can often give therapists vital clues to underlying relationship dynamics. For example, if one partner doesn't have control of the checkbook or makes less money than the other, that person may always feel required to defer to the other person. Likewise for decisions about sex: Who gets to decide when it happens? Who gets to decide what happens? Who's needs get met, and whose don't? These are all important indicators of who has power and who feels like they don't have power in the relationship.

There is a dark side to this, however. This occurs with people who are conflict averse and tend to avoid confrontations. In these cases, the issues get stonewalled or ignored. At best, there is stony silence, which brings up feelings of awkwardness or embarrassment and increases the distance between the partners. At worst, however, the issues repeatedly come up and won't go away. Many times, these are issues related to parenting, lifestyle choices, religion and spirituality, and, underlying all of these, personal values.

Values conflicts are at the heart of some of the most persistent and divisive conflicts in relationships. When there is a power imbalance, at least one person will feel required to compromise their values. However, working through the issues, and understanding the deeper values, can provide a clarity for both the individuals in the couple and the couple itself. This means shedding old ways of looking at yourself, others, or the world around you. It means becoming more self-confident ("I deserve to allow myself to ask for the things I want, rather than demand them or expect them. On the other hand, I may not be able to get them . . ."). It means being more self-reliant ("I am sufficient. I am worthy and do not need to rely on the validation of others."). In virtually each type of affair, if the power issues are able to be balanced and (most) decisions are made jointly, couples can go from a problematic dynamic to a more fulfilling one:

Type of Affair	*Resolved and Improved Outcome*
Conflict-Avoidance	Conflict Resolvers
Intimacy-Avoidance	Deeper Intimacy
Sexual Addiction	Sexual Integrity
Split-Self	Living Whole

The only type of affair that is not reflected prior is the Exit Affair. In the Exit Affair, the goal is to end the relationship. Any attempt to try to bring about a resolved outcome is usually futile. As Brown (2007) notes, the ideal outcome is resolving the issues around ending the relationship. This is not to say that a counselor should give up on these couples but, rather, that the counselor should take a realistic approach when treating them (however, it is unlikely that a couple intent on ending the relationship would have moved past the step of creating a new wish, dream, or fantasy for the relationship).

What if one of the couple can't choose between the relationship and the lover (as in the case of Split-Self Affairs)? Is it possible to continue without giving up the relationship with the other person? In truth this is very difficult. It is not impossible, but it is difficult. Consider the following example from the world of politics.

The Case of President Franklin Delano Roosevelt

The relationship of Franklin Delano Roosevelt, the 32nd president of the United States, and his wife, Eleanor Roosevelt, was unique in the history of the US. FDR presided over the tumultuous eras of the Great Depression and World War II, while Eleanor became a champion for the rights of others and helped shape the United Nations. Stricken with polio in the 1920s, which left him paralyzed, FDR relied on Eleanor to be his "eyes and ears" and travel to places he could not go. In this respect, she became a partner like no other political spouse had ever been. However, their marriage was something altogether different. First, FDR's mother did not approve of Eleanor. Sara Delano Roosevelt was a dominant and powerful figure in FDR's life. She lived with Franklin and Eleanor frequently, and they built two houses side by side in New York City (with connections on each floor). She helped paint and decorate the houses with FDR. Eleanor never participated or felt the house was hers.

In terms of their sexual relationship, Eleanor did not like sexual intercourse and considered it "an ordeal to be endured." In 1914 (about 11 years after they were married), Eleanor hired Lucy Mercer to be her secretary. She became a fixture in the household and was close with the family. It is believed that around 1916, FDR and Lucy began a sexual relationship when Eleanor and the children were away. As a commentary on the state of the marriage, both FDR and Eleanor's cousin (and daughter of President Theodore Roosevelt), Alice (who encouraged the romance), was reported to have said: "He *deserved* a good time . . . He was married to Eleanor!" It was clear to many people that this marriage was not a good "match."

Lucy stopped working for Eleanor in 1917 and went to work for the Navy, where FDR was the assistant secretary of the Navy. She began to work for him directly. In addition, he brought her along to many of his yachting parties because Eleanor refused to go. Eleanor eventually discovered the affair in 1918 when she found love letters between FDR and Lucy that he had kept. For

Eleanor, it was a crushing blow to her already low self-esteem. She felt that she was "unattractive" based on her mother's criticisms of her as a girl. Early in her marriage to FDR, Eleanor broke down crying to her cousin that she was afraid she would not be able to keep FDR because he was "too attractive." Now, just because she did not understand his wants in terms of sexuality or companionship, and Lucy seemed to, she was devastated. In the letters from Lucy, she saw that FDR had deeper feelings for her. She offered to grant him a divorce and "set him free," but it was FDR's mother, Sara, who intervened—not out of care for Eleanor, but for fear of FDR's political career—and forbade a divorce. After this, according to James Roosevelt (Eleanor and FDR's son), the Roosevelts' marriage was "an armed truce that endured until the day he died." Eleanor seemingly confirmed this later in life, saying: "I have the memory of an elephant. I can forgive, but never forget."

Despite Franklin's promise to Eleanor, he kept in contact with Lucy Mercer (who was now Lucy Rutherfurd after her marriage to a wealthy businessman), corresponding with her by letter throughout the 1920s. At the same time, FDR employed another personal secretary, Missy LeHand, who would serve as the hostess for many functions when Eleanor was not around (or did not want to participate). She shared many of the same hobbies (stamp collecting, card playing) and social activities as FDR (Eleanor did not like alcohol, while FDR engaged in daily cocktail hours that included guests). Throughout FDR's illness and recovery, and then his term as governor, Missy continued her professional and personal relationship. However, unlike with Lucy Mercer Rutherfurd, this relationship was tolerated by Eleanor. While Missy and FDR were said to have a close personal relationship, there is some doubt about whether the relationship was (or even could have been) sexual due to the president's paralysis following his bout with polio in 1921. Once FDR won the presidency, Missy became his chief of staff and lived in the White House.

At the same time, the relationship with Lucy did not go away, but it did go underground. FDR wrote her letters, and some speculated these letters may have been the cause of a purported nervous breakdown of Missy in 1927. In 1941, Missy suffered a stroke, and Lucy's husband was likewise incapacitated by illness (interestingly, both Missy and Lucy's husband died in 1944). At this point, FDR began to reconnect with Lucy, enlisting his daughter, Nancy (who was now acting as FDR's social secretary and hostess at White House functions because of Eleanor's frequent absences), to arrange for private meetings with her. Eleanor did not know about these meetings. Nancy was upset to be put in this position but reportedly began to like Lucy and arranged for private diners with other guests at the White House. On April 12, 1945, Lucy was at FDR's "Little White House" in Warm Springs, Georgia, when he complained of a sharp pain in the back of his head. He suffered a fatal stroke and died with her by his bedside. When Eleanor learned of this, she was devastated. And when she discovered Nancy's role in arranging for Lucy to be there (over 27 years after she forbid FDR to see her again), they were estranged for many years.

One of the more important factors is context. First, this was a relationship that occurred a century ago, when the idea of divorce was inextricably intertwined with ruin and scandal. However, the scenario is not as far-fetched as one might think. The case of the Roosevelts is interesting for several reasons. They had several "perpetually gridlocked" issues (sex, alcohol, entertaining, mother-in-law) they could not *navigate* or *negotiate* (see the following for details), so the affairs (one secret, one tolerated) filled a need in the relationship. However, perhaps one of the best perspectives on this comes from Eleanor Roosevelt herself. In one of her later books, she wrote that she occasionally failed to "meet the need of someone whom I dearly love," stating, "You must learn to allow someone else to meet the need, without bitterness or envy, and accept it." We can speculate about the dynamics of the relationship based on some of the historical accounts. It was a partnership, but not one with much affection or passion. FDR and Eleanor shared some ideals in common, but not many personal interests. They were able to forge a new vision or dream for the relationship, and they found a way to share power in the relationship (albeit after FDR's paralysis at the hands of polio). As Napier (2007) wrote:

> The sense of defeat at the hands of the other is interlocking; and of course each tends to see the other as the source of his or her despair. Neither sees the collusive nature of their patterns, or the ways in which they both have failures of courage when they might instead push through to greater honesty or intimacy. And they do not know about the powerful weight of transference pushing down on them both, the sense that *of course* they can't speak up or ask for something or risk sharing a vulnerability—because they couldn't do so in their families of origin. And of course true intimacy, perhaps a lifelong stranger to them both, is frightening.
>
> (pp. 296)

As a result, FDR sought the company of two women who filled the role Eleanor could not.

Return to the See-Saw and Imbalances of Power

Recall from Chapter 4 the metaphor of the see-saw and power imbalances. If one person is too heavy (have all the power), they never go in the air (have all the responsibility and no fun). If, on the other hand, a person is too light (no power), they are afraid they'll never get down or the other person will get off and send them crashing (at the whim of the other person, with no ability to affect decision making). Balancing the see-saw (and the power) is the key. However, it is not as easy as it sounds. This is primarily because *who* has the most power is based in part on perception. Each person may feel they are at the mercy of the other person. Another element in balancing power in a couple is understanding *where* each person's role models for power distribution in a couple come from. That means looking into each person's family of origin. The best (and quickest) method for obtaining this information is through the use of genograms.

Family-of-Origin and the Use of Genograms to Understand Power in the System

Utilized by family therapists, genograms were first introduced by Murray Bowen in the 1950s as an assessment tool for family therapy (McGoldrick, Gerson, & Petry, 2008). They are a simple, graphic way to trace multi-generational influences on a couple's current level of functioning. The basic symbols used to represent individuals and classify relationship issues are in shown in Figures 8.1 and 8.2. Recall from Chapter 2 that family processes tend to repeat themselves, particularly with regard to unresolved emotional issues (McGoldrick et al., 2008). Genograms can be used to trace recurring patterns of addictions, intimate partner violence, divorce, and even chronic diseases within a family (Hardy & Laszloffy, 1995; McGoldrick et al., 2008). Exploring the couple's history in relationship to their families of origin often yields useful information in clarifying some issues and bringing them into the therapeutic arena. Basic information reported on the genogram includes names and ages of family members (usually for three generations), marital statuses, divorces or separations (if appropriate), and deaths (Hardy & Laszloffy, 1995; McGoldrick et al., 2008).

In addition, genograms provide information about boundaries, intimacy, and power (hence their inclusion in this chapter!). First, any inter-generational patterns of how these elements were demonstrated in a couple's families of origin can be graphically displayed. Many times, when this is laid out in front of a couple, the

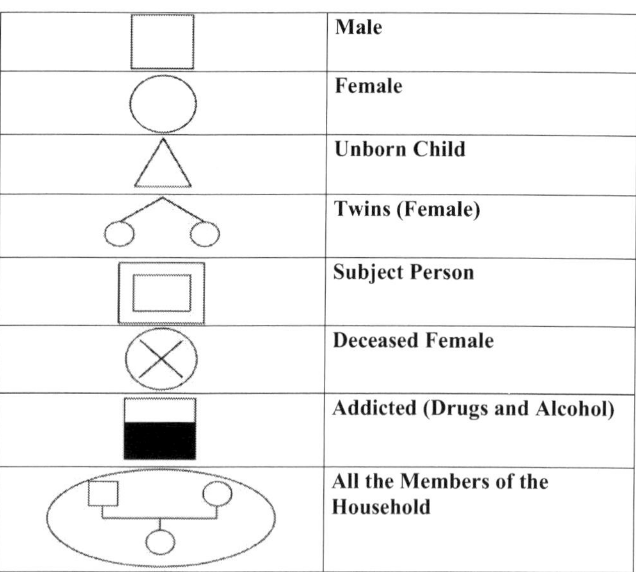

Figure 8.1.: Defining a genogram: Symbols

Defining a Genogram: Relationships

m. 1982	**Marriage**
m. 1985 d.1999	**Divorce**
	Romantic Relationship
	Enmeshed Relationship Between Mother and Son
	Conflict Between Father and Daughter
	"Cut Off" or No Relationship Between Father and Son

Figure 8.2.: Defining a genogram: Relationships

direct impact of these family "legacies," expectations, or habits becomes clearer. Recall from Chapter 2 that boundaries are important elements in systems theory. For structure or boundaries, questions to be answered include: Who else is considered part of the couples system? Do parents or children have a closer relationship to one of the partners than the partners have with each other? Is the family patriarchal or matriarchal? Has this been a pattern over generations? How are these things intruding into the couples relationship? For intimacy, some questions are: What was the quality (closeness or distance) in other relationships across generations? How do the spouses tolerate or respond to each other's needs and desires for intimate contact and closeness? How do spouses use emotional and geographical distance when struggling with their need for closeness? Ultimately, these question lead to questions of power How is it balanced in the relationship? Who is in charge? How do the partners decide who gets to do what? Answers to such questions provide significant data for the therapist in assessing how power is shared in the couples system (Sperry & Peluso, 2018). Let's take a look at an example from a couple.

The Case of Ted and Nancy

Ted and Nancy had been married for 7 years prior to entering couples therapy. Nancy initiated the therapy after her discovery of a recent affair between Ted and a co-worker. The couple have a 5-year-old daughter and a 3-year-old son, and both state that they want to stay together, primarily for the children, if possible. Nancy stated that she had been at her mother's house on an extended trip with the children. She arrived home earlier than expected because she was suspicious of Ted and discovered a Ted's co-worker in her robe. Ted defended himself by saying that he and Nancy had not had sex in more than a year and that they had been growing apart since the birth of their son 3 years earlier. Ted stated that the problems between them actually started at the beginning of their marriage because Nancy was "attached at the hip" to her mother.

Exploration of the couple's families of origin produced a genogram (see Figure 8.3) which revealed that Nancy's parents had divorced when she was young. She was not particularly close to her father but was close with her step-father (the man her mother had an affair with before divorcing Nancy's father). Several years later, when Nancy was in her teens, Nancy's mother divorced her step-father (after a series of affairs), and she resented her mother for "making him go away." Her mother later remarried and divorced. Nancy vowed not to have a marriage like her mother's but admitted to being somewhat enmeshed with her mother: "She is like my best friend, rather than my mother. I know that sounds weird, but it is true." She admits that usually calls her mother several times a day and at least every night (usually when Ted was home), at which time they would talk at length. Ted complained that Nancy "would always make time for her mother but never put in that type of effort with me." Nancy indignantly retorted that her mother needed her, "and besides, I like her. Is there anything wrong with being friends with your mother?"

Ted's family of origin revealed that his mother and father had been married until his father's death 5 years earlier but that the relationship between his parents was very tumultuous. Frequently, he had defended his father, which created tension between he and his mother. He was also the only son, and he had four sisters. He was closest to his oldest sister ("She was more of a mom to me than my mom!"), and he currently had no relationship with his youngest sister (a year younger than him), saying that she was "attached at the hip" with his mom, just like he described Nancy and her mother. Ted recalled that he admired his father as strong and decisive compared to his mother's apparent "high-strung" nature and wondered why they never divorced.

As for their marriage, Ted and Nancy did not do a good job planning time for each other. They were each devoted to their careers first, their children second, then other things (family, religion, friends), and, finally (a distant fourth), their relationship. They deluded themselves into thinking they were prioritizing each other, but to people close to them, it was obvious they weren't. Her mother even told her: "I am concerned for you. You need to spend time together. Go out on a date." And despite having the financial resources to travel, go out to dinner, and so on, they always spent time at home. They hadn't gone on a vacation alone together for years. Even when they had the time to do so, they just couldn't agree on a place to go that would interest them.

In terms of her sexuality, Ted described their sex life as "lifeless" while Nancy reported feeling that her sex drive had diminished since the birth of her children, which concerned her. Nancy stated that she doesn't really miss sex and was kind of relieved when Ted stopped pestering her for it all the time. She did admit that she does periodically want Ted sexually but that it never seems to happen at a convenient time (kids, mealtime, etc.). Nancy confessed that she had suspicions Ted may have been seeing someone else, which compounded her feelings of sexual inadequacy.

Ted reminisced that in the beginning their sex life was "hot" and that, before the kids were born, they would frequently make love spontaneously, watch adult movies and attempt different positions, or even engage in masturbatory fantasy on the phone with each other during the day while at work. Nancy dismissingly stated that it was "fun for a while, but then it got old. I grew up." This seemed to hurt Ted, although he didn't voice the feeling. He felt that Nancy had engaged in what could have been termed an "emotional affair" with her boss. He was an older, charismatic, and self-assured man. He flattered her at every opportunity. He frequently told her that she was "the best junior partner I ever had" and that she was destined to succeed him in his job.

In discussing his affair, Ted defended himself by saying that he and Nancy had not had sex in more than a year and that they had been growing apart since the birth of their son. Ted claimed that he only started the affair at work after he had been abandoned by Nancy in the marriage and only after repeatedly being rejected by her until he stopped trying to initiate sex. He recalled that he had bought her a negligee and underwear from Victoria's Secret ahead of a "getaway" they were supposed to have. However, she never opened it, and 6 months later, it remained in her closet, unopened. "That to me was a real symbol of where we were. I spent time and thought to get that for her, and had hopes for what it would 'spark,' and she left it unopened and in the closet." Shortly after that, he began the affair with his co-worker.

As mentioned earlier, sex is power. In a couple, it only takes one person to veto the other, particularly with sex. However, there is something deeper about sex. It is care. Who has the power to make the other feel good? Who has the power to make the other person feel bad or ashamed? Do both partners see to the other's needs, or does one always seem to be satisfied while the other is frustrated? And are they aware when this happens? In the aforementioned case, the couple suffered from neglect. Their sex life ceased, which created great dissatisfaction, and their fantasies about the relationship died. In terms of power, Ted felt that Nancy's relationship to her mother and over the children left him as the "odd man out," and with her "emotional affair," he felt even more justified in getting his needs met. The

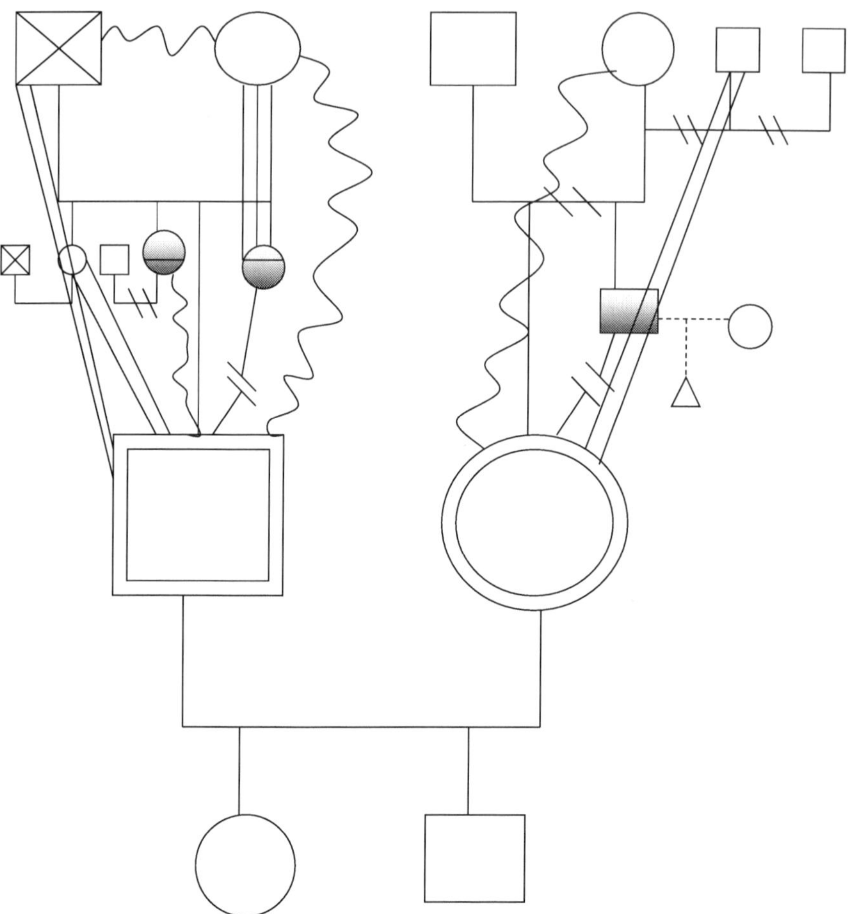

Figure 8.3.: Genogram for Ted and Nancy

affair became a way to affect all three elements of the model (satisfaction, power, and fantasy). But once it was discovered, the reality of the state of their relationship had to be confronted. In the following section, techniques for helping couples address the balance of power in the relationship will be reviewed and applied to the case of Ted and Nancy.

Techniques to Share Power and Balance the See-Saw

So once you understand the power imbalances and know the system dynamics that shape them and the family-of-origin issues that contributed to them, how can you help the couple begin to balance the power between them? There are two principles. First, there are some things that will not be balanced. This is because there are some things that one person may just be *better* at (either because of talent, practice, or passion). Some people are better at cooking, others at cleaning. Some people enjoy yardwork, while others may enjoy "tinkering" and fixing things around the house. Likewise, while both partners may work, one partner may (by virtue of their career choice or because they are very good at it) simply earn more than the other person. As mentioned prior, this can cause many conflicts. So the question is how to *navigate* around this imbalance. The second principle is that there are things that can be shared more equally and balanced. This might be in the area of parenting or other joint decisions. This requires the couple to make a commitment to sharing the power and decision making and not forcing a choice when there is not agreement. It also means committing to not capitulating to the other person and abdicating responsibility. And while it can lead to stalemates, it can also foster opportunities for the couple to learn to *negotiate* with one another, honestly and openly. The next section of the chapter presents techniques to help clients learn how to *navigate* and *negotiate* these issues, in the service of sharing power equally (or approaching a more equal power distribution). The first is a technique that is good for helping couples *navigate*.

Navigating (Doubling) Technique

Doubling is a therapeutic technique created by couples therapist Dan Wile as a part of Collaborative Couple Therapy (Wile, 2002; 2008; 2011; 2017). A primary goal is to solve the problem of the moment by turning the couple's immediate concern into an intimate conversation. Related to the doubling technique pioneered in psychodrama, doubling in couples therapy is the process of the therapist speaking as if they were one of the partners talking to the other. It allows for the therapist to help the couple have the conversation they *need* to have, but can't, rather than the (destructive) conversation they often have. It is a tool for navigating some of the more difficult and unsolvable conflicts that couples have while keeping a commitment to balance power.

Initially, Wile sought to create an approach that would replace a partner's inflammatory or angry comments for those that were less so. When doubling, the counselor takes on the voice of each of the partners, speaking out loud the "replacement" statement while checking in with the person being spoken for. Then, the counselor checks with the other partner to see how the re-formatted message was received. Wile often will move around the room to crouch or kneel next to the person he is speaking for in order to seem less threatening and to appear "on their side." Along the way, he created six core principles for doubling that will be discussed here.

1 Changing the Tone

This principle is focused on both verbal and nonverbal communications. As Virginia Satir (1967) wrote, it is a way to take statements that are potentially positive in their denotation (*what* is being said) but negative in their connotation (*how* it is being said). For example, if someone says, "You know I love you," but it is in a flat tone, it may be received as insincere and not really heartfelt. By changing the tone, and repeating the same words, but with a softer or more emphatic tone, the counselor can either: (1) ask the partner who is experiencing it to reflect on how he or she perceives it, or (2) ask the partner who the counselor is doubling to reflect on if this is what he or she *means* to say, but lacks the ability to do so.

Changing the tone can also take an ambiguous statement and re-interpret it to give it a new meaning. For example, if someone says, "I guess that's okay," they may either mean they are truly agreeing with what the other partner is saying or wants to do, or they may mean they don't agree but don't know how to directly say that. Again, having the counselor make a statement (one way or the other) to clear up the ambiguity allows each partner to experience an unambiguous statement and then react to that. This is an important part of *navigating* and is particularly important when working with couples who are conflict-avoidant.

2 Confide Vulnerable Feelings/Turn Complaints Into Wishes and Fears

Much like Gottman and Gottman's (2017) "Dreams Within Conflict" technique (discussed in Chapter 7), confiding vulnerable feelings or turning complaints into wishes and fears is a way to get at the emotional core of statements that may be made in anger (or fear) and "soften" them. This is particularly salient when one or both partners are withdrawing away from each other. It can help re-engage them by revealing what might be underlying their more sensitive feelings. Again, with couples dealing with an infidelity, this can be especially helpful when working with intimacy-avoidant couples who may use conflict to disengage with one another. Confiding vulnerable feelings and turning complaints into wishes and fears is a way to address deeper attachment longings as well, which helps couples navigate around these conflicts.

3 Make Acknowledgments

According to Wile (2017), during a fight, neither partner is generally willing to concede anything to the other, even if the partner makes a valid point. Often they are afraid that, if they do, it will undermine their argument, and they will lose. A typical strategy is to re-state their position as if they hadn't even heard their partner. Unfortunately, this also means that opportunities to come to a consensus and navigate difficulty disagreements are lost. Making acknowledgments (and teaching this to couples) is a way to dissipate the most common tactics that shut down conversation, namely criticism, blaming, accusing, and defensiveness (i.e., many of Gottman's (2011) "Four Horsemen").

When counselors make acknowledgments (and, again, have each partner "check" the validity and reaction to the response), the counselor is not saying, "I'm entirely right and you're entirely wrong," which prolongs the power imbalance. Rather, the counselor is saying, "Maybe we both have a point here" or "I can see that you have a point" or "You're right that . . ." in the hopes that hearing an acknowledgment of acceptance of each other's perspectives will get the couple to feel less frustrated with one another and back away from defensive positions. Combining this with "changing the tone" is also very helpful as well.

4 Report Rather Than Unload Anger

When couples are in a conflict, anger is the predominant emotion. As mentioned previously, many couples counselors view strong emotion (like anger) as destructive and attempt to tamp it down at all costs. However, this can be counterproductive as emotion is the fuel for systemic change, and "tamping it down" often sends the message from the counselor that "I can't deal with your strong feelings, they are not welcome here." Partners may then begin to disengage from the therapy, which leads to treatment failure. At the same time, raw, unchecked emotion that is unproductive *does* have the ability to sabotage a conversation or a session. In these cases, helping couples take a "middle path" is necessary. By using the principle of reporting, rather than unloading, anger, the emotion is given its rightful expression, but it is also put into its proper context. Examples of this include "As you can see, I am very frustrated" and "I am devastated by what you just told me," which are better alternatives to name-calling, shouting, or stunned silence/stonewalling. For the couple, hearing the counselor speak from these vantage points allows someone who is emotionally flooded to hear *their highly* emotionally charged thoughts come out of another person's mouth while they can take a detached perspective on it ("Yeah, that's what I wanted to say" or "Wow, I really sound like that?"). In this approach, it is important for the counselor to actively voice both partner's viewpoints on this and provide a calm brokering for their perspectives. This is the trickiest water to navigate, but it can also teach the couple how to do this properly.

5 Describe the Couple Predicament

This principle is used to help the couple see their joint situation or predicament. It is a way of explicating the system dynamic, particularly if it is an old or negative one that is trying to assert homeostasis (Chapter 2). This is particularly useful in helping couples who are trying to navigate a power imbalance to seek a more even distribution of power. For example, if a couple are getting gridlocked in a frustrating conversation about their disagreements about money, where one person usually asserts dominance (either because they are the higher earner or the better saver), and the other acquiesces but becomes sullen or withdrawn, the counselor may describe their predicament by using a "Look at us . . ." or "Here we are again . . ." statement. For the couple being described the counselor may say, "Look at us, we are back to our old fight where you are trying to do what you think is best for us financially, and I am feeling powerless to have any influence. This never goes well for us." Making a statement like this gets the couple to commiserate. It is akin to the Narrative Therapy approach of "externalizing the problem" and, at the same time, also shows mutual awareness. The best outcome would be if the couple could do this themselves, but in the heat of the battle it is tough. Thus, doubling provides the modeling behavior to help clients navigate this, begin to re-define the system dynamic, and come to a place where they can both share in the power or decision making.

6 Turn Monologues Into Dialogues

In the Disney/Pixar animated superhero movie *The Incredibles*, when the villain catches himself talking at length to the hero he has captured, he stops himself and laughs, saying: "Oh, ho ho! You sly dog! You got me monologuing! I can't believe it!" Previously, the heroes had made fun of super-villains who undo themselves by talking at length about the brilliance of their plans (which are ultimately foiled)! In the same way, when partners begin to monologue (go into long descriptions of their position or lengthily diatribes where they detail their—often long—history of gripes or complaints), all the oxygen gets sucked out of the conversation. Often these tangents are used by partners who feel they have power and use it to "run out the clock" or filibuster during a therapy session. By using doubling, turning monologues into dialogues is the counselor's way of breaking the monologue and getting the other partner's voice into the conversation. This might be in the form of stopping the person monologuing, summarizing and adding a question at the end. Or it might be saying, "You know, when I listen to you talk, here is what I hear." It may also be a place to add in a "report" of anger (principle 4) or a description of the couple's predicament (principle 5). The goal is not to shut the partner up, but to build in space for the other partner to get his or her point of view into the conversation in order to spark a dialogue.

How Doubling Helps a Couple Navigate Power Issues

Wile (2017) discusses how, when he uses the doubling technique, he is acting like a Cyrano de Bergerac (the fictional character who feeds lines to a would-be suitor of the woman he loves). He lends his voice and his understanding to the couple in the hopes of getting them to be able to be more honest and vulnerable. For couples dealing with the aftermath of an infidelity, as they are navigating the issues of shared power, it is an important tool.

In using doubling, the counselor acts like the director of a play (hence the original use in psychodrama) and guides the "action" in the session. There are three strategic approaches that are used to direct the conversation: *going within*, *going between*, and *going above*. These navigating tactics can be thought of as either being a "first-person" narrator of a story, creating character dialogue, or taking a "third-person" narrative position. As with any novel or story, if an author wants you to know the character's inner thoughts, the narrative takes a "first-person" perspective. With doubling, "going within" is the counselor's attempt to take both partners inside the head or heart of the person the counselor is speaking for. For example, "When I hear you say that, it makes me wonder if I am really that important to you." Or, "I can't help but think, 'Are you really going to be there for me?'" When the counselor "goes between" the couple, the conversation is guided more directly. This is more transactional, in order to shape the conversation or navigate it away from distraction or destruction, and less revelatory. Finally, going above is the "third-person" narrative that takes a "30,000 foot" view of the situation. It gets couples out of the "street-level" conflict and breaks impasses by either universalizing their struggle ("See, everyone else goes thought this") or proving feedback on their systems dynamics ("And here is where you get dragged back into your same pattern . . ."). The goal is to help the couple navigate the power issues that perhaps cannot be balanced by allowing each person to be able to be more authentic in their statements and more vulnerable in their feelings. In this way, it often can allow them to connect on the wish, dream, or fantasy level and keep in the spirit of their new explicit goals for the relationship.

One of the pitfalls of doubling is that one partner may feel the counselor is not on his or her side. However, if done properly, each person's perspective will feel equally and fairly represented. It does require the counselor to be highly active and shift positions (literally and figuratively) throughout the session. The net result, however, is to turn the conflict into a conversation. Let's go back to Ted and Nancy and see where doubling might help them navigate an impasse related to a disagreement about time they spend together.

Nancy: I want to bring up an area of conflict that I have with you, and I know you are going to get defensive about it . . . your drinking. You know that when you drink too much, you walk around the house and don't remember it. It worries me. I have found you out on the patio and in the garage and you don't remember the next day. I think you have a real problem with alcohol.

Ted: I know it gets beyond my control sometimes, but I don't think *that* is the root cause of my problems. I think it is a symptom.

Nancy: I just don't understand why you have to let yourself get that far.

Ted: I think it is because I am lonely. We don't do much of anything together. You are either asleep or working most nights or on the phone to your mom! On weekends, you don't ever want to go out. I think that I use alcohol to relax, and then because I am lonely, I just don't want to stop.

Nancy: I am *always* saying that I want to do things together, as a family.

Ted: Yes, but when it comes to actually doing them, I am the one who has to plan them, and then half the time you say "no." You have something else to do, either with the kids, or your family, or with work. I'm not in the mix at all.

Nancy: Okay, but I am not the only one who gets caught up in my work. You do too. You disappear into it and go off on long trips or writing up your reports. You take up evenings and weekends with that as much as I do! Only you don't see that.

Now, at this point, the counselor can see this is an area that needs to be navigated. The clients are talking *at* each other and not *to* each other. The counselor chooses to employ a doubling technique to help turn the conflict into a conversation.

Counselor: Okay, I can see that we are getting into an impasse here with this conversation, and I would like you to not get stuck in the topic, but I don't want to see you avoid and bury it altogether. We discussed how avoiding conflicts was one of your system dynamics, and that it helped create the conditions where the affair happened. So, I am going to use the doubling technique to see if we can't navigate through this toward an open conversation where you can both get your positions heard on this, okay?

Both: Okay.

Counselor: Great. First, I will start with Ted. Ted, you responded to Nancy's concern about alcohol intake that you did see her point. So let me come over here (*moves next to Ted*). "Nancy, you are right about that, it does get out of control, but there is something deeper than just how much I drink. For me it is *why* I drink to excess." Is that right, Ted?

Ted: Yes, that was pretty much what I said.

Counselor: Okay, and Nancy, how do you hear this? What comes to you.

Nancy: Well, I think that he just drinks too much, and he needs to stop it before he gets hurt.

Counselor (*moving to Nancy's side*): Can I say it like this? "You may have a point about *why* you drink, and I think it's valid. At the same time, it really scares me when I find you wandering, and I worry that you will get hurt. (*softening tone*) I don't want anything to happen to you."

Ted: I know . . . I know . . .

Counselor (*moving to Ted's side*): What if I said, "I'm afraid too, but I don't know what to do about it"? Ted, is that accurate?

Ted: Yes, it is.

Counselor: Nancy, what is it like for you to hear that?

Nancy: I am glad to hear that he is afraid too. I don't think he's an alcoholic, I don't think he needs treatment, and I don't think *he* thinks he needs treatment. He just needs to know—

Counselor: Wait. Can you stop and let that sink in?

Nancy: Okay.

Counselor: I don't think I could have said it better than her: "I am glad to hear that he is afraid too. I don't think he's an alcoholic, I don't think he needs treatment." How do you hear that, Ted?

Ted: Like she listens to me. Like she is hearing me.

Counselor: And that is better—that feels better—than being afraid that she doesn't hear you?

Ted: Yes, yes it does.

Counselor: I want to go back to something you said a while ago, Ted. And that was how you felt lonely and that you think that maybe that is a part of why you drink to excess sometimes.

Ted: Okay.

Counselor (*moving to Ted's side*): "There are times when I feel lonely. There are times when I miss you. And even though I see you there, I see you are engaged in doing something else, and I can't break through that, and I just want you." Is that close, Ted?

Ted: Yes, yes it is.

Counselor: Nancy, what is it like for you to hear that?

Nancy: It makes me feel guilty. I don't want to push him away. But then it makes me feel angry. I feel like I have no control, and the only way I can control things is to get on top of them at work.

Counselor: So, can I try? (*Nancy nods her head.*) Again, I think you stated it great, and I would add, "I don't want you to be pushed away. It hurts me to hear you say that. And then at the same time, I feel so overwhelmed with work that I don't know how to keep the demands of that world from colliding with our world."

Nancy: Yeah, I just don't know how to do that.

Counselor: Maybe we can discuss some ways you can solve this together?

Ultimately, the doubling technique got the couple out of the destructive conversation cycle and into a more productive one where they could navigate the complexities of their work-life balance. Now we will look at a negotiating technique developed by Gottman (2011).

Negotiating (Gottman-Rapoport) Technique

Gottman created a technique for advanced active listening that couples can use *before* trying to persuade their partner that their approach is correct. It borrows from the work of mathematician and systems thinker Anatol Rapoport. Rapoport believed that in order to successfully persuade someone that his or her views are *wrong*, the other person needs to feel he or she is fully understood. Therefore, the Gottman-Rapoport technique instructs couples to have a conversation about an area of gridlocked conflict (or conflict in general) where the goal, before providing any persuasion about their point of view, is that they must be able to state (to their partner's satisfaction) their partner's position. There are two "roles" to be played, the role of the speaker and the role of the listener:

The Speaker: Requires a Mental Transformation and Shift to The Partner's Point of View

- No blaming, no "you" statements.
- Talk about your feelings.
- Only use "I" statements about a specific situation.
- State your positive need. Remember that behind every negative emotion there is a longing, and a wish, and therefore a recipe for your partner to be successful with you. That is your positive need. What do you want and need from your partner?

The Listener: Don't Respond Defensively

- Postpone your own agenda. Hear and repeat the content of the speaker's needs and perspective (the story).
- Listen to your partner's pain with compassion.
- Hear the speaker's affect (name the affects, and feel a bit of them).
- Validate the speaker by completing a sentence like, "It makes sense to me that you would feel that way and have these needs, because . . ."
- Okay to ask questions.

Source: The Gottman Institute (www.gottman.com).

This gives the listening partner the power to ensure he or she is being understood before being asked to consider an alternative point of view. If done correctly, it also can provide both the listener and the speaker with a new appreciation of their partner's viewpoint and can often lead to areas of compromise because of the accurate empathizing they do while going through this exercise.

Let's return to Ted and Nancy. As you will recall in their case, Ted had an affair with a co-worker. And while he has agreed to break off the relationship, he still has to interact with her at work. Nancy has admitted that there have been times when she had flashbacks and has felt extremely vulnerable, jealous, and anxious when Ted is away or staying late at the office. In the past, this has led to fights and inevitable deadlock. In the couples session, the counselor worked with them to negotiate the issue of the relationship with the co-worker using the Gottman-Rapoport technique.

Nancy: I thought that I was over this, but it just drives me nuts whenever I see that you get an email from her. I just think to myself: "Why does he have to be in contact with her?"

Ted: I know how much it bothers you that I have to see Kelly virtually every day. I wish that I could change jobs, but there just aren't any out there that wouldn't make us move or wouldn't require me to take a big pay cut.

Nancy: I still don't think that it is good for us. It's not.

Ted: What do you want me to do about it? Quit my job, is that it? Be real, Nancy. We'd lose the house for sure.

Counselor: Okay, wait a moment here. Let's not lose the positive momentum we have been building. It is clear that you guys are at an impasse. Nancy, you feel powerless to do anything about it and believe that Ted should. Ted, it sounds like you also feel powerless to change the situation as well, right? (*Ted nods.*) Okay, then, let's try the Gottman-Rapoport technique to try to negotiate this between you. Ted, I would like you to be the speaker. I want you to try to state Nancy's position to her satisfaction. Remember to use "I statements" as if you were Nancy.

Ted: I feel that you don't seem to try hard enough to put distance between yourself and Kelly. When you are not around, I can't see what you are doing at work, and that makes me nervous.

Counselor: Nancy, how is that for starters?

Nancy: Good.

Counselor: Ted, now that you have her "go ahead" please try to state what her positive need is. What is she wishing for underneath her request?

Ted: I think it is, "I want you to be more transparent with me. I want you to reassure me when I get into my anxious moods. I don't want you to run away or feel like I am accusing you."

Nancy: I don't want you to feel responsible for my moods. I just want you to understand them. And I don't want you to run away. And when you react defensively, it puts me on the defensive as well.

Ted: Even though it has been nine months since I ended it with her, I still try to avoid her whenever I can. I've got to confess that I feel relief when she is out sick or on vacation. I don't feel like I have to be on my tiptoes then. Honestly, I am not sure how much more of this I can take. Maybe we should start thinking about options to possibly move if a position comes open?

Here you can see how engaging in the Gottman-Rapoport technique helps steer the couple from conflict to negotiation. The issue of power imbalance now becomes one where the couple can make a decision jointly and share the power in making the choice. One more helpful suggestion that Rapoport made, and that Gottman encourages, is that each person should agree to the following: If you find yourself attributing a positive trait to yourself, try to see some of this trait in your partner. If you find yourself attributing a negative trait to your partner, try to see some of this trait in yourself as well (Gottman, 2011). Napier (2007), seemed to echo this sentiment:

> From the clinician's perspective, we can assume that the affairee has almost invariably symbolized his or her spouse with negative attributions, and organized on the lover more positive connotations. The spouse is seen as dominating, or weak, or cold, or unloving, or inattentive, or unspontaneous, or some combination thereof. These perceptions are grounded both in the character traits of the spouse, and in the affairee's symbolizing of these traits.
>
> (p. 301)

Conclusion: Go Back to Sharing Power, Balancing the See-Saw

Remembering the metaphor of the see-saw, where, in both cases, the systems dynamics of the couple—where no one is to blame, and each are responsible for creating the conditions that allowed the infidelity to occur—are captured. If the set points of the system are to be changed, the old way of one person being "up" and the other person being "down" has to go away. Truly sharing power means seeing one's partner's negative traits in one's self and seeing one's positive traits in one's partner. That is the key to effectively navigating the issues that cannot be changed, and negotiating over the issues that can be change is dependent on this ideal.

The next chapter revisits the idea of riding the ups and downs of relationship satisfaction. The methods for working through these issues are considered. Following from creating a new, shared, and explicit dream, fantasy, or wish for the relationship, and learning to effectively navigate and negotiate the power elements of the relationship, couples must learn how to deal with the emotions that come when their level of satisfaction in the relationship dips (as it invariably does).

CHAPTER 9

Increasing Satisfaction and Learning to Ride the Ups and Downs of Relationships

"I don't like secrets" "She sees things one way and one way only!" "I am single-minded." "I am mad at you because for eight years I asked you and you did nothing to help the situation. Then when it got so bad, it couldn't be easily fixed. If you had only listened to me!"

In some ways, this chapter is deceptive. It comes as the last of the three steps in the treatment model, but it is not the end of the process. In fact, in many ways, it is the beginning of a new process for the couple. As such, there are important skills the couple must learn in order to keep and maintain the changes they initiated by creating a new dream, wish, or fantasy for themselves, as well as changes to the power dynamic between them. This chapter is about managing the day-to-day routines of life, where the stressors and challenges will threaten to "rip the Band-Aid off" the wounds from the infidelity. These stressors and challenges will test the couple and sometimes send them back to an earlier (and more raw) emotional state as they test out whether or not they will be able to keep and maintain the gains they started.

Recall from Chapter 3 the "stock market" metaphor of relationship satisfaction (Gottman, 2011). Positive and negative feelings about the relationship inevitably go up and down. The key is deciding which perspective to take about the relationship. If, like some investors, they decide that when their satisfaction is that it will never come back up, they are likely to bail out on the relationship and leave. However, if they decide they are in the relationship for the long-term, if they decide the fundamentals of the relationship are strong (there is a shared dream for the relationship and a commitment to share power), they will decide to "stick it out" in the belief that any dissatisfaction is temporary and that the positive feelings of satisfaction will eventually rise up. In stock trading circles, this is called a "buy and hold" strategy, and this is what most investors advocate that most non-professionals use. However, with couples (particularly when there has been an infidelity), it is not as simple as just waiting it out. Couples who want to remain committed to the relationship need to find ways of understanding the ups and downs of satisfaction and also the tools for working together when the inevitable lows come.

This chapter discusses issues of daily life and satisfaction. The emphasis for couples counselors is to help couples see the importance of protecting the bond. This chapter presents some of the longer-term healing issues (such as being sensitive to the "healing wound" and not doing things that might inflict more damage). In addition, this chapter addresses the issue of flashbacks and fears, as well as handling the ebb and flow of satisfaction and frustrations.

Satisfaction With Sex and Communicating About It

As discussed in Chapter 3, sexual satisfaction and relationship satisfaction are strongly related. In fact, expressing sexual dissatisfaction was more indicative of a potential infidelity than was overall dissatisfaction with the relationship, although the two are highly correlated (Scott et al., 2017). As a result, helping a couple communicate about their sexual desires, particularly when they feel disappointed or feel that their wishes or ideas haven't been heard or validated by their partner, is crucial.

Communicating About Sexual Desires

Communicating about sex, and particularly one's *comfort* talking about sex, increases the chances that a couple will feel more satisfaction and fulfillment with their sexual relationship (Scott et al., 2017). At the same time, the ability to communicate about their sexual desires is a separate form of communication within the relationship than other communication (Mark & Jozkowski, 2013). As a result, even couples who are "good" communicators (overall) may actually be poor communicators when it comes to sex and their needs and wants. This is particularly true for couples where there has been a Conflict-Avoidance, Intimacy-Avoidance, or Split-Self Affair. In the former two, there are often times that one or both partners in the couple have tried to communicate about their sexual needs. However, in the Split-Self Affair, it is more likely that the couple has given up trying to express their needs or desires. As Napier (2007) described it:

> Out of the couple's desperation, they develop an unconscious "plan" to break the impasse. There may be almost-explicit conversations that signal the collusive decision to escalate their schism, but usually the "agreements" are half-conscious and largely inferential. In one couple, the tough-guy husband, who was a marathon runner and weight-lifter, risked asking his wife, as they turned to go to sleep one night, to hold him. Frightened by his sudden vulnerability, she replied, "You'll have to find somebody else to do that." Deeply hurt by the remark, he did find someone else to hold him. In another marriage, the wife said, only half-joking: "If you ever decide to have an affair, don't tell me about it," a remark which the husband took as implicit permission. In other instances the evidence which the betraying partner uses to justify the decision to have an affair is inferential: "If I'm gone this much and she doesn't complain, she must not love me."
>
> (Napier, 2007, p. 296)

So the "cost" for not being able to successfully communicate about one's sexual needs and desires can be assumptions made or confusion about the sexual norms for the relationship. According to Scott et al. (2017), when couples cannot communicate about their needs, it leads to a loss of closeness, which may be an indicator "that sexual encounters no longer provide emotional connection or that sex is a stressful experience which could lead some individuals to seek sexual contact with other people to fill emotional voids from their primary sexual relationship" (p. 396).

So why is this so difficult? First, openly communicating about one's sexual needs and desires is an emotional risk. Individuals open themselves and feel vulnerable when talking about their sexual preferences, and while it can lead to greater satisfaction and closeness, there is a chance of rejection, and this can often be one of the most humiliating and emotionally hurtful types of rejection. It also taps into attachment needs for each person, and the wounds due to rejection can be just as deep (Johnson, 2008). If a partner or couple do not feel comfortable communicating about sex, they are less likely to try to communicate their needs, which can also lead to an eventual decrease in even initiating sexual contact (due to fear or discomfort). This is often where an infidelity creates an opportunity for a betraying partner to talk about their needs to a new partner in ways the other partner won't accept. Thus, helping a couple increase their comfort and skill in discussing their sexual needs becomes a preventative measure against future infidelities as well (Scott et al., 2017).

At the same time, being comfortable talking about their sexual desires and wants can lead to increases in sexual satisfaction and can also initiate a deeper type of bonding and closeness. It ties in with underlying fantasies, wishes, and dreams about the relationship in general and therefore is an important part of helping maintain those shared dreams. It also helps the couple share power equally, particularly with regard to when sex is initiated and how bids for sexual contact are received. And while sexual satisfaction and relationship satisfaction are two separate constructs (Birnie-Porter & Lydon, 2013), helping couples communicate openly about their sexual needs, and feel comfortable about it, provides the opportunity for a sense of connectedness and closeness that is associated with overall relationship satisfaction (Scott et al., 2017). Let's take a look at how this might work in an excerpt from a session with Adam and Martina (who were introduced in Chapter 4).

Interaction From Adam and Martina

Recall from Chapter 4 that Adam and Martina who were in couples therapy after Martina had been engaging in an emotional affair with the pastor of her church. Adam, over the course of their 15-year marriage, had been growing aloof and distant, and Martina was not engaging in sex with Adam. This, coupled with her attention to her pastor, Dave, increased Adam's jealousy. In this excerpt, Adam talks about his frustrations with Martina over their sex life.

Adam: I think we are good partners. We work well together most times, managing our daily routines, etc. We are great parents. I think we are even great lovers (when *you* want to be). But I don't think that we are good friends anymore. I am sad to say that, but I think that is true.

Counselor: Why do you think that?

Adam: I don't trust her. Well, that's not entirely true. There is a lot that I trust her with—

Martina: So what don't you trust me with? That's rich after what you did.

Counselor: (*to Adam*) Before you answer. (*to Martina*) Did you notice what you did there?

Martina: Yeah.

Counselor: It sounds like maybe his question made you feel defensive and you felt that you had to lash out?

Martina: Yeah.

Counselor: Let's take a step back. How do you think he will react?

Martina: Defensively?

Counselor: And what was he about to share?

Martina: The things that he doesn't trust me with.

Counselor: And now what do you think he will do?

Martina: Well, he said that we are only lovers when I want to be, that was a cheap shot.

Counselor: It sounds like you heard it as that, but remember what we discussed about not getting sidetracked from some of the deeper issues. We know that he feels that you controlled the sex. Whether you agree or not with that won't change his feeling. Only deeper connection and building trust will. But now, we have bled that energy off and are on a different topic. We could continue this, but we all know where it will lead: frustration and gridlock. Or you two can make a choice to go back to the deeper issue. (*silence*) So why don't you start by asking him about what he doesn't trust you with?

Martina: Why don't you trust me?

Counselor: Wait. Are you sure you want to ask the "why" question? You know what his answer is going to be.

Martina: "I don't know."

Counselor: Probably correct. That is why—

Martina (*laughs*): You just did that there, asking a "why" question.

Counselor: Maybe! But it is the *reason* that "what" questions are better than "why" questions. So try it again.

Martina: What is it that you don't trust me with?

Adam: I forgot what I was going to say.

Counselor: We did get sidetracked. And that is one of the dangers when you get close to some deeper meaning and deeper truths. And I think you might have gotten a little flooded here. But you were saying that your relationship was good in a lot of ways, but that you didn't feel that you were friends anymore. And that there were some things that you didn't feel you could trust her with . . .

Adam (*sighs*): That's true.

Martina: So what can't you trust me with?

Adam: I have always had problems trusting people. I have always had problems when I say what I am feeling, that I get it wrong, or it gets misunderstood.

Martina: What do you mean?

Adam: I mean that when I share things, even with you, I am afraid that you will take it wrong. That you will judge me, you will look at me funny, and I will know that you don't like it.

Martina: So what do you do?

Adam: I just don't say anything. I keep it to myself.

Martina: Why— (*catches self*)? Wait. I mean, What else? What else don't you trust me about?

Adam: I am not sure I can trust you to be there for me. That you will take care of me. I just think that in the end, when I need you the most, you won't be able to do it. Or you won't be there.

Martina: Why would you think that? Uh, I mean, what makes you think that?

Adam: You don't really *know* me. You don't really know what I want, what I need. I try to tell you, but you just reject me.

Martina: What do you mean?

Adam: I am talking about sex, but it is also more. For example, do you know how many times you reject me? How many times I feel like I am "dirty" or "perverted" because I want you sexually? You either stay up too late doing work or go to bed too early because you are tired. There is no room for me. Until *you* want to have sex. That is usually once a month, if I'm lucky. Then we are great together. You are willing, and it is good. So I hold out for those times. But everything in between, I have to take care of myself. I have to take care of my own needs. Every once in a while I beg you to do something to give me a release, but I hate begging for it.

Martina: It's just that I am not in the mood, and my mind isn't "there."

Adam: Yeah, but *mine* is. And all I want is for you to just spend two or three minutes to take care of my needs. Hell, we don't even have to have sex! You could just jack me off in the shower every once in a while and I would be ecstatic. But you won't even do *that* for me unless I really beg. And it makes me think: "Am I not worth the effort to her?" "Does she really not care?" I mean, I would do that for you. If I knew that would give you that much pleasure (and it usually does when we make love), and you *wanted* me to do that, I would do that, and I would *love* doing that for you. But you don't. You don't want that for you (which is fine), but you don't even want to give me the pleasure. Especially when I really need it. So I just take care of my own needs.

Martina: So I am just supposed to drop everything and tend to your needs just because you have a hard-on?

Counselor: Martina, Adam is trying to communicate something important here about his needs and how it plays into his trust issues.

Martina: Yeah, but am I just going to have to forget about what I want? Do I have to serve him?

Counselor: No. But if you want to get to the deeper reasons for his lack of trust, something you said you wanted to earn, you have to be willing to hear him out without jumping in to defend yourself. If you want to know about his needs and the reasons for his needs, then you do have to listen. Whether you agree to change how you act with him is still up to you. You don't give that up just by listening. But when you shut him down like you were about to do by getting defensive, you risk him not opening up to you for a long time. So why don't you try it again? He has made himself vulnerable to you. Why don't you start with what you heard from him, check it out for accuracy, and then tell him what you are feeling about it.

Martina (*sighs*): Okay . . . You want me to be more attentive to you when you are wanting to have sex, instead of me dismissing you, is that right?

Adam: I want you to know that it's not easy for me to ask you to be with me sexually. Whenever we do, I always feel closer to you, don't you feel closer to me?

Martina: Sometimes . . . I guess.

Adam: I am just saying that when you reject me, it really, really hurts, and I just shut down. I don't even want to try anymore.

Counselor: Martina, try to summarize what Adam is saying and see if it is accurate with him.

Martina: It takes a lot for you to approach me when you are feeling sexually aroused, and you are afraid I will reject you. And when I say no, it is a rejection for you that makes you feel like you can't trust me with your needs. Is that it?

Adam: Yes, that is pretty good, pretty accurate.

Counselor: Okay, now, Martina, since he has agreed that you have accurately summarized his position, why don't you share your feelings about it? What happens to you, emotionally, when he comes to you?

Martina: Well, it is never the right time—

Counselor: Wait right there. Start with the emotions, then go to the reasons. It will cause less defensiveness.

Martina: Okay. Sometimes when he approaches me in the morning, I feel annoyed. I feel like, "Not now, I have to get up." Or, "Not now, I have to get ready for work," you know, mentally.

Counselor: What is it that annoys you?

Martina: I feel like he can't see that I am not ready for sex. I need to be in the mood.
Counselor: So you feel annoyed. What else?
Martina: I feel flustered, frustrated. I mean, I don't want to tell him no but I can't tell him yes, at least not at that moment.
Counselor: So you feel like you are caught in the middle? You can't do it, but you don't want to say no.
Martina: Yeah.
Counselor: In addition to frustrated, I'm thinking that might make me feel sad, like, "I hate to disappoint you . . ."
Martina: Maybe.
Counselor: Okay. That doesn't look like I hit the mark. Let me try again. Does it make you feel a little worried? Does it make you feel like you are somehow inadequate because he wants sexual contact and you don't? That might feel overwhelming . . .
Martina: Yeah, that's more like it. I feel overwhelmed. Like I just *can't* do it, and I am being forced to.
Counselor: And it sounds like you then send some of that overwhelmed and frustrated feeling Adam's way because you know it will get him to stop.
Martina: Oh, it does! It shuts him right down. And he shuts me out. Won't talk to me sometimes for days.
Counselor: So, good news, he stops. Bad news, you send him far away emotionally. Is that what you really want to happen?
Martina: No, I don't want him to shut me out. I want to be closer, but . . .
Counselor: But you are scared of being overwhelmed, and you are scared of being punished by his cold shoulder.
Adam: But I don't want to shut you out, it's just that it is so hard for me.
Martina: In more ways than one! (*giggles*)
Adam: Martina! (*starts to laugh*) Yeah, that's the problem!
Counselor: So, how can Adam ask for what he wants without feeling rejected and Martina not feel so overwhelmed?
Martina: If he can.
Counselor: Okay, but start with what *you* will do, rather than what you want the other person to do. For example, what can you tell yourself about his communicating to you about his sexual needs?
Martina: Okay, if I tell myself that he is feeling really sensitive and vulnerable, and if I tell him that I hear that in what he is saying, maybe that would be a good first step?

In the case here, a modified version of the Gottman-Rapoport technique was used (see Chapter 8) to help the couple be able to communicate about their needs. The counselor needed to intervene to keep the couple on topic and not get sidetracked when the emotions began to run high. Martina and Adam were able to begin to have an honest conversation about their dissatisfaction with their sex life, their deeper feelings about it, and some of their larger concerns regarding the relationship.

According to Scott et al. (2017) and Markman and Rhoades (2012), increasing communication skills and using common approaches for training couples in communication can be an effective preventative intervention for infidelity. In their research, Scott et al. (2017) found that men who increased their expression of sexual preferences and concerns to their partner were at greater risk of an infidelity. Interestingly, however, they did not find differences in sexual frequency in couples with an infidelity compared to couples that did not experience an infidelity. Therefore, training couples to be able to discuss their preferences in a safe context, and not necessarily encouraging any significant changes in the frequency of sex, may be more effective. If each person experiences acceptance and understanding, rather than criticism, this might be able to help couples weather the ups and downs of satisfaction.

Relationship Satisfaction and Life Satisfaction

Stanley et al. (2012) found that interventions that increased an individual's satisfaction with life had a positive effect on relationship satisfaction as well. It is believed that when individuals are satisfied with other aspects of their life (work, friends, etc.), they are more likely to approach their romantic relationship with openness and a willingness to explore, rather than with suspicion or negativity. It is not certain whether the relationship is uni-directional (life satisfaction causes relationship satisfaction or vice versa) or bi-directional (each influences the other to an equal extent). Therefore, incorporating techniques to help each individual member of the couple increase their own well-being may prove to be just as effective as helping the relationship (Robles et al., 2014).

In fact, several studies across the socio-economic spectrum have shown that increasing individual well-being, facilitating couples' communication, and increasing relationship satisfaction also have the benefit of decreasing negative psychological behaviors: "a recent randomized relationship education intervention among low income couples, demonstrated higher levels of relationship satisfaction, lower psychological abuse from partners, enhanced positive communication and reduced negative behaviors during marital conversations compared to a control intervention at 12 months" (Robles et al., 2014, p. 177). The effect size for their findings were comparable to interventions that target health promotion (like exercise or diet).

Last, there are benefits to assessing relationship quality for overall health quality. From chronic diseases that are negatively impacted by chronic stress, to exposure to stress hormones (i.e., cortisol), to unhealthy behaviors that are known to exacerbate poor health (e.g., obesity, smoking, diet), poor relationship quality can be a significant contributing factor. Another study found a link between relationship satisfaction and medical treatment adherence. In other words, if patients were highly dissatisfied with their relationship, their adherence to a medical regimen would be poor. Thus, medical personnel should consider routinely assessing for relationship quality as a health indicator. "Fostering greater understanding and awareness in health care providers of the relational context in which health problems often occur may eventually increase the development and dissemination of couples-based interventions" (Robles et al., 2014, pp. 177–178). Indeed, in the context of medical and couples treatment, focusing on relationship satisfaction as a source of intervention and prevention may have a long-lasting and wide-ranging positive impact.

Mindfulness Techniques to Help Couples With Relationship Satisfaction

One of the critical issues that couples healing from an infidelity have to contend with during periods when their satisfaction with their relationship is not good is the powerful emotions that arise. Several clinical approaches have incorporated the concept of mindfulness to help individuals cope with their emotional reactivity. These are particularly salient for couples who are trying to learn to deal with their emotions without damaging their relationship.

Definition of Mindfulness

While mindfulness is rooted in ancient Buddhist traditions, it has recently been incorporated in clinical approaches in a major way. In 2004, Bishop and his colleagues defined mindfulness as follows:

> The first component involves the self-regulation of attention so that it is maintained on immediate experience, thereby allowing for increased recognition of mental events in the present moment. The second component involves adopting a particular orientation toward one's experiences in the present moment, an orientation that is characterized by curiosity, openness, and acceptance.
>
> (Bishop et al., 2004, p. 232)

Practitioners who utilize a mindfulness-based approach focus on the present and work with clients to also become aware of their own experiences. The aim is to help the clients remain present in their experience, without a need to distract or run away from it. Bishop et al. (2004) state that mindfulness is "a kind of non-elaborative, non-judgmental, present-centered awareness in which each thought, feeling, or sensation that arises in the attentional field is acknowledged and accepted as it is" (p. 232). There are three essential elements in this process: (1) being in a relaxed state by focusing on one's breathing, (2) practicing *choiceless awareness* as distractions occur to the client (which they inevitably will), and (3) gently returning to the breathing and breath focus. In these approaches, the therapist models this stance toward his or her own feelings. Sometimes, client feelings can be overwhelming, as with couples dealing with an infidelity. It is often difficult for them to nonjudgmentally accept them without reacting to them (Mozdzierz et al., 2014a). *How* to employ this with couples will be discussed in the following using two major mindfulness-based approaches: Acceptance and Commitment Therapy and Dialectical Behavioral Therapy.

Using Elements of Acceptance and Commitment Therapy to Therapeutically Work With Emotions

Acceptance and Commitment Therapy (ACT) was developed in the 1980s and 1990s by Steven C. Hayes and his colleagues. It was one of the first approaches to place mindfulness as part of its core constructs. They started with the central concept that pathology is due to psychological inflexibility. According to Hayes, Luoma, Bond, Masuda, and Lillis (2006), individuals who experience psychological problems have a lack of values or clarity on their values; tend toward impulsivity; and avoid certain unpleasant experiences or emotions. In addition, clients' problems are the result of being fused with a dominant thought or conceptualization of their past that they are "damaged" somehow and that the future is certain—and is going to be bad (Mozdzierz et al., 2014a). Again, for couples who are dealing with an infidelity, particularly when satisfaction dips down, it is difficult to move forward positively and believe they can recover if this belief persists. Unlike cognitive-behavioral approaches that try to teach people to just control their thoughts, feelings, and behaviors, ACT teaches clients to increase their psychological flexibility by noticing, accepting, and embracing their internal thoughts and feelings without judging them. These are considered "positive psychological skills, not merely a method of avoiding psychopathology" (Hayes et al., 2006, p. 8). There are several core clinical principles that ACT clinicians utilize: acceptance, cognitive diffusion, being present, values, and committed action. These will be discussed in the following.

Acceptance

In ACT, *acceptance* is the first skill that is taught as an alternative to avoiding experiences, thoughts, and emotions. "Acceptance involves the active and aware embrace of those private events occasioned by one's history without unnecessary attempts to change their frequency or form, especially when doing so would cause psychological harm" (Hayes et al., 2006, p. 8). When individuals can do this, they are able to be in synch with, and accept, their feelings, both positive and negative (Mayer & Stevens, 1993). For example, if a partner in a couple is having a "flashback" and feeling anxious after the other partner is late coming home, he or she is taught to feel anxiety, as a feeling, fully and without feeling defensive. In other words, thoughts are allowed to come and go without struggling with them.

Cognitive Diffusion

According to Mayer and Stevens (1993), individuals who consistently feel flooded or swamped by their emotions, like the emotions are taking control, are considered to be "engulfed." These engulfed individuals usually cannot easily identify their feelings and don't feel that they can influence or control their emotions (sometimes called alexithymia; see Jordan & Smith, 2017, for details). It is as though they are chronically stressed and feeling emotionally out of control, but without being consciously aware of it. Indeed, many couples with an Intimacy-Avoidance Affair come to therapy with this style. In ACT, the core principle of cognitive diffusion is the "antidote" for this engulfed style of emotional reaction. According to Hayes et al. (2006):

> Cognitive diffusion techniques attempt to alter the undesirable functions of thoughts and other private events, rather than trying to alter their form, frequency or situational sensitivity. Said another way, ACT attempts to change the way one interacts with or relates to thoughts by creating contexts in which their unhelpful functions are diminished.
>
> (p. 9)

Functionally, this could mean helping clients catch themselves and just observe their feeling state—such as, "I am thinking that he is late because he is with someone . . ."—which would weaken the strength of the particular thought or feeling that made the client feel bad about him- or herself.

Values and Committed Action

In ACT, clients who have a high level of psychological inflexibility tend to not be clear on what their values are and how to achieve them. According to Hayes et al. (2006): "Values are chosen qualities of purposive action that can never be obtained as an object but can be instantiated [exemplified] moment by moment" (p. 9). ACT uses a variety of exercises that shortcut cognitive processes that might lead a person to make choices based on avoidance, social compliance, or fusion rather than from their own values (e.g., "I *should* be like . . ." or "A 'good' person would . . ." or "My parents would want me to . . ."). In ACT, the goal is to be able to act in a way that is consistent with one's values. When this occurs, the emotions that come with disappointment do not have devastatingly negative consequences for the client. According to Hayes et al. (2006):

> ACT encourages the development of larger and larger patterns of effective action linked to chosen values . . . ACT looks very much like traditional behavior therapy, and almost any behaviorally coherent behavior change method can be fitted into an ACT protocol, including exposure, skills acquisition, shaping methods, goal setting, and the like. Unlike values, which are constantly instantiated but never achieved as an object, concrete goals that are values consistent can be achieved, and ACT protocols almost always involve therapy work and homework linked to short, medium, and long-term behavior change goals. Behavior change efforts in turn lead to contact with psychological barriers that are addressed through other ACT processes (acceptance, diffusion, and so on).
>
> (pp. 9–10)

In working with a couple dealing with an infidelity, the jointly created and agreed to dream, wish, or value would be an important component in clarifying the values of both people, as well as for the couples system. Now, let's look at a case from Chapter 4 (Maria and Jim) to show how some of these ACT mindfulness-based techniques might be utilized.

They had worked through a lot of issues. Maria struggled to work through her issues of setting boundaries and not trying to please Jim or others. She would say: "I don't trust myself . . . or others." They agreed to separate for a while during treatment. Maria stated that she wanted to work on herself first. She admitted, "I don't feel safe" around Jim, and she worried that she would use sex with him to get love from him. Using some mindfulness techniques, she was able to accept her feelings of distrust (especially in herself) rather than act on them. She made particular use of cognitive diffusion so that whenever she was starting to react to Jim, or when she was feeling unsure of herself, she would not lose control while still honoring her feelings. Eventually, she was able to say (of Jim), "I know he has my back, though." She eventually ended her relationship with her dermatologist.

Jim, for his part, was nervous when they separated and worried that Maria would go pursue her relationship with her doctor. He felt that learning about "acceptance" was especially helpful whenever she would go to see him. But when Maria saw him again, she said she felt no attraction for him, just "sad." The emotion had discharged from the relationship. Jim also learned how to be "lonely" and feel it rather than just try to deny it or push it away (short-circuit). "I re-created my own abandonment that I felt in my childhood. It was familiar and awful. But if I 'put myself out there' I run the risk of being used and abandoned." However, he is fighting it, as he says, "so I can do genuine caring things." He grew to become more tolerant of his distress.

Dialectical Behavioral Therapy and Mindfulness

Mindfulness is also one of the core concepts of another modern approach, called Dialectical Behavioral Therapy (DBT). It serves as the foundation for the other skills taught to clients in DBT because it helps them accept their emotions when they are faced with upsetting situations and ultimately tolerate them (Mozdzierz et al., 2014a). Just as with other mindfulness approaches, the capacity to nonjudgmentally attend to the present moment and experience one's emotions and senses fully, without distortion, is critical for the success of DBT (Linehan, 1993).

The central part of mindfulness training in DBT comes in the form of skills acquisition. Clients are taught *what* skills and *how* skills. According to Mozdzierz et al. (2014a):

> The *what* skills include teaching clients to *observe* (nonjudgmentally) what is going on in a given circumstance); *describe* (explain simply what has been

> observed); and *participate* (becoming fully focused and involved in the events around them). The *how* skills give instruction about *nonjudgmentally* (describing the facts and not thinking about what's good or bad, fair or unfair, which helps to get the point across in an effective manner to someone else); *one-mindfully* (maintaining focus without becoming distracted by the emotional reactions that may be occurring); and *effectively* (doing what works and avoiding what does not).
>
> (p. 282)

The primary purpose of both of these categories of skills is to help clients determine if the emotions they are recognizing and experiencing are adaptive or maladaptive. If emotions are adaptive, they are accepted and supported because they are authentic. However, if they are maladaptive, as in the case of intense negative emotions, they must be subjected to a process of examination. For example, with couples dealing with an infidelity, if one partner is feeling extreme guilt about cheating on the other partner, those feelings are examined to see if they are adaptive or not. If it is because of a "dip" in satisfaction, the feelings may not be adaptive and would be discussed as so.

Distress Tolerance

Distress tolerance skills are one of the more important mindfulness skills in DBT. Distress tolerance is the ability to accept both oneself and the current situation in a nonjudgmental and non-evaluative way. Acceptance and tolerance are not signs of approval or rejection but acknowledge the reality of a situation as it is. This is important for couples dealing with an infidelity, as often the fear (in the early stages) is that "acceptance" is synonymous with accepting or endorsing behavior. Rather, the goal is to help clients become capable of calmly recognizing when they find themselves in negative situations, and their potential impact, rather than hiding from or becoming overwhelmed by them. DBT works with client to help them learn how to be able to bear pain and not make poor choices about how to take action (or whether to as well). Taking action based on an inability to tolerate distress and painful emotions is often a common reaction that creates more problems than it solves (Linehan, 1993).

A primary distress tolerance skill that clients are taught is distraction. Distraction entails recognizing the unpleasant reaction or situation and then distracting one's attention temporarily, rather than acting out. In order to remember the skills, DBT counselors teach clients the acronym ACCEPTS, which stands for:

Activities: Use positive activities that you enjoy.
Contribute: Help out others or your community.
Comparisons: Compare yourself either with people who are less fortunate or to how you used to be when you were in a worse state.
Emotions (other): Cause yourself to feel something different by provoking your sense of humor or happiness with corresponding activities.

Push away: Put your situation on the back-burner for a while. Put something else temporarily first in your mind.

Thoughts (other): Force your mind to think about something else.

Sensations (other): Do something that has an intense feeling other than what you are feeling, like a cold shower or a spicy candy.

(taken from Linehan, 1993)

So, for a couple dealing with an infidelity, when dissatisfaction with the relationship creates tension between the partners, each person can be coached to utilize one of the techniques from this list in order to distract themselves and tolerate the distress without lashing out at the other person.

Another distress tolerance technique that DBT therapists teach is *self-soothing*. Although other approaches utilize self-soothing, in DBT it is a powerful tool to teach clients who have difficulty handling powerful or strong emotions. The process of learning self-soothing begins in childhood and is facilitated by good parenting. It requires that a person takes responsibility for his or her feelings and reactions and must find ways to calm him- or herself down. It is a skill in which a person behaves in a comforting, nurturing, kind, and gentle way to him- or herself. If spite of poor or inconsistent parenting, individuals can learn to self-soothe, but it is more difficult. The objective of self-soothing is to provide feelings of emotional comfort to one's self as a counter-point to negative thoughts, urges, and feelings. DBT methods of self-soothing include promoting a "dialogue" with one's self and engaging in a healthy feeling experience (e.g., a warm bath, listening to favorite relaxing music, or engaging nature through a walk). Promoting self-soothing allows for a disengagement from emotions that are temporarily overwhelming.

Self-soothing also shows clients that they have control over their emotional life. For example, if one member of a couple is having difficulty handling his or her emotions because he or she is upset with the other partner or not feeling very satisfied with the relationship, rather than lash out at the partner and damage the bond between them, the person may decide to go to the gym and work out or take the dog for a walk. This allows both partners time to consider their reactions and decide what they want to do about them.

Interpersonal Effectiveness

All of these DBT skills (mindfulness, distress tolerance, and emotion regulation) are important for the individual to help manage his or her emotions. However, there is one more, interpersonal effectiveness, which is particularly salient for couples. Specifically, interpersonal effectiveness is the choice of behaviors the client makes in relation to another person and their choice of behaviors. People get themselves into a bad emotional state because they either compromise their values or give up their power to someone else, hoping for a good result. Many times, people may even know they will not get their needs met by their partner but will still make bad decisions. Interpersonal effectiveness focuses on teaching skills to handle situations when a person needs to make a request of someone, ask someone to do something, request that someone make a change, or say no to someone. The purpose of these skills is to help clients achieve their desired outcome for a particular situation, while simultaneously not damaging the relationship. Three acronyms encapsulate the skill sets that are taught to increase interpersonal effectiveness. They are DEARMAN, GIVE, and FAST.

First, DEARMAN is an acronym used to help clients remember the steps they need to do in order to be successful in making a request of another person. They are:

Describe your situation.
Express why this is an issue and how you feel about it.
Assert yourself by asking clearly for what you want.
Reinforce your position by offering a positive consequence if you were to get what you want.
Mindful of the situation by focusing on what you want and ignoring distractions.
Appear confident even if you don't feel confident.
Negotiate with a hesitant person and come to a comfortable compromise on your request.

(from Linehan, 1993)

GIVE is the next acronym, and it focuses on steps for maintaining relationships when making requests. They are: *gentle* (being courteous and nonjudgmental; using appropriate language), *interested* (asking questions of the other person, etc.), *validate* (communicating verbally and nonverbally that you are engaged with the other person), and *easy manner* (being clam, using humor, not pressuring, etc.). Finally, FAST is an acronym for a series of skills that help clients maintain self-respect when engaging interpersonally with another person (and is used in combination with the other two skill sets). It stands for *fair* (to one's self and others), *apologies* (don't apologize more than once for something or for something that was effective), *stick to your values* (don't allow others to manipulate you to do something that goes against your values), and *truthful* (lies will only damage relationships and self-respect). These interpersonal effectiveness skills are very similar to assertiveness skills classes that help individuals appropriately advocate for what they need. (Linehan, 1993; Lynch, Chapman, Rosenthal, Kuo, & Linehan, 2006; Mozdzierz et al., 2014a). Now, let's look at a case example that illustrates some of these skills in action.

Going back to the case of Martina and Adam from Chapter 4 (and earlier in this chapter), we can see some of the DBT techniques in action.

Martina: And that is why you don't trust me.
Adam: It's because it makes me think of other things. It makes me think that you really don't think of me at all. You don't think about what it is like to

be me. I think that you *think* that you consider me, but you really don't. Instead, you put your work first—

Martina: I do not!

Adam: You do. You really do. I notice it and the kids do. They make fun of you always being on your phone or computer. They see it, and you know they do.

Martina: They don't understand, my job—

Adam: We *all* know how stressful your job is. You tell us all the time!

Martina: That's not fair!

Adam: I know. But it is not fair to us that you are not there. Even when you are at home, you are not really there. And you haven't been for a while. And I get it. You are stressed. You are in a new position with work, and you have to be available, but I think you take it too far. Even when you were in better positions, it took a lot of your time and attention. And when you were in worse positions, it was the same thing. I think that it is you. You put work first, kids second, God and religion third, and I am a somewhat distant fourth.

Martina: I do not!

Adam: But that is how *I* see it. That is how it feels to *me*. Even right now, I feel like I should have kept that to myself. I mean, why should I even bother? You will just deny it!

Counselor: Well, let's go back to the dream you both agreed to for your relationship: Each person feeling loved, each person being at peace with themselves and each other. Now, Adam, how do you think that holding onto the resentment you are hanging onto works with that dream?

Adam: Not very well.

Counselor: And Martina, what about you, do you feel at peace with yourself when you feel yourself retreating into your job responsibilities?

Martina: No, no I don't.

Counselor: Now remember what we discussed in terms of asking each other for what you need and want? First, you have to be able to soothe yourselves when you feel your fears kicking in.

Adam: Okay, yeah.

Counselor: And then you have to accept your feelings without judging them.

Martina: That is still tough for me. It's mostly the guilt that I feel when Adam brings it up, because I know he is right. I don't want to admit it, and that is when I get defensive.

Counselor: Okay, so what if instead you worked on just accepting the feeling? In the moment, as it is happening. And Adam, how can you ask Martina to be more present with you? I think that is what you're asking.

Adam: It totally is!

Counselor: What about DEARMAN? *Describe* your situation. *Express* why this is an issue. *Assert* yourself and ask for what you want, clearly. And the other steps. Remember when you did that successfully last week?

Adam: Okay, Martina, your "disappearing"—like when you are on your phone at dinner—is hard for me. I get upset because I want our family time to be just us, and I am concerned that the kids get the wrong idea.
Martina: I understand, although sometimes I need to respond to emails, and other times it just makes me feel relieved to not have it piling up.
Adam: I know, but I think that you can wait at least until dinner is over. I am happy to clean up the dishes and give you your time to catch up immediately after, but can you at least commit to not having the phone at dinner?
Martina: Okay, I see your point, and I will do that. And if there is a time when I am expecting something—an email or a call that is work related—I will tell you ahead of time so that you will know *that* is why I have my phone with me and that it is important.
Adam: Thank you, I really appreciate it!

Using Recollections to Assist Clients to Recognize and Reflect on Emotional Processes

Often the emotional reactions of clients and couples are not rooted in the present moment, but have a link to past experiences. This is particularly true when the emotional reactions are not proportional to the situation and seem like an overreaction. Bitter (2008) derived a variation of the early childhood recollection technique described in Chapter 7. He tied in some of the emotional processing work of noted family therapist Virginia Satir and Gestalt pioneers Erving and Miriam Polster (Bitter studied with all these individuals). Specifically, Bitter directs a client's attention to experiencing the physical sensations (both the affective expressions and internal feelings) as a means of helping the client to connect to the emotional state deeper personal dynamics that underlie the emotional reaction. The technique is briefly described here:

1. A client describes in detail the feeling that he wants to work on.
2. The therapist asks the client to describe any feelings that he is aware of regarding the issue.
3. Then the therapist asks about the client's internal feelings. Specifically, the therapist asks the client to create as many *sensory connections* as possible to the feeling in order to strengthen his recognition of the feeling, and also asks the following:
   a. Where is the feeling located on the client's body?
   b. Does the feeling have a particular shape?
   c. Does the feeling have a particular texture? Is it smooth, coarse, rough, sharp, or the like?
   d. Does the feeling have a particular temperature to it (hot, cold, etc.)?
4. Once the client has a clear visual and verbal picture of the feeling, the therapist asks the client to recall the earliest memory he has of feeling this way. Clients

generally associate the present concern to the early childhood memory as well as the emotional processing surrounding it.

5. The therapist will then help the client recognize the impact of his emotions and invite him to reflect on the connections to help with the original presenting concern.

As described in the discussion of early childhood recollections previously, there is an important relationship between what someone is feeling in a recalled memory and what about the circumstances that he described prompted him to feel that way. For example, if a client is trying to work on his or her rage at the other partner, the recalled memory will often help the counselor direct the client's focus to the deeper, underlying principle or value that is either being expressed or violated. Let's return to the case of Maria and Jim from Chapter 4. In one segment, Jim talked about his anger at Maria whenever she would start to cry during an argument:

Jim: I just can't seem to win! See, she starts crying, and I am helpless to do anything. In the past, I would try to comfort her and get her to stop, but now I just don't care! Now, I just get angry and walk away.

Maria: I hate it when you don't let me just *feel* what I am feeling! I always have to hide it or bottle it up.

Counselor: Jim, I want to try something with you. I would like for you to think about that feeling that you get when Maria starts to cry. Can you do that?

Jim: Oh yeah.

Counselor: Okay, first, can you tell me where the feeling is located on your body?

Jim: My fists. Definitely in my clenched fists.

Counselor: Does it have a particular shape?

Jim: Mmm, no. Not really.

Counselor: That's okay. Does it have a texture? Is it smooth or rough . . .

Jim: Hard. Like a big stone.

Counselor: Okay, is it hot, cold, or no temperature at all?

Jim: It's cold. Also like a stone.

Counselor: Okay. Now I want you to feel that very clearly. Can you do it? (*Jim nods yes*) Great. Now I want you to think back, and I would like me to tell you about a time in your past, possibly from your childhood, when you felt this feeling like you are now. (*pause*) Is anything coming to your mind?

Jim: I remember my mother yelling at me because I had hit my sister. She had taken away a model plane that I was building and she broke it. I was so mad!

She broke it and I swatted at her, but she yelled and started crying and all of a sudden my mother came in and just went off on me. I tried to explain it to her, but she wouldn't hear it. She just kept telling me that hitting was wrong, and she didn't care about what I was angry at. That used to happen a lot. I would get mad, particularly at my sister when she would come in my room and wouldn't get out. Mom would always punish me, and never my sister. She said because I was the older one that I had to be more considerate.

Counselor: It sounds like you didn't feel that it was fair. That it was right. So when you have this similar reaction with Maria, it is because you are worried that you won't be able to have your needs met and that you won't be understood. Is that right?

Jim: Absolutely! It's like once she starts to cry, all of the oxygen is sucked out of the conversation and it can't go any further. I don't want to see her upset, but I know that it means that I lose!

Using the recollection technique, the counselor was able to help Jim see how his reactivity to Maria's moods was tied to a sense of fairness. Jim went on to say that in the past, he would feel guilty that he hurt her, and rather than "stand his ground" he would cave in or placate her to get her to stop crying and for him to be back in her good graces. But the resentment would build, and he would be dissatisfied for days.

Conclusion: Back to the Stock Market

It might be helpful to re-introduce the couple to the figure of the Dow Jones Industrial Average from 1900–2010 (Figure 3.2, reprinted here as Figure 9.1). Invite the couple to look at the area around 1929–1938, which is the period of time from the Crash of 1929 through the Great Depression. Clearly, it was a time of great struggle and tremendous difficulty. And it is unmistakable when one looks at the chart. However, when you look at the progress after the Depression to the present day, you see unimaginable growth. It doesn't erase the reality of the Depression, or its significant impact, but the result afterward is a lot of positive developments. A relationship that is in recovery from an infidelity can function in the same way. There is no erasing the devastation of the event, but there can be good that comes after it if the couple can ride the waves of the ups and downs of satisfaction. Looking at the figure, after the Depression, there are still several periods of time when the market went up and also went down. There was even a period from 1964–1982 where the market was relatively *flat*! The point is that if couples are willing to "be in it for the long haul" and develop the skills that allow them to take a mindful perspective on their relationship, the potential for a happy, satisfying (overall), and healthy relationship is greatly increased. This is discussed in the next chapter.

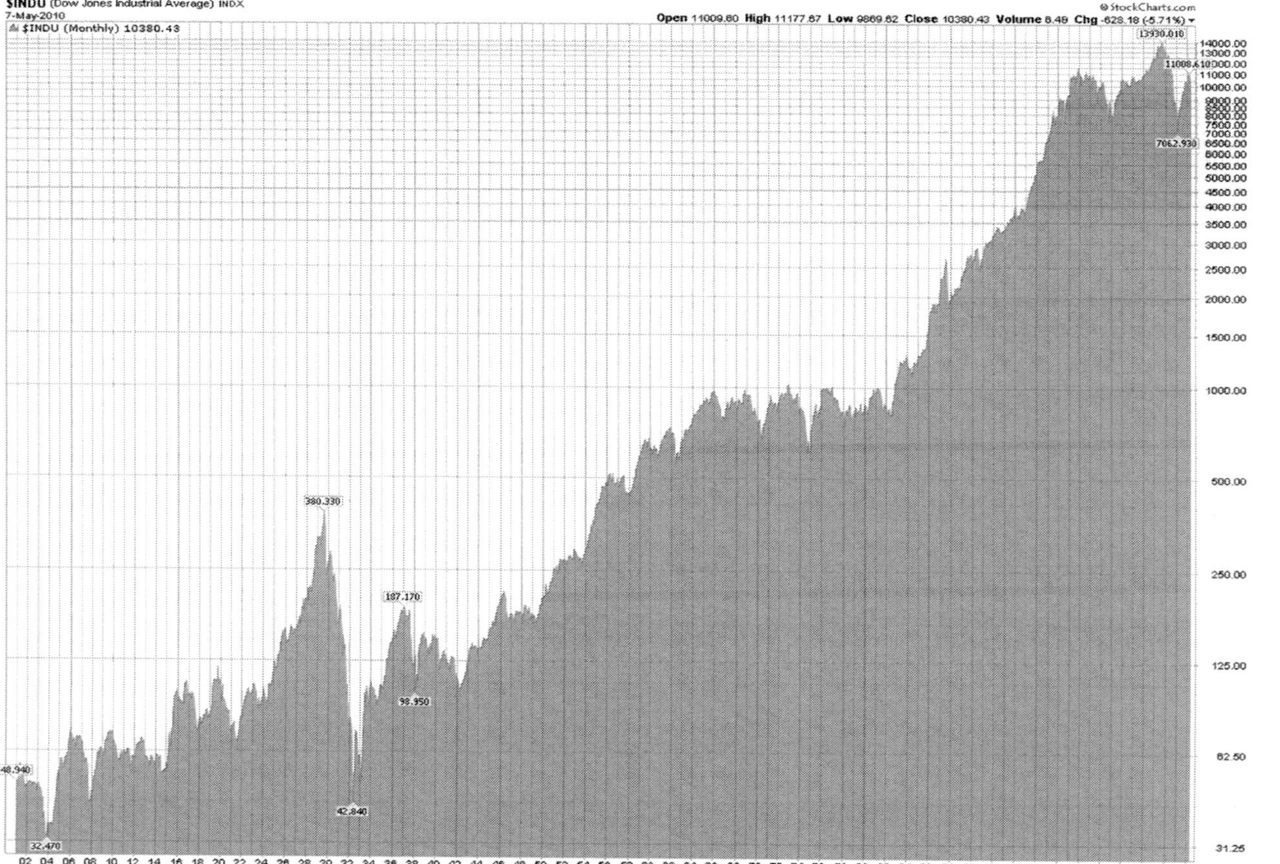

Figure 9.1.: Dow Jones Industrial Average from 1900–2010 (Chart courtesy of StockCharts.com)

CHAPTER 10

Affair Proof! How to Help Couples Make Sure An Infidelity Isn't Happening or Won't Ever Happen Again

The last three chapters presented the three steps of the treatment model to help couples work through the issues of re-capturing or creating a new dream, wish, or fantasy for the relationship; learning to share power and balance out each other's strengths; and dealing with the emotional ups and downs in satisfaction that accompany a relationship. Couples who are able to work through these issues and adopt the skills and attitudes contained within will be in a much better position to maintain a healthy relationship. However, this chapter discusses prevention exercises and techniques that can be shared with couples in order to strengthen their relationship and head off any potential problems. These exercises and concepts are focused on both the individual and the systemic level. Suggestions derived specifically for couples that have worked through an infidelity are discussed, and suggestions from successful couples are also discussed as a guide to continue their success.

Couples and Infidelity—What Next?

The main question that most couples want to know when they finish (or get near the end of) treatment is: What can we do to make sure this doesn't happen again. And while utilizing the three-step model presented in this text will go a long way toward helping couples change the dynamics of their couples system so that the conditions where an infidelity can arise are changed to create a system where an infidelity is not likely to occur, there are some additional, practical measures that couples can take. For example, noted infidelity researcher Sheryl Glass (2003) suggested the following seven tips to couples for preventing infidelity.

1. Maintain appropriate "walls" and "windows" [recall these from Chapter 6]. Keep the windows open at home. Put up privacy walls with others who could threaten your marriage.
2. Recognize that work can be a danger zone. Don't lunch or take private coffee breaks with the same person all the time. When you travel with a coworker, meet in public rooms, not in a room with a bed.
3. Avoid emotional intimacy with attractive alternatives to your committed relationship.

4. Protect your marriage by discussing relationship issues at home. If you do need to talk to someone else about your marriage, be sure that person is a friend of the marriage.
5. Keep old flames from reigniting. If a former lover is coming to the class reunion, invite your partner to come along.
6. Don't go over the line when you're on-line with Internet friends. Discuss your on-line friendships with your partner and show him or her e-mail if he or she is interested. Don't exchange sexual fantasies on-line.
7. Make sure your social network is supportive of your marriage. Surround yourself with friends who are happily married and who don't believe in fooling around.

(p. 381)

Eckstein (2002) also borrowed the concept of "walls" and "windows" from Glass to describe appropriate boundaries for couples. He uses the following questions for couples in which infidelity has been an issue:

1. What has been your successful previous history on the concept of walls (boundaries) that you have set between you and someone or something (i.e., addictive behavior)?
   a. Cite examples of when and how you successfully created a needed wall.
   b. Cite examples of walls that needed to be set that were not. What were the challenges and resistances that interfered?
2. Now focus on your past personal interpersonal history between you and your partner and/or family.
   a. Cite examples of when and how you successfully created a needed wall.
   b. Cite examples of walls that needed to be set that were not. What were the challenges and resistances that interfered?
3. Lastly, consider your present relationship.
   a. Cite examples of when and how you successfully created a needed wall.
   b. Cite examples of walls that needed to be set that were not. What were the challenges and resistances that interfered?
4. Discuss how walls and windows can be applied to you now.
5. Develop an action plan, a series of beginnings, intermediate, and long-range strategies to use the concept of walls (closings) and of windows (openings) in your relationship.

(p. 343)

Jenkins (2005) used a similar metaphor to Eckstein's by citing various *hedges* to describe healthy boundaries that can help protect marriages. He wrote specifically with *men* in mind as the partner most likely to engage in an infidelity. His suggestions have been modified to include any partner. His belief was that no matter how mature people are, they will always find other people attractive. His point was not to avoid attraction, but instead to put up hedges against *acting* on the attraction. These seven hedges are:

1. Not to dine or travel with a person you find attractive alone unless an unavoidable complication makes this impractical, and then to tell your partner first.
2. To only ever hug a person you find attractive in front of others.
3. To never compliment a person you find attractive on their looks.
4. To avoid any kind of flirting except with one's partner and to engage in as much flirtation as possible with your partner.
5. To remind one's self often of their wedding vows orally and in writing (if applicable).
6. To get home early and spend time with the children, if there are any, every day before bed.
7. To share their story of their relationship often.

Glass (2003) seemed to echo some of Jenkins's sentiments with regard to attraction, writing:

> Chemistry plus exclusivity equals an affair. If you are spending time alone with someone you are attracted to for the sole purpose of getting to know this person or because it is enjoyable, you are playing with fire. Privacy allows for intimate conversation and activities that otherwise would be limited. One tip-off that you are starting down the slippery slope is a desire not to let your spouse know how much you think about this fascinating individual.
>
> (p. 88)

Although touched on in the last chapter, let's revisit the situation where one of the partners must be in contact with the person they had the affair with (as in the case of co-workers). Traditionally couples counselors try to look at issues of dealing with the "other person" solely in light of the affair, making it a negative thing: "Can't you see that this hurts your partner . . . ?" This can back the individual into a corner and bring up defensiveness. However, if it is taken from the perspective of the fantasy level, the question can be reframed from the perspective of the three-step model. For example, the couple can be asked, "When he still is in contact with that person, what part of the fantasy does that violate, what part of the fantasy does that call into question?" The other partner might say "safety" or "security" or "trust." You can then ask the other partner, "What part of the fantasy does it violate for you?" He or she might say. "I see myself as a good guy. I don't want to see myself as the bad guy. Of course, I don't want to hurt my partner, but I also don't want to be a jerk at work!" The dilemma can be re-phrased in terms of a choice: "Do you want to be a bad guy at work or a bad guy at home?" Doing so doesn't let the individual shirk from the responsibility to the relationship, but it does offer an avenue of discussion (shared dream, fantasy, or wish) that they have agreed upon.

It also can allow for a discussion of the power differentials as well. While one partner might feel it is unfair for the other to be so demanding in relation to the other person in the infidelity, the other partner might feel it is unfair and cruel that it seems the other person's needs at work are being valued over his or her needs. This becomes an opportunity for *navigating* and *negotiating* the issue and using a collaborative approach to balance the power in deciding what to do about continued contact with the other person. Finally, the couple can work on the timing of the feelings of insecurity by considering the "stock market" of satisfaction. In other words, is there a *particular* reason or trigger for why this is an issue right now? Has something not been attended to?

The Role of Loneliness

In their book *Never Be Lonely Again*, noted couples counselors Pat Love and Jon Carlson (2011) talk about the role of loneliness plays in a number of personal and psychological problems in life. Often people don't talk about their feelings of being lonely and how it drives isolation and despair. Loneliness is not the same as being alone, as each recounted how, in their own lives, they externally had many friends and activities to surround them but still felt alone with no one to understand them. Based on their decades of counseling work with couples and individuals, and after an encounter with the Dalai Lama, they came up with an adaption of the Four Noble Truths from Buddhism and applied them to loneliness:

1. Loneliness is a fact of life. Noting is permanent; there is loss and frustration.
2. The cause of loneliness is an attachment to transient things and a false vision of reality. In the real world, you can't hold on to what can't be held.
3. The cessation of loneliness is attainable.
4. There is a path to the cessation of loneliness when attachment stops and the world is accepted as changing or impermanent (Love & Carlson, 2011, p. 63).

In order *not* to be lonely, Love and Carlson suggest a path of discovery by asking several questions. The first is discovering what your core values are and then looking at your connections to other people (are they fulfilling?) Next, are you living in (and participating in) community? This is followed by: Are your talents being put to use in meaningful work? Finally, they ask: Are you living out the purpose of your life? The answers to these questions can often help identify where in a person's life they are not fulfilling their potential or living up to their expectations. This may be an opportunity for each partner to share with the other and look to support one another.

What About Guilt and Forgiveness?

There are libraries full of books about both guilt and forgiveness, and they are important factors to touch on here. First, guilt and moral values are critical to forgiveness. Love and Carlson (2011) noted:

> Guilt occurs when your actions do not line up with your core values. If your core value is to be a faithful wife and you are not faithful, you will feel guilty. This guilt, by the way, is a sign of mental health. People who have no sense of guilt have no moral compass and ultimately cannot be trusted. Guilt is corrective; it is designed to bring you back to your core values. So what can you do with the past deeds about which you feel regret, remorse or guilt? First, let the feelings guide you back to your core value. In the example of infidelity, you would ask yourself, "What would a faithful wife do? How can I demonstrate my fidelity?" Then do it over and over until your behavior lines up with your core values and the person you want to be.
>
> (Love & Carlson, 2011, p. 63)

Recall from Chapter 6 that guilt is what generally brings a partner to "confess" the infidelity to the other partner when disclosing the affair. And the hope for these individuals is that the "confession" will relieve the guilt. However, the other partner's hurt and anger usually do not provide much relief. Therefore, tied into this guilt, and the true remedy that is sought, is forgiveness. Unfortunately, there is often a rush to forgiveness, as Fincham, Hall, and Beach (2005) wrote:

> As any marital therapist can testify, marital interactions are often overlearned, unfold at an astonishing speed, and appear to proceed without much thought. This does not deny the importance of forgiveness for marital interactions; it simply suggests that the kind of deliberate and effortful judgments of forgiveness that we have studied thus far will provide an incomplete picture of its role. For example, it is not uncommon to come across a spouse who says and believes that he or she has forgiven the partner, only to discover that resentment or a desire for revenge is instigated by the slightest cue during interaction with the partner. If we are to understand how forgiveness in marriage influences marital interaction, we will also need to study forgiveness at this implicit level. Unlike explicit forgiveness that can be adopted quickly, implicit forgiveness, like any automatic process, requires extensive practice to develop.
>
> (p. 222)

Johns, Allen, and Gordon (2015) found that there is a negative dimension of forgiveness (where one partner harbors negative thoughts and feelings about the other, is dysregulated emotionally toward the partner, and tends toward withdrawing from the partner) and positive dimensions of forgiveness (having a balanced perspective on the partner and the partner's actions without the intense feelings of resentment or hurt toward them). This is particularly true if the forgiveness process is rushed. Ortega and Fleming (2005) agreed with Fincham et al. and Jones et al., stressing that:

1. Forgiveness is not given because it is deserved. It cannot be earned. It is given by faith. The motivation does not come from the character qualities of the offender.
2. Forgiveness is not a feeling. It is a decision. Feelings follow as the healing process is worked out.
3. Forgiveness is not a process; healing is a process. Once forgiveness has been declared it has taken place. It does not need to be repeated. *When the angry or hurt feelings reoccur, they do not indicate a lack of forgiveness.* They indicate that further healing still needs to take place. Part of the healing process is reminding oneself that these infractions have been forgiven. Answering the pain with a reminder will lessen the pain, and eventually it will be gone.

(pp. 120–121, italics added for emphasis)

Successful attempts at forgiveness have been empirically related to increased relationship satisfaction, increased quality of life, decreased aggression, and increased empathy between partners, as well as increased trust (Burchard et al., 2003; Fincham & Beach, 2002; Fincham, Paleari, & Regalia, 2002; Fincham, Beach, & Davila, 2004; Karremans, Van Lange, Ouwerkerk, & Kluwer, 2003; Sells, Giordano, & King, 2002). Failing to forgive, or forgiving too soon, can lead to negative consequences (the "negative dimension" of forgiveness) and may be seen through the lens of ambivalence regarding the relationship (recall "THE Question" from Chapter 6). In fact, Kachadourian, Fincham, and Davila (2004) and Paleari, Regalia, and Fincham (2005) found that lack of forgiveness and ambivalence were related to rumination about past transgressions, which, in turn, led to poor relationship qualities.

Ruminating Versus Thinking?

As discussed in Chapter 6, when couples are working through an infidelity, particularly in the early disclosure phases, partners will have traumatic flashbacks. In their anxiety, they will think endlessly about minute details. This is often the hallmarks of traumatic stress and the associated disorders. For the most part these flashbacks are normal and to be expected. However, as time and treatment passes, these should lessen. For some couples, they do not. With couples, I often contrast the idea of *thinking* with the idea of *ruminating*.

In the science fiction program *Doctor Who*, the Doctor (main character) is trying to convince an alien to back away from a conflict that will involve mass destruction (and possibly self-destruction). He says to the character: "I *just* want you to think. And do you know what thinking is? It's just a fancy word for changing your mind." I contrast this with the idea of rumination. Rumination is the process where cattle will regurgitate some undigested grass back into their mouth and continue to chew on it over and over again. It is also used to describe the process of continuing to churn over emotional upsets (hence the term "chewing the cud"). I pose the question to the couple: "Is what you are doing more in the spirit of thinking (changing your mind) or ruminating (barfing up undigested thoughts and going over them again and again)?" Often this can help shake individuals out of habitual patterns and engage them in ones more productive for the relationship.

Tied into this rumination is the idea of "checking" on the other person. Usually this is in a negative way, stemming sometimes from an innocent oversight by one partner or built off the anxieties of the other partner. There may be demands for accountability and methods for keeping tabs on the other person (giving passwords to social media and emails, accessing text and phone data, etc.) that feel intrusive or contrary to rebuilding a sense of trust. Much of this gets derisively labeled as "spying" on a person. I have created an exercise that takes the negative connotation and turns it into a positive, called "spy on the relationship," which is included in the following.

Exercise: "Spy on the Relationship!"

Often there are concerns about one partner fearing the other is not truthful and the other partner not being believed. There is a desire to know what the other person is doing or thinking. This can lead to "negative mind reading" and other negative interactions. Many times one partner wishes to "spy" on the other person. This can be used to positive effect by "spying" on the relationship or, more specifically, on each person's interactions *with* each other. The assignment is to write down specific instances when one partner is telling the truth and when the other partner *believes* him or her. This is a way of decreasing the focus on the number of times a person lies (or is accused of lying) and increasing the focus on the number of times a partner tells the *truth* and is believed by the other! This continues to build trust with each other. It also helps for couples to be able to talk more constructively about the issue of insecurity (which is almost always underlying issues of trust).

The Normality of "Dating" Each Other Again

Often it is difficult for a couple dealing with the aftermath of an infidelity to even contemplate that they might want to "return to normal" activities. But once the bulk of the work of couples counseling has been completed, it is time to symbolically begin the process of a return to normalcy. One of the more outward ways to do this is to "go on a date" like they did in the beginning of the relationship, when they were courting each other. For some couples, this might be harder than others (especially if they did not have a tradition of going on dates or if the relationship deteriorated to the point they didn't want to go on dates with each other). Table 10.1 has an easy three-step approach for planning a date night for couples that have been dealing with the aftermath of an infidelity.

Table 10.1.: The three steps in planning a date night

Step 1: Make a Date List
This is a collaborative step to take together. If couples have gone through the three steps of the treatment model, they should have the necessary skills to work through this together. The goal is to work with your partner and brainstorm date ideas. In the brainstorming phase, there are no right or wrong answers. In fact, you can even see who can come up with the silliest or "out of the realm of possibility" scenarios ("We could have dinner at the top of the Eiffel Tower!"). This will loosen up creativity and increase the sense of "play" between the partners. Sometimes, the silly ideas can lead to better ones. The key is to get out as many ideas as you can together.

Step 2: Select and Plan a Date
From the list you and your spouse have created, select one date idea that both partners can commit to, and put it on the calendar. Think about any logistics that need to be accomplished in order to make this happen (i.e., babysitters, transportation, reservations, etc.) and who will be responsible for what—make it collaborative (i.e., "I'll do this . . . You do that . . ."). In order to rebuild your marriage, you need actions that will propel the relationship forward. Setting the date and having the plans in place shows a commitment and prioritization for the relationship. It also gives the couple something positive to look forward to.

Step 3: Set Conflict Aside for Length of the Date
This may be the most important step of all. And while it doesn't erase any feelings of residual hurt or betrayal, it is a commitment to begin a new phase of the relationship that is built on shared dreams and wishes, a sharing of power, and an ability to deal with the ups and downs of satisfaction with each other. Agree that, for this date, each person will commit to relax and not bring up any conflicts or points of contention during the time that has been set aside. Partners should be mindful of hot-button issues that could sabotage the evening and avoid them. While there may be some tension or nervousness in the first date, it is an opportunity to begin to build positive memories.

Then follow the plan and go on the date!
Reflection Questions for Your Date Night

These questions might be helpful to de-brief one another or bring into the next couples counseling session.

1. Did you develop the date plans together? How did you negotiate that? Was it easy or it difficult? In what way? Were you able to follow through on actually going on the date? What were the obstacles (if any)?
2. How did you feel on your "first" date?
3. Did you and your spouse set ground rules in what you would discuss/not discuss on the date? Were you able to stick to them?

Source: Adapted from infidelityrecoveryinstitute.com.

What Do Well-Functioning Couples Do?

While there are many infidelity-related issues that couples recovering from the impact of an affair need to attend to, there are things that well-functioning couples (what Gottman, 2011, calls the "masters" of relationships) do that can be instructive for couples counselors to share with their clients. Carlson and Dinkmeyer (2003) highlighted 10 components that are present in couples who have satisfying relationships. These couples:

1. Individually accept responsibility and develop self-esteem.
2. Encourage each other.
3. Identify and align their relationship goals.
4. Communicate their feelings with honesty and openness.
5. Listen empathically when feelings are being expressed.
6. Seek to understand the factors that influence their relationship.
7. Demonstrate that they accept and value each other.
8. Choose thoughts, words, and actions that support the positive goals of the relationship.
9. Solve relational conflicts.
10. Commit themselves to the ongoing process of maintaining an equal relationship.

According to Carlson and Dinkmeyer, couples who have a deficit in one or more of these areas can be taught these skills. They believe that small, incremental changes can lead to larger changes in the relationship over time. As a result, couples counselors don't feel like they have to make a "home run" with a couple in terms of "breakthroughs" or insights. Tiny but noticeable changes by either partner are important. They also believe that even if the couple feels that their feelings of love and caring have diminished over time (recall the conversation about relationship satisfaction from Chapters 3 and 9), these can return. However, this is not something that is done automatically. It accompanies mindful and purposeful behavior change. Last, they believe that change for couples takes time (and patience) and begins with each partner making a choice. This gives both partners the power to decide for themselves and to keep making decisions. This choice leads to changes in the couple's system dynamics as well. For couples that are struggling to cope with an infidelity, where they may feel powerless and out of control, these qualities can be a guide toward a more positive relationship.

Many of these qualities are echoed in other approaches, like Gottman and Gottman (2017) and their idea of a "Sound Relationship House" (which was first presented in Chapter 7). The elements of their house include: building love maps, sharing fondness and admiration, turning toward one another, taking a positive perspective, managing conflict, making life dreams come true, and creating shared meaning all within a framework of trust and commitment (for a wider discussion of these elements, see Gottman's *The Science of Trust* or *What Makes Love Last?*).

Gillet (2017) in an article for *Business Insider* took Gottman's work and looked at so-called "power couples" (couples where both partners are highly successful in their careers) that are successful in maintaining their relationships and the nine things they seem to have in common. She found the following of these power couples:

1. *They prioritize spending time together.* Time is the most precious of resources, and this is especially true of power couples. As a result, they have to be deliberate and mindful of their choices with regards to their free time. What they choose signals what they prioritize. Successful power couples are mindful in

choosing each other. Gillet (2017) cites the example of Mark Zuckerberg and Priscilla Chan, who drew up an agreement where he committed to spend 100 minutes of alone time with her each week (outside of the office or apartment) and take her on a date once a week. While this might seem mechanistic or formulaic to some people, it is the commitment of the resource of time that matters. It is the vehicle for meaningful connection, regardless of the way it is arranged.

2. *They outsource tedious chores.* Again, because time is such a precious commodity, it can have a monetary value attached to it. It is the basis for everyone's salary ("time is money"), and it can be the basis for valuing the relationship, too. Gillet (2017) cites Laura Vanderkam's work where she looked at successful women's habits and found that they "outsource" many of the chores they have to spend their off time doing so they can spend time with families (and partners). While it might seem like an expensive and frivolous use of money, she states the following: "If you make $45,000 annually and work 40 hours a week (that's 2,080 work hours a year), that means your time is potentially worth about $22 an hour ($45,000 divided by 2,080)." Therefore, anything that you can pay someone around $20 an hour to do is potentially worth the hour of your life that you can get back and spend with your partner.
3. *Their time is spent doing good.* Again citing the example of Zuckerberg and Chan, or Bill and Melinda Gates, these power couples have created entities whereby they can work together to do good in the community. Now, if (like most of us) your clientele is slightly less prosperous than these billionaires, creating a foundation may not be ideal. But the *idea* of working together to help out in the local community, or sometimes overseas, can build an intrinsic sense of positivity together. It gets individuals outside of themselves (or their egos) and back in touch with a deeper spiritual purpose that they can share together (i.e., "Sound Relationship House"). It can also tie into the new, explicit and shared dream, wish, or fantasy they have about the relationship.
4. *They listen and empathize.* As discussed in Chapters 8 and 9, there are a number of ways for couples to be able to listen, and empathize, with their partners. Listening to a partner who is having a difficult time solving his or her own problems, without necessarily trying to solve the problem, can be a great tool (in other words, being a sounding board). The problem is that highly successful people spend a lot of time solving problems of their own during the day. This means there are one of two pitfalls they can fall into: (1) rushing in to offer a solution, which is a problem because it may make the other person feel *unable* to solve his or her own problem, or (2) feeling so overwhelmed themselves with listening and solving their own problems at work that when they come home they do not have the capacity listen to their partner's problems. Therefore, those power couples that are able to avoid the two pitfalls have found ways to work together and understand each other's needs and communicate about them.
5. *They speak up about problems before it's too late.* Again, because these couples are aware of the value of time, they do not waste it with grudges or unspoken

hurts. Instead, they make their concerns known at a very early stage. This may be borne out of their work experiences where problem solving is valued and correcting errors is "good for business." As a result, these individuals tend not to be conflict avoiders. Instead, they see conflict as an opportunity to make things better. Therefore, in their own relationships, they "cut to the chase" and make sure to air their grievances in a manner that is efficient but also sensitive to the needs of their partners.

6. *They express their appreciation.* This can be done with grand gestures (e.g., a giant bouquet of flowers sent to the office), but the most powerful expressions of appreciation are usually the small, timely ones. This can be in the form of text messages or conversations by phone during the middle of the day. While general expressions of appreciation are helpful, the most effective expressions are ones where one partner notices something small the other person does that is appreciated. It should be noted that appreciation does not have to be for things the partner does for *him or her personally*; it can also be noticing and appreciating what the partner does for kids, family, community, and so on, as well.
7. *They agree upon important issues from the get-go.* Much like the shared and explicit wish, fantasy, or dream the couple creates for the relationship, the so-called power couples also are "up front" about their needs and expectations from the other person. Especially if two very successful people are each expecting the other person to submit to their needs or will, the *what* and *how* of that needs to be explicit. And much like the issues of power sharing or power imbalances that have been discussed in this book, many expectations and agreements about issues like money and sex can stave off misunderstandings and disappointments later. Again, coming from the world of business, these agreements may take the form of a negotiated contract that is written down, with periodic reviews for re-negotiation as times and circumstances warrant.
8. *They commit to one another overall.* This may be easier said than done, but the idea of commitment is crucial. It is the sense that the other person "has their back." If the partners in the couple feel this is the case, they will not feel anxious when distance or business keep them apart for a time. Of course, the other skills mentioned are the building blocks for this implicit trust and commitment. Commitment also provides the basis for supporting one another in a way that others cannot. Highly successful people have a lot of people around them who seem like they are trustworthy, committed, and supportive of them, but who (in reality) want something from them. By having a "safe harbor" with their partner, they know they have someone they can wholly rely on and do not have to question the validity of their support or commitment.
9. *They work somewhere that understands family comes first.* This is easier for successful people who are the entrepreneurs and owners of their business than for people who work for firms or companies where they have high positions. However, many companies today are realizing the importance of having a corporate culture that supports their employees. This can include

a "family-friendly" environment which allows for a good work-life balance. Ultimately, this has a beneficial impact on the corporations' bottom line because impaired workers (due to problems at home) can have a negative effect at work. This is especially true for people in upper management or who are very important to the company's mission.

Emotional ATTUNEment

Another finding from Gottman and Gottman's (2017) work is related to the functioning of successful relationships. According to Gottman (2011), there is a critical set of skills that successful couples (and parents) demonstrate. These skills are a "blueprint for building trust in long-term committed relationships" (p. 178). Couples who can do this are called "emotion coaching" couples because they don't take responsibility for their partner's negative emotion but do help understand and empathize with their partner. By contrast, couples who can't do this are called "emotion dismissing" because in the face of their partner's negative emotion, they took responsibility for it, and if they couldn't (or didn't want to) "fix" it, they dismissed it out of hand as "stupid" or somehow wrong. This dismissing often leads to feelings of being disregarded and uncared for and is a good indicator of an imbalance of power as well as eventual dissatisfaction in the relationship.

The series of skills Gottman (2011) discovered that emotion coaching couples do was something he called "ATTUNEment." ATTUNE is an acronym that stands for the following six skills: *awareness* of the emotion; *turning toward* the emotion; *tolerance* of the emotional experience; *understanding* the emotion; *nondefensive listening* to the emotion; and *empathy* toward the emotion (Gottman, 2011). These are skills that can be learned, but for emotion-dismissing couples it requires a "shift" in their thinking. In other words, it requires that the couple's system dynamics be changed (recall "second-order change" from Chapter 2) in order to create new "set points" for the couple around negative emotions. Each of the six skills will be described in the following.

1. *Awareness of the emotion*. This skill is designed to have individuals assess their partner's emotional state without blaming or judging the partner. It means accurately labeling and identifying the emotion. It also requires some soothing of the partner by processing the emotion and helping them "air out" their emotion by letting them talk. The negative emotion in question may be about external forces or entities (work, boss, family, kids), or it may be internally focused (irritation with the partner, or something the partner did or did not do).
2. *Turning toward the emotion*. When the negative emotion is about someone or something else, this is an easier skill to master, but when it is focused on the partner, this is more difficult and requires skill in self-soothing (as well as soothing the partner!). By turning toward the (negative) emotion, the partner looks for the "positive" need underlying the complaint or criticism that is the

impetus for the negative emotion. "In general, in sadness something is missing. In anger there is a frustrated goal. In disappointment there is a hope, and expectation. In loneliness there is a desire for connection" (Gottman, 2011, p. 193). Once the need is found, the couple can work toward providing for that need, rather than argue about being blamed for the negative feeling.

3. *Tolerance of the emotional experience.* The idea of "tolerance" for their partner's (negative) emotional experience is not the same as agreeing with the emotion (especially if the negative emotion is directed at them). It also means they do not try to change the emotion or persuade the partner to stop having the emotion as well. Tolerating one's partner's emotion also does not mean they have to feel the same way as their partner. Instead, it means to "sit with" the partner in the midst of the negative emotion and be present with him or her.
4. *Understanding the emotion.* This skill incorporates both eliciting information from the partner about his or her experience and being able to intuit the underlying issue or motivations behind the negative emotion. According to Gottman (2011), "they postpone their own agenda in a search for understanding their partner's point of view" (p. 194). Individuals go on a "mission" to seek out what their partner's experience is and how *their partner* understands it (rather than base it on their perspective). Again, when directed externally, it is easier to do in a calm and nonjudgmental way. When it is directed at *them* it can be very challenging (although ultimately rewarding).
5. *Non-defensive listening to the emotion.* Proceeding from the understanding skill, non-defensive listening is the process by which individuals can listen to their partner in a fully present way (especially when they may be the target of the negative emotion) without reacting or "jumping to conclusions." There are several methods to help achieve this. The first is to regulate one's emotions through self-soothing and deep breathing. The second is to cognitively reframe their experience and their partner's experience. This might take the form of "self-talking" where the individual says to themselves: "I have to listen as if this is not about me" or "I know this is upsetting to hear, but I don't have to get upset because of it."
6. *Empathy toward the emotion.* The final skill in *attunement* is empathy. Empathy is the ability to "see with the eyes of another" and not just view their experience as they see it, but feel their experience as they feel it. In doing so, individuals are able to resonate compassionately with their partner's experience and accurately reflect back to their partner that they understand it. It is not the same as saying, "I know how you feel, because I once felt like . . ." but rather, "If I were in your shoes, and that happened to me, I would probably feel (like you are feeling now)." It validates the partner's experience and interpretation of his or her own experience, and it builds trust in the other person.

The skill set in attunement is powerful for any couple, but for couples dealing with the aftermath of an infidelity, these skills can be vital. They build up a sense of "you get me" between the partners and encourage each person to feel that their partner will be able to help *them* work through the feelings, rather than solve the problem for them. It allows them also to make *choices* about how to react to their partner (similar to the work of Carlson and Dinkmeyer, 2003, mentioned prior). This is especially true when the conflict is centered between the couple (as in the case of an infidelity), as opposed to a conflict with an external context or person (i.e., work, friends, school, kids, etc.). Last, attunement helps couples build trust as they competently work through difficult situations, harsh negative feelings, and the inevitable ups and downs of living life together.

Conclusion

While the focus of this chapter has been on the "after" part of treatment (that is, what to do after the three steps have been worked on), the reality is that since this is a systems-based approach, these skills presented at the "end" can (and possibly *should*) also be introduced in the beginning! And while skills that many successful couples seem to employ were also presented, the purpose in presenting these was not to suggest there are such glaring differences between well-functioning relationships and relationships where an infidelity has occurred. Rather, the goal was to show that *no relationship is perfect*. Every couple has to work hard to be successful, and often the difference between successful relationships, and ones where there is an infidelity, comes down to choices, skills, and the system dynamics the couple has created.

The last chapter discusses several controversies that are not explicitly addressed in this book. The system-wide changes made by effective treatment of infidelity will also be covered. Finally, two high-profile public cases that have been successful in recovering from infidelity, and who acknowledged that couples counseling helped them, are discussed.

CHAPTER 11

Conclusion and Wrap-Up

This chapter provides a recapitulation of the explanatory and treatment model and its systemic "roots." Some of the more controversial and pressing issues related to the treatment of infidelity are also considered. Finally, some closing examples of high-profile couples who found success in coping with an infidelity in their relationship with the help of couples counseling are presented.

Controversies Not Covered

While no one text can cover the totality of clinical issues that counselors must face related to the treatment of couples trying to recover from an infidelity, this book attempts to create an overview of a systems-based approach that will help couples counselors work with these couples. As a result, there are a number of issues that did not get a full treatment but are discussed briefly here.

Should Couples Counselors Keep an Infidelity a Secret?

Quite possibly, one of the most divisive issues amongst couples counselors is the question of what to do if one partner confesses to having an affair, and is in counseling, but does not want to disclose it to his or her partner. As a result, the couples counselor must make a choice about what to do with the information. Does a couples counselor respect the autonomy of the individual partner and continue to work with the couple knowing there is this secret? Or does the counselor refuse to work with the couple unless or until the partner confesses the infidelity (and offer to help him or her disclose it).

The reality is that some practitioners believe that to keep the secret is to collude with one partner against the other partner, which would compromise the treatment. Many systems-oriented couples counselors believe the *couple* is the client, not the individuals. Therefore, if the actions of the individual (hiding the infidelity) are against the health of the client (couple), ethically it must be disclosed. Other practitioners feel that individuals are the clients. Finally, noted couples counselors who are infidelity specialists have recently stated that they have changed their position on the *absolute* need for immediately disclosing the secret (Weiner-Davis, 2017; Sachs, 2008). Part of their reasoning is that, in their clinical experience, they are not sure that all couples *benefit* from disclosure, particularly if the infidelity has occurred in the past, the affair has definitively ended, and the individual is committed to improving the relationship. So which is the best way? This is an issue for each couples counselor to make based on their best clinical judgment and informed by the best clinical research. The "take away" for couples counselors is that whatever your policy, it should be made clear to the couple before working with them.

How Should Couples Counselors Deal With the "Other Person"?

Technically, this has been explored in Chapters 7, 8, and 9 in some form. This is another issue that has created some controversy for couples counselors. Author and couples counselor Esther Perel (2017) has advocated a position where the perspective of the "other person" should be considered in the treatment of couples. She (and others who agree with her approach) don't *necessarily* believe the relationship with the other person needs to end. In some cases, they also advocate that the other person should be included in the couple's sessions. It is not surprising that there are strong feelings that this is antithetical to an approach that is trying to help the couple heal and make the kind of systemic changes that are implicit in the three-step model here and elsewhere.

What About Lesbian, Gay, Bisexual, and Transgendered Populations?

This text attempts to look at the impact of an infidelity on committed relationships (regardless of marital status). In the last decade (since the publication of my book *Infidelity: A Practitioner's Guide to Working With Couples in Crisis*), there have been tremendous changes in the state of marriage, particularly with the federal recognition of gay and lesbian marriages. In fact, in my previous book, I invited two authors to contribute two separate chapters on working with gay couples (Shernoff, 2007) and working with lesbian couples (Burch, 2007) because I felt there were unique and distinct cultural and contextual issues that required expertise from within those communities from practitioners who worked with those communities. In addition, I knew I was not the expert in those communities (I did have experience working with gay and lesbian couples but felt I did not have the expertise to adequately do justice to these important communities).

There have also been continuing and evolving areas of understanding for polyamory and diverse configurations of sexual fidelity that will continue to impact popular understanding of infidelity. In addition, there has been an explosion of support and tolerance of transgendered couples over the last decade that is also going to continue to push forward the field of couples counseling and impact our conceptualization of couples, couple functioning, and the nature of infidelity. Since this is the first book in a *series* of books, I am hopeful that a future volume in this series will be devoted to exploring these specific populations and evolving areas of couples counseling.

What About Research?

This text has attempted to include as many research findings as possible while keeping the clinical focus of this book for practitioners. The reality is that there needs to be substantially more research conducted on the prevalence and understanding of infidelity, as well as the treatment of infidelity in couples counseling (Hertlein & Piercy, 2008; Moller & Vossler, 2015). While several practitioners (Doug Snyder, Sue Johnson, and Dave Atkins) have conducted some of the most important work in this area (McIntosh et al., 2007; Kessel et al., 2007; Snyder et al., 2008), more work needs to be done to increase the evidence base for couples counseling work with couples dealing with the aftermath of an infidelity. Currently, I am involved in a nation-wide randomized clinical trial along with John and Julie Gottman that is looking to provide empirical support for the Gottman Method Couples Therapy applied to couples in therapy for infidelity. Results of this work should hopefully become available within the next 2 years.

Speaking of "controversies," one of the more controversial figures in the late 20th and early 21st century is presented here as one of our last high-profile cases. This couple has shaped political life over the last 25 years, and for them not only was an infidelity publicly disclosed, but they, by their own admission, were helped by couples counseling.

President Bill Clinton and Secretary Hillary Clinton

"I did not have sexual relations with that woman." Those words uttered by the 42nd president of the United States, Bill Clinton, provide possibly one of the most monumental examples of infidelity and the price to be paid by a president. In 1999, he was only the second president in the history of the United States to be impeached by the US Senate (Andrew Johnson was the other). And while he was not found guilty (of either perjury or obstruction of justice), it was his attempts to hide an infidelity with then intern Monica Lewinsky that brought about the dire consequence of impeachment.

However, the story neither started nor ended there. Bill Clinton married Hillary Rodham Clinton in 1975 after meeting at Yale Law School. Hillary Clinton admitted that she turned him down twice because he was focused on a political career. As she recounted in her autobiography, she "knew marrying him would be like hitching a ride on a comet." She later became aware that he was not faithful in their marriage. She would later come to explain his infidelity as something that arose from his childhood (trying to please his demanding mother and grandmother) and that she had thought (or hoped) he had conquered it in the 1980s. However, in 1992, on the eve of the New Hampshire primary, a story broke that a former Arkansas state worker named Gennifer Flowers had evidence of a decade-long affair with Bill. At the time, the Clinton campaign had planned for this, with Hillary reportedly acknowledging that "there was something to it." They famously went on *60 Minutes*, where Hillary stated: "I'm not sitting here—some little woman standing by my man like Tammy Wynette. I'm sitting here because I love him, and I respect him, and I honor what he's been through and what we've been through together."

In private, many friends and close associates wondered whether the marriage had reached its breaking point. In her book *Living History*, she wrote that after Bill had admitted what had happened, she was left "feeling dumbfounded, heartbroken and outraged that I'd believed him" (p. 456). She would later blame herself that she had not attended to his emotional needs, especially when he was under great stress. This would come about again during the Monica Lewinsky relationship in the late 1990s, when Bill would eventually admit to having an affair with her. Hillary reportedly felt that the sexual relationship was "meaningless" and a personal lapse, although she acknowledged the deep hurt and pain that resulted. In 2017, she reflected in her book *What Happened?*:

> There were times that I was deeply unsure about whether our marriage could or should survive. But on those days, I asked myself the questions that mattered to me: Do I still love him? And can I still be in this marriage without becoming unrecognizable to myself—twisted by anger, resentment, or remoteness? The answers were always yes. So I kept going.
>
> (p. 228)

For their part, the Clintons got marriage counseling. Bill described marathon sessions where he would do full-day sessions examining his life and his choices. According to him, it lasted for over a year, and he admitted on Oprah Winfrey's show that it was a worthwhile experience:

> Let's suppose it hadn't worked out, and we'd gotten a divorce . . . I would still be profoundly grateful that I did the counseling, because I think what happens is a lot of people who love each other a lot, still they fall into routines and patterns and habits in their relationship.

They remained married, with Hillary Clinton stating: "We've had many, many more happy days than sad or angry ones . . . I love him with my whole heart. That's more than enough to build life on."

There are a number of people who feel that the Clintons' marriage is a political arrangement and that the statements and displays of affection are all "show" for the public. And there are others who believe that Bill and Hillary's public statements about their marriage and infidelity are an honest and accurate reflection of their relationship. I cannot determine which of those perspectives is correct, and since I know neither of them (except what I see on TV and read), I have presented their case with two thoughts in mind: (1) it was one of the most public (and well-documented) accounts of an affair in the White House, and (2) the people involved discussed their treatment by a counselor and have remained married 20 years after the events unfolded. And as of the writing of this book, they remain so. In addition, there have not been any additional reports of an infidelity in the Clinton relationship, which indicates that perhaps the treatment they received *helped* them. The point is that if such a high-profile case can be helped (admittedly by the couple) with couples counseling, it provides a measure of encouragement to the field of couples counseling for the treatment of couples working through an infidelity.

Return to the Three-Step Model and Systems Dynamics

As you have read this book, I hope one thing has become clear. A model for explaining how an infidelity occurs, and one that also explains the way to help couples recover and make changes in light of an infidelity (i.e., a treatment model), is not only *useful*, but critical. And while the three-step model presented here does have a linear, stepwise flow, it is more appropriate to think of the "steps" as sequential and inclusive, and not exclusive and completely distinct. I hope that, throughout the last few chapters, it has been clear that even after the couple has created a new, explicit, and shared dream, wish, and fantasy for the relationship, it must be carried forward into discussions about sharing and balancing power, and what is learned about both of those areas plays into coping with the changing nature of relationship satisfaction.

In addition, it is my hope that this text has helped make the case for the two systems-oriented principles for the outlined in Chapter 2, namely: (1) that the infidelity is *not* the central issue of concern in the relationship, it's a symptom, and (2) that both partners had a contributing role in creating the conditions that led to the infidelity. Again, this is one of the more important and profound "shifts" both counselors and couples must make in their thinking related to infidelity. However, it is my contention that success in treating these couples is dependent on this shift. I want to conclude with another high-profile case where an infidelity was acknowledged, and where the couple sought couples counseling and found it to be highly successful, that makes this case.

Jay-Z and Beyoncé

There has been no greater "power couple" in the early 2000s than recording artists Beyoncé and Jay-Z. They began collaborating together in 2002 and were married in 2008. They enjoyed commercial and financial success, earning them a top place in *Forbes* magazine's Top Earning Couples list several years in a row. They were notorious for not talking about their relationship in public (even hiding that they had been married). Jay-Z was quoted as saying that they specifically do not comment about their marriage in interviews.

However, in 2015 there were rumors of infidelity. A surveillance video in an elevator showed Beyoncé's sister physically attacking Jay-Z, which fueled speculation about his infidelity due to the suddenness and ferociousness of the attack (like she had heard some shocking and infuriating news). Finally, in 2016 Beyoncé released an album, *Lemonade*, that featured songs with themes of betrayal and infidelity. In one song, she sang: "You know I give you life, if you try this s—t again you're gonna lose your wife."

Then, in 2017, Jay-Z released an album entitled *4:44*, which seemed equally autobiographical and had songs that were seemingly an apology to his wife. Finally, Jay-Z opened up about his album and relationship with Beyoncé in an interview in the *New York Times*. He admitted that he had an affair with someone and that he and Beyoncé had been in therapy to deal with the aftermath. He said:

> I grew so much from the experience. But I think the most important thing I got is that everything is connected. Every emotion is connected and it comes from somewhere. And just being aware of it. Being aware of it in everyday life puts you at such a . . . you're at such an advantage.
>
> Baquet (2017)

He stated that he had been bullied and had bullied others as a child. He discussed growing up in a housing project in the Bedford-Stuyvesant neighborhood of Brooklyn, without a father, and he talked about emotionally being in survival mode: "and when you go into survival mode what happen? You shut down all emotions. So even with women, you gonna shut down emotionally, so you can't connect . . . And then all the things happen from there: infidelity" (Baquet 2017). However, through therapy, he and Beyoncé began the process of healing. Jay-Z expressed how difficult it was: "The hardest thing is seeing pain on someone's face that you caused, and then have to deal with yourself." They remained committed to their marriage: "You know, most people walk away, and like divorce rate is like 50 percent or something 'cause most people can't see themselves." They also used their art to work through their issues. They had intended to release both albums simultaneously, but Beyoncé's was ready sooner. During this time, Jay-Z reflected on the process:

> And that's where we were sitting. And it was uncomfortable. And we had a lot of conversations. You know. [I was] really proud of the music she made, and she was really proud of the art I released. And, you know, at the end of the day we really have a healthy respect for one another's craft. I think she's amazing.
>
> Baquet (2017)

As of the writing of this book, they have remained married, and in 2017 they announced that Beyoncé had given birth to twins.

Again, while Beyoncé and Jay-Z have the luxury of being wealthy, and of being able to use their art to express their inner turmoil and recovery from infidelity, Jay-Z's acknowledgement of the role of effective couples counseling in helping them is important. He acknowledged that his family-of-origin issues played into how he emotionally expressed himself (or *didn't* express himself, i.e. "walled off") to his wife. He discussed how couples counseling helped him see himself and his wife in a new way (forge a new fantasy or dream for the relationship?) and allowed them to find ways to work together (literally on their albums—sharing power—as well as their relationship?). Finally, their ability to communicate (having a lot of uncomfortable conversations) seems to suggest they have found the skills to be able to cope with the variable nature of relationship satisfaction and ultimately see an upward trajectory over time to their overall relationship story.

Conclusion

The goal after all of this, of course, is that a systems-wide change will take place for the couple. This system-wide, second-order change will change the way the couple relates to each other on a profound and structural level. Last, the purpose of this book is to show that *any* couple—and that *all* couples that start out with love, hope, and trust, regardless of what happens in between—can find love and unity again if they are willing to take the steps to do it together.

References

Abrahms Spring, J. (with Spring, M.). (1996). *After the affair: Healing the pain and rebuilding trust when a partner has been unfaithful.* New York: Harper Collins, Inc.

Adler, A. (1931/1998). *What Life Could Mean to You.* Center City, MN: Hazelden.

American Psychiatric Association. (2013). *Diagnostic and statistical manual of mental disorders: DSM-5* (5th ed.). Washington, DC: American Psychiatric Association.

Atkins, D. C., Eldridge, K. A., Baucom, D. H., & Christensen, A. (2005). Infidelity and behavioral couple therapy: Optimism in the face of betrayal. *Journal of Consulting and Clinical Psychology, 73,* 144–150.

Atkins, D. C., Marin, R. A., Lo, T. T. Y., Klann, N., & Hahlweg, K. (2010). Outcomes of couples with infidelity in a community-based sample of couple therapy. *Journal of Family Psychology, 24,* 212–216.

Baquet, D. (2017, Dec. 3). Jay-Z and Dean Baquet. *New York Times.* Retrieved on-line from https://www.nytimes.com/interactive/2017/11/29/t-magazine/jay-z-dean-baquet-interview.html

Baucom, D. H., Snyder, D. K., & Gordon, K. C. (2009). *Helping couples get past the affair: A clinician's guide.* New York, NY: Guilford Press.

Baumeister, R. F., & Leary, M. F. (1995). The need to belong: Desire for interpersonal attachment as a fundamental human motivation. *Psychological Bulletin, 117*(3), 497–529.

Birditt, K. S., Miller, L. M., Fingerman, K. L., & Lefkowitz, E. S. (2009). Tensions in the parent and adult child relationship: Links to solidarity and ambivalence. *Psychology and Aging, 24*(2), 287–295.

Birnie-Porter, C., & Lydon, J. E. (2013). A prototype approach to understanding sexual intimacy through its relationship to intimacy. *Personal Relationships, 20,* 236–258.

Bishop, S. R., Lau, M., Shapiro, S., Carlson, L., Anderson, N. D., Carmody, J., . . . Devins, G. (2004). Mindfulness: A proposed operational definition. *Clinical Psychology: Science & Practice, 11*(3), 230–241.

Bitter, J. R. (2008). *Theory and practice of family therapy and counseling*. Pacific Grove, CA: Brooks/Cole.
Bowen, M. (1978). *Family therapy in clinical practice*. Baltimore, MD: Aaronson.
Brown, E. (2001). *Patterns of infidelity and affairs: A guide to working through the repercussions of infidelity*. New York: Jossey-Bass.
Brown, E. (2007). The affair as a catalyst for change. In P. R. Peluso (Ed.), *Infidelity: A practitioner's guide to working with couples in crisis* (pp. 149–165). New York: Routledge.
Burch, B. (2007). Lesbian couples: The infidelities of women sexual and otherwise. In P. R. Peluso (Ed.), *Infidelity: A practitioner's guide to working with couples in crisis* (pp. 229–248). New York: Routledge.
Burchard, G. A., Yarhouse, M. A., Kilian, M. K., Worthington, E. L., Berry, J. W., & Canter, D. E. (2003). A study of two marital enrichment programs and couples' quality of life. *Journal of Psychology and Theology*, *31*, 240–252.
Carlson, J., & Dinkmeyer, D. (2003). *Time for a better marriage*. Atascadero, CA: Impact Publishing.
Carlson, J., Watts, R. E., & Maniacci, M. (2006). *Adlerian therapy: Theory and practice*. Washington, DC: American Psychological Association.
Castonguay, L. G. (2013). Psychotherapy outcome: An issue worth re-revisiting 50 years later. *Psychotherapy*, *50*(1), 52–67. doi: 10.1037/a0030898.
Christensen, A. (1988). Dysfunctional interaction patterns in couples. In P. Noller & M. A. Fitzpatrick (Eds.), *Perspectives on marital interaction* (pp. 31–52). Philadelphia, PA: Multilingual Matters.
Clark, A. J. (2002). *Early recollections: Theory & practice in counseling and psychotherapy*. New York, NY: Brunner-Routledge.
Clinton, H. R. (2017). *What Happened*? New York, NY: Simon and Schuster.
DeMaris, A. (2009). Distal and proximal influences on the risk of extramarital sex: A prospective study of longer duration marriages. *Journal of Sex Research*, *46*, 597–607.
Depaulo, L. (2010). Hello America, my name is Rielle Hunter. *GQ Magazine*, https://www.gq.com/story/rielle-hunter-john-edwards-exclusive-interview.
Eckstein, D. (2002). Walls and windows: Closing and opening behaviors for couples and families. *The Family Journal: Counseling and Therapy for Couples and Families*, *10*, 343–344.
Eldridge, K. A., & Christensen, A. (2002). Demand-withdraw communication during couple conflict: A review and analysis. In P. Moller & J. A. Feeney (Eds.), *Understanding marriage: Developments in the study of couple interaction* (pp. 289–322). Cambridge, UK: Cambridge University Press. doi: 10.1017/CBO9780511500077.016.
Fincham, F. D., & Beach, S. R. (2002). Forgiveness in marriage: Implications for psychological aggression and constructive communication. *Personal Relationships*, *9*, 239–251.
Fincham, F. D., Beach, S. R., & Davila, J. (2004). Forgiveness and conflict resolution in marriage. *Journal of Family Psychology*, *18*, 72–81.
Fincham, F. D., Hall, J. H., & Beach, S. R. H. (2005). "Til lack of forgiveness doth us part": Forgiveness and marriage. In E. Worthington, Jr. (Ed.), *Handbook of forgiveness* (pp. 207–225). New York, NY: Routledge.
Fincham, F. D., Paleari, G., & Regalia, C. (2002). Forgiveness in marriage: The role of relationship quality, attributions, and empathy. *Personal Relationships*, *9*, 27–37.
Garry, M., & Polaschek, D. (2000). Imagination and memory. *Current Directions in Psychological Science*, *9*(1), 6–10.
Gillet, R. (2017, February 13). Power couples who stay together have 9 things in common. *Business Insider*. Retrieved December 18, 2017.

Glass, S. P. (2003). *Not "just friends": Protect your relationship from infidelity and heal the trauma of betrayal.* New York: Free Press.

Gordon, K. C., & Baucom, D. H. (1998). Understanding betrayals in marriage: A synthesized model of forgiveness. *Family Process, 37*(4), 425–449. doi: 10.1111/j.1545-5300.1998.00425.x.

Gordon, K. C., Baucom, D. H., & Snyder, D. K. (2004). An integrative intervention for promoting recovery from extramarital affairs. *Journal of Marital and Family Therapy, 30*, 1–12.

Gottman, J. M. (2011). *The science of trust: Emotional attunement for couples.* New York, NY: Norton.

Gottman, J., & Gottman, J. (2017). The natural principles of love. *Journal of Family Theory & Review, 9*, 7–26. doi: 10.1111/jftr.12182.

Gray-Little, B., Baucom, D. H., & Hamby, S. L. (1996). Marital power, marital adjustment, and therapy outcome. *Journal of Family Psychology, 10*(3), 292–303.

Greenberg, L., Warwar, S., & Malcolm, W. (2010). Emotion-focused couples therapy and the facilitation of forgiveness. *Journal of Marital and Family Therapy, 36*, 28–42.

Hardy, K. V., & Laszloffy, T. A. (1995). The cultural genogram: Key to training culturally competent family therapists. *Journal of Marital and Family Therapy, 21*(3), 227–237.

Hawkins, D. N., & Booth, A. (2005). Unhappily ever after: Effects of long-term, low-quality marriages on well-being. *Social Forces, 84*, 451–471. doi: 10.1353/sof.2005.0103.

Hayes, S. C., Luoma, J. B., Bond, F. W., Masuda, A., & Lillis, J. (2006). Acceptance and Commitment Therapy: Model, processes and outcomes. *Behaviour Research and Therapy, 44*(1), 1–25. doi: 10.1016/j.brat.2005.06.006.

Hendrix, H. (1996). *Getting the love you want: A guide for couples*, by H. Hendrix, 1988. New York: Henry Holt.

Hertlein, K. A., Wetchler, J. L., & Piercy, F. P. (2005). Infidelity: An overview. *Journal of Couple and Relationship Therapy, 4*, 5–16.

Hertlein, K. M., & Piercy, F. P. (2008). Therapists' assessment and treatment of Internet infidelity cases. *Journal of Marital and Family Therapy, 34*(4), 481–497.

Jenkins, J. (2005). *Hedges: Loving your marriage enough to protect it.* Wheaton, IL: Crossway.

Johns, K. N., Allen, E. S., & Gordon, K. C. (2015). The relationship between mindfulness and forgiveness of infidelity. *Mindfulness, 6*, 1462–1471. doi: 10.1007/s12671-015-0427-2.

Johnson, S. (2008). *Hold me tight.* New York: NY: Little Brown, & Co.

Jordan, K. D., & Smith, T. W. (2017). The interpersonal domain of alexithymia. *Personality and Individual Differences, 110*, 65–69.

Juhnke, G. A., Coll, K. M., Evans, M., Sunich, M. F., Hanson, K. D., & Valadez, A. (2008). A modified infidelity debriefing process for couples who have recently experienced infidelity disclosure. *The Family Journal: Counseling and Therapy for Couples and Families, 16*(4), 308–315. doi: 10.1177/1066480708323202.

Kachadourian, L. K., Fincham, F. D., & Davila, J. (2004). The tendency to forgive in dating and married couples: The role of attachment and relationship satisfaction. *Personal Relationships, 11*, 373–393.

Karremans, J. C., Van Lange, P. A., Ouwerkerk, J. W., & Kluwer, E. S. (2003). When forgiving enhances psychological well-being: The role of interpersonal commitment. *Journal of Personality and Social Psychology, 84*, 1011–1026.

Keim, J., & Lappin, J. (2002). Structural-strategic marital therapy. In A. S. Gurman & N. S. Jacobson (Eds.), *Clinical handbook of couple therapy* (3rd ed., pp. 86–117). New York: Guilford Press.

Kern, R. M., Belangee, S. E., & Eckstein, D. (2004). Early recollections: A guide for practitioners. *Journal of Individual Psychology, 60*(2), 132–140.

Kessel, D. E., Moon, J. H., & Atkins, D. C. (2007). Research on couple therapy for infidelity: What do we know about helping couples when there has been an affair? In P. R. Peluso (Ed.), *Infidelity: A practitioner's guide to working with couples in crisis* (pp. 55–70). New York: Routledge.

Kroger, C., Reißner, T., Vasterling, I., Schutz, K., & Kliem, S. (2012). Therapy for couples after an affair: A randomized-controlled trial. *Behaviour Research and Therapy, 50*, 786–796. http://dx.doi.org/10.1016/j.brat.2012.09.006.

Kübler-Ross, E. (1969). *On death and dying*. New York, NY: Macmillan.

Labrecque, L. T., & Whisman, M. A. (2017). Attitudes toward and prevalence of extramarital sex and descriptions of extramarital partners in the 21st century. *Journal of Family Psychology*. Advance online publication. http://dx.doi.org/10.1037/fam0000280.

Lavner, J. A., & Bradbury, T. N. (2012). Why do even satisfied newlyweds eventually go on to divorce? *Journal of Family Psychology, 26*(1), 1–10.

Linehan, M. M. (1993). *Skills training manual for treating borderline personality disorder*. New York, NY: Guilford Press.

Love, P., & Carlson, J. (2011). *Never be lonely again*. Deerfield Beach, FL: Health Communications, Inc.

Love, P., & Shulkin, S. (2001). Imago theory and the psychology of attraction. *The Family Journal: Counseling and Psychotherapy for Couples and Families, 9*(3), 246–249.

Luquet, W. (1998). The relational paradigm. In W. Luquet & M. T. Hannah (Eds.), *Healing in the relational paradigm: The imago relationship casebook* (pp. 1–18). New York: Brunner/Mazel.

Lynch, T. R., Chapman, A. L., Rosenthal, M. Z., Kuo, J. R., & Linehan, M. M. (2006). Mechanisms of change in Dialectical Behavior Therapy: Theoretical and empirical observations. *Journal of Clinical Psychology, 62*(4), 459–480.

Maddox Shaw, A. M., Rhoades, G. K., Allen, E. S., Stanley, S. M., & Markman, H. J. (2013). Predictors of extradyadic sexual involvement in unmarried opposite-sex relationships. *Journal of Sex Research, 50*, 598–610.

Marcus, R. (2009, June 30). Jenny Sanford, role model. *Washington Post*. Retrieved from http://www.washingtonpost.com/wp-dyn/content/article/2009/06/30/AR2009063003046.html.

Mark, K. P., & Jozkowski, K. N. (2013). The mediating role of sexual and nonsexual communication between relationship and sexual satisfaction in a sample of college-age heterosexual couples. *Journal of Sex and Marital Therapy, 39*, 410–427.

Markman, H. J., & Rhoades, G. K. (2012). Relationship education research: Current status and future directions. *Journal of Marital and Family Therapy, 38*, 169–200.

Mayer, J. D., & Stevens, A. (1993). *An emerging understanding of the reflective (meta) experience of mood* (Unpublished manuscript).

McDaniel, B. T., Drouin, M., & Cravens, J. D. (2017). Do you have anything to hide? Infidelity-related behaviors on social media sites and marital satisfaction. *Computers in Human Behavior, 66*, 88–95. http://dx.doi.org/10.1016/j.chb.2016.09.031.

McGoldrick, M., Gerson, R., & Petry, S. (2008). *Genograms: Assessment and intervention* (3rd ed.). New York, NY: Norton.

McIntosh et al. (2007). Forgive and forget: A comparison of emotionally focused couples therapy and cognitive behavioral models of forgiveness and intervention in the context of couple infidelity. In P. R. Peluso (Ed.), *Infidelity: A practitioner's guide to working with couples in crisis* (pp. 127–148). New York: Routledge.

Moller, N. P., & Vossler, M. (2015). Defining infidelity in research and couple counseling: A qualitative study. *Journal of Sex & Marital Therapy*, 41(5), 487–497. doi: 10.1080/0092623X.2014.931314.

Mozdzierz, G., Peluso, P. R., & Lisiecki, J. (2014a). *Principles of counseling and psychotherapy: Learning the essential domains and nonlinear thinking of master practitioners* (2nd ed.). New York: Routledge.

Mozdzierz, G., Peluso, P. R., & Lisiecki, J. (2014b). *Advanced principles of counseling and psychotherapy: Learning, integrating, and consolidating the nonlinear thinking of master practitioners*. New York: Routledge.

Napier, A. Y. (2007). Reflections on the affair: An experiential perspective. In P. R. Peluso (Ed.), *Infidelity: A practitioner's guide to working with couples in crisis* (pp. XX). New York: Routledge.

Ortega, A., & Fleming, M. (2005). *The dance of restoration: Rebuilding marriage after infidelity*. Chattanooga, TN: Living Ink Books.

Paleari, F. G., Regalia, C., & Fincham, F. D. (2005). Marital quality, empathy, and rumination: A longitudinal analysis. *Personality and Social Psychology Bulletin, 31*, 368–378.

Peluso, P. R. (2007). *Infidelity: A practitioner's guide to working with couples in crisis*. New York: Routledge.

Peluso, P. R., Watts, R. E., & Parsons, M. A. (2013). *Changing Aging, Changing Family Therapy: Practicing with 21st Century Realities*. New York: Routledge.

Perel, E. (2017). *The state of affairs: Rethinking infidelity*. New York, NY: Harper Collins, Inc.

Pittman, F. (2007). Reflections of a master an interview with Frank Pittman. In P. R. Peluso (Ed.), *Infidelity: A practitioner's guide to working with couples in crisis* (pp. 279–290). New York: Routledge.

Rassmussen, P. R., & Kilbore, K. J. (2007). Sex in intimate relationships: Variations and challenges. In P. R. Peluso (Ed.), *Infidelity: A practitioner's guide to working with couples in crisis* (pp. 11–30). New York: Routledge.

Roberto-Forman, L. (2002). Transgenerational marital therapy. In A. S. Gurman & N. S. Jacobson (Eds.), *Clinical handbook of couple therapy* (3rd ed., pp. 118–150). New York: Guilford Press.

Robles et al. (2014). Marital quality and health: A meta-analytic review. *Psychological Bulletin, 140*(1), 140–187. doi: 10.1037/a0031859.

Rowe, J. O., Hailing, S., Davies, E., Leifer, M., Powers, D., & van Bronkhorst, J. (1989). The psychology of forgiving another: A dialogal research approach. In R. S. Valle & S. Hailing (Eds.), *Existential-phenomenological perspectives in psychology: Exploring the breadth of human experience*. New York: Plenum.

Sachs, A. (2008, July 8). *Why we have affairs-and why not to tell*. Retrieved October 25, 2017, from http://content.time.com/time/artists/article/0,8599,1820942,00.html.

Satir, V. (1967). *Conjoint family therapy*. Palo Alto, CA: Science and Behavior Books.

Scott, S. B., Parsons, A., Post, K. M., Stanley, S. M., Markman, H. J., & Rhoades, G. K. (2017). Changes in the sexual relationship and relationship adjustment precede extradyadic sexual involvement. *Archives of Sexual Behavior, 46*, 395–406. doi: 10.1007/s10508-016-0797-0.

Seal, M. (2010, May). The temptation of Tiger Woods. *Vanity Fair*. retrieved from https://www.vanityfair.com/culture/2010/05/tiger-woods-article-full-201005

Sells, J. N., Giordano, F. G., & King, L. (2002). A pilot study in marital group therapy: Process and outcome. *The Family Journal: Counseling and Therapy for Couples and Families, 10*, 156–166.

Shackelford, T. K., & Buss, D. M. (1997). Cues to infidelity. *Personality and Social Psychology Bulletin, 23*, 1034–1045.

Shaw, A. M., Rhoades, G. K., Allen, E. S., Stanley, S. M., & Markman, H. J. (2013). Predictors of extradyadic sexual involvement in unmarried opposite-sex relationships. *Journal of Sex Research, 50*, 598–610. http://dx.doi.org/10.1080/00224499.2012.666816.

Shernoff, M. (2007). Male couples and monogamy: Clinical and cultural issues. In P. R. Peluso (Ed.), *Infidelity: A practitioner's guide to working with couples in crisis* (pp. 207–220). New York: Routledge.

Silva, A., Saraiva, M., Albuquerque, P. B., & Arantes, J. (2017). Relationship quality influences attitudes toward and perceptions of infidelity. *Personal Relationships*, 1–11. doi: 10.1111/pere.12205.

Snyder, D. K., Baucom, D. H., & Gordon, K. C. (2007). Treating infidelity: An integrative approach to resolving trauma and promoting forgiveness. In P. R. Peluso (Ed.), *Infidelity: A practitioner's guide to working with couples in crisis* (pp. 99–126). New York: Routledge.

Snyder, D. K., Baucom, D. H., & Gordon, K. C. (2008). An integrative approach to treating infidelity. *The Family Journal: Counseling and Therapy for Couples and Families, 16*(4), 300–307.

Softas-Nall, B., Beadle, M., Newell, J., & Helm, H. M. (2008). Spousal disclosure of extramarital relationships: Attitudes of marriage and family therapists. *The Family Journal: Counseling and Therapy for Couples and Families, 16*(4), 328–337.

Sperry, L., & Peluso, P. R. (2018). *Couples therapy: Theory and effective practice* (3rd ed.). New York, NY: Routledge.

Stanley, S. M., Ragan, E. P., Rhodes, G. K., & Markman, H. J. (2012). Examining changes in relationship adjustment and life satisfaction in marriage. *Journal of Family Psychology, 25*(1), 156–170. DOI: 10.1037/a0026759.

Starratt, V. G., Weekes-Shackelford, V., & Shackelford, T. K. (2017). Mate value both positively and negatively predicts intentions to commit an infidelity. *Personality and Individual Differences, 104*, 18–22. http://dx.doi.org/10.1016/j.paid.2016.07.028.

Stone, E. A., & Shackelford, T. K. (2006). Marital satisfaction. In R. F. Baumeister & K. D. Vohs (Eds.), *Encyclopedia of social psychology*. Thousand Oaks, CA: Sage.

Tafoya, M. A., & Spitzberg, B. H. (2007). The dark side of infidelity: Its nature, prevalence, and communicative functions. In B. H. Spitzberg & W. R. Cupach (Eds.), *The dark side of interpersonal communication* (2nd ed., pp. 201–242). Mahwah, NJ: Lawrence Erlbaum Associates.

Valenzuela, S., Halpern, D., & Katz, J. E. (2014). Social network sites, marriage wellbeing and divorce: Survey and state-level evidence from the United States. *Computers in Human Behavior, 36*, 94–101. http://dx.doi.org/10.1016/j.chb.2014.03.034.

Walton, F. X. (1998). Use of the most memorable observation as a technique for understanding choice of parenting style. *Journal of Individual Psychology, 54*(4), 487–494.

Watzlawick, P., Weakland, J., & Fisch, R. (1974). *Change: Principles of problem formation and problem resolution*. New York: Norton.

Weiner-Davis, M. (2017, April 1). Two contradictions that can help couples on the brink restore connection. *Psychotherapy Networker*. Retrieved December 19, 2017, from www.psychotherapynetworker.org/blog/details/1166/affair-repair.

Weiser, D. A., & Weigel, D. J. (2015). Investigating experiences of the infidelity partner: Who is the "other man/woman"? *Personality and Individual Differences, 85*, 176–181. http://dx.doi.org/10.1016/j.paid.2015.05.014.

Whisman, M. A., Dixon, A. E., & Johnson, B. (1997). Therapists' perspectives of couple problems and treatment issues in couples therapy. *Journal of Family Psychology, 11*, 361–366.

Whisman, M. A., Gordon, K. C., & Chatav, Y. (2007). Predicting sexual infidelity in a population-based sample of married individuals. *Journal of Family Psychology, 21*, 320–324.

Wile, D. B. (2002). Collaborative couples counseling. In A. S. Gurman & N. S. Jacobson (Eds.), *Clinical handbook of couple therapy* (3rd ed., pp. 281–307). New York: Guilford Press.

Wile, D. B. (2008). *After the honeymoon: How conflict can improve your relationship* (rev. ed.). Oakland: Collaborative Couple Therapy Books.

Wile, D. B. (2011). Collaborative couple therapy. In D. K. Carson & M. Casado-Kehoe (Eds.), *Case studies in couples therapy: Theory-based approaches* (pp. 303–316). New York: Routledge.

Wile, D. B. (2017). *Doubling in collaborative couple therapy: Chapter 3 from solving the moment: Theory and method of collaborative couple therapy* (in preparation). Retrieved December 2, 2017, from http://danwile.com/writings/downloadable-articles/.

Williamson, M. E., & Brimhall, A. S. (2017). A journey of remembering: A narrative framework for older couples experiencing infidelity. *Journal of Couple & Relationship Therapy, 16*(3), 232–252. doi: 10.1080/15332691.2016.1253516.

Worden, J. W. (2009). *Grief counseling and grief therapy*. New York, NY: Springer.

Index

Made in the USA
Columbia, SC
06 November 2018